ARTISTS IN THE MAKING

ARTISTS IN THE MAKING

FRANK BARRON

Professor of Psychology
University of California, Santa Cruz
and
Research Psychologist
University of California, Berkeley

With the collaboration or assistance in particular chapters of:

Wallace B. Hall, Ph.D., Robert H. Knapp, Ph.D., Phebe Cramer, Ph.D., Marvin Rosenberg, Ph.D.
Diane Denman, M.A., Jerrell Kraus, M.A., Judy Alter, M.A., Susan Hopkin, M.A.
Isabel Conti, Cynthia Marlowe

 SEMINAR PRESS   New York and London   1972

SEMINAR PRESS, INC.
111 Fifth Avenue, New York, New York 10003

United Kingdom Edition published by
SEMINAR PRESS LIMITED
24/28 Oval Road, London NW1 7DD

LIBRARY OF CONGRESS CATALOG CARD NUMBER: 72 - 77220

PRINTED IN THE UNITED STATES OF AMERICA

To

THE REPUBLIC OF IRELAND

*for the following magnanimous Act in
practical recognition of*

THE ARTIST

Finance Act, 1969

REPUBLIC OF IRELAND

*providing "complete tax relief on earnings from a book or other writing,
a play, a musical composition, a painting or sculpture . . ."*

"The purpose of this relief is to help create a sympathetic environment here in which
the arts can flourish. . . . This is something completely new in this country and . . . in the
world."

Mr. Charles J. Haughey, T.C.

*Minister of Finance
Republic of Ireland*

and in memory of

GUY HAMILTON CROOK

in art and in psychology

AN ORIGINAL

"The four artistic careers which excel serious writing in difficulty are, in order of hardship, poetry, sculpture, serious music, and painting. Bells should be rung and the entire village should meet for prayer when a young man or woman dedicates himself to one of those fields, and it is proper that a nation should prize above most things its genius in any of those endeavors. As a man who has knocked about in the arts for some time, I can only say that in the presence of a poet I am struck with awe that I should behold so courageous a man. I never felt that way about generals or admirals, for our society is organized to protect the warrior."

JAMES A. MICHENER
. . . The Chances Against the Beginning Writer.
In "The Writer's Book" (*Helen Hull, ed.*), *Barnes & Noble, New York, 1956.*

Contents

PART THREE

A MISCELLANY

Preface

As everyone knows, art is unnecessary to the survival of the human species. In this it differs from war, which, as everyone knows, is an essential instrument of national policy and the ultimate guardian of national honor.

It is only fitting, then, that national budgets do not provide for battalions of artists, who might if unleashed change the very face of the nation—the face of their own nation, that is, not the faces of other nations. I am reminded of a mordant sign erected in March, 1945, along the road leading into the heart of Munchen Gladbach, Germany. On it were the words of Adolph Hitler, spoken in 1939 when he made clear his plans for military conquest by the Third Reich: "Give me five years and you will not recognize the face of Europe." Beyond the sign stretched mile upon mile of rubble, the leveled remains of the city, a part of the face of Europe, altered as only bombs and artillery shells can alter.

The naked ape, as Desmond Morris has chosen to call himself and the rest of us, has war deep in his heart. But as Morris himself showed in an earlier book "The Biology of Art," even the hairy ape will create visual art if given the opportunity. An exhibition of the paintings of an assortment of anthropoids, from the famous Congo to lesser lights of more recent years, is presented to show that the basic artistic forms are within reach of the skill of our primate relatives. The creation of patterns of beauty is an intrinsic impulse of intelligence in its higher forms of development, as deeply implanted as the ancient instincts to defend territory and to kill the enemy.

Yet the impulse to create in art is not widely honored in the observance. The heavy weight of the world and its routines make drudges of us all. In the words of Henri Bergson, "Psychic creation is a stone thrown uphill against the downward rush of matter." Implied in this, however, is art's great value, for it is an instrument of the evolution of mind, of consciousness.

That which would remain dark does not seek the light. The collectivity does not seek the free individual. Virginia Woolf once said in concluding an appraisal of the artist's situation:

> Accentuating all these difficulties is the world's notorious indifference. It does not ask people to write poems . . . it does not need them.
> . . . Here the psychologists might come to our help. For surely it is time that the effect of discouragement upon the mind of the artist should be measured.

Virginia Woolf's bitter statement to the girls of Newnham College was later made part of the essay[1] in which she fantasies the fate of a female Shakespeare who goes to the grave not just unknown but unexpressed. It was in part a complaint against the world of men who do not value the songs of women. Still, there is a general truth in it as it stands. By the mass of men art is valued very little, and when it does receive high valuation in the coin of the realm it is usually in the service of a nonartistic purpose, such as ornamentation, conspicuous consumption to elevate the status of the buyer, or bald trade.

I am touched by the expression, "Here the psychologists might come to our help." That a great artist should have seen the possibility of an alliance between the arts and psychology, especially in those days when a wrong-headed antihuman behaviorism was dominating academic psychology, is to me a source of encouragement. I have myself experienced psychology as a vocation in the way I imagine artists to experience their calling. The present work arose from my conviction that psychologists do in fact have something

[1] "A Room of One's Own," Harcourt, New York, 1929.

to contribute to the understanding, recognition, and encouragement of art and artists; indeed, of artistic interests and aesthetic values in general. All of us, whether we go all the way as an artist or not, may cultivate our own creative potential by honoring the artistic impulse within ourselves. We do this by expressing it, even in small ways if larger ways are not within the range of our means.

This book is about artists or potential artists in various stages of personal and professional development. It approaches its subject matter in an empirical spirit, applying simple and usually familiar techniques of psychological research to the task of understanding artistic development. Most of the persons studied by these means were young adults, and most were beginners in art, students at recognized art schools or in university departments of art, at the time they took part in the research. "Artists in the Making," then, may be taken to refer to patterns of development in artists and potential artists.

Not all readers, of course, will find the research techniques simple and familiar, and in fact some of the applications and results should seem quite novel even to the experienced professional psychologist. The chapter on role conceptualization and the projection and discernment of character in theatrical performances, e.g., and the chapters on the possibility of genetic influences in aesthetic judgment and creativity, the correlates of formal modes of expression in the plastic arts, and the relationship of nonrational experience to creative imagination, all contain novelties of method or surprising results. The specific psychometric techniques employed in the research are generally widely known within the field of psychology, however. Yet even these are introduced in such a fashion that the reader unfamiliar with the psychological literature and current practice in testing may learn as he goes along, so that in some passages the book may seem almost like a primer of psychological testing for the student or the professional from another field. (Some of the descriptions are drawn from the Appendix of my earlier and now out-of-print book "Creativity and Psychological Health.") Teaching the reader about psychological tests is certainly not the purpose of the book, which aims rather to present the results of research and to suggest further problems for investigation; nevertheless for some it may be an incidental benefit, even though for others it is old stuff and perhaps unduly simplified. Since my desire was to accommodate a readership that might include artists and art educators as well as psychologists and educational researchers, I felt constrained to include much preamble that I might otherwise have omitted, to stick as much as possible to simple percentages or probabilities and to provide ample illustrative material in the actual words of the student artists themselves.

The book ends with a description of the new college devoted to aesthetic education on the Santa Cruz campus of the University of California. When the chapter was written, the college was just emerging from the rather chaotic early stage of creation. Its baptism of fire seems now to be past, and the aesthetic studies major has firmly taken hold and gives promise of sound growth.

Thus the college now has an identity, though it still lacks a name. It does have a number, however; since it was fifth in the order of initiation of the new colleges on this experimental campus, it is known, affectionately, as College V. The seal of its "fiveness" was placed upon it this fall by one of the members of its art faculty, the sculptor Fred Hunnicutt, who designed a massive V-shaped fountain, made of stainless steel cylinders and colored Plexiglass, to complete the faculty quadrangle.

The aesthetic education research program continues of course to have ties with the San Francisco Art Institute, as well as with the Institute of Personality Assessment and Research at Berkeley; but both the research and this novel experiment in aesthetic education have clearly settled down together in a new home.

Acknowledgments

The research reported here has taken place over a period of ten years, although most of it has been accomplished quite recently and may be viewed as the first step in a program of basic research in aesthetic education. The later stages of the work have been supported by a grant from the United States Office of Education.

My own interest in aesthetic education began with a general interest in the psychology of creativity. As part of the general program of research at the Institute of Personality Assessment and Research, I initiated a study of creative writers by conducting a psychological "assessment" of student writers, feeling that the place to begin was with beginners. That assessment produced a number of case studies in some psychodynamic depth, and crucial questions concerning the relationship of artistic promise to the realization of talent in mature artistic achievement were posed by the study. Two of the case studies are reported for the first time in this volume.

The research with student actors was carried out in collaboration with Professor Marvin Rosenberg, of the Dramatic Arts Department of the

University of California. The later stage of this research, specifically the study of role conceptualization and enactment by student actors, was supported by a grant from the Institute of Social Science at the University. This study has been published in the *Journal of Theatre Education*; permission to include it in this volume is gratefully acknowledged.

My research with student painters began in 1960, when I took part in a study at the Rhode Island School of Design, under the sponsorship of the Carnegie Corporation. We were interested in the effect of motivation upon creative performance, and also in the effect of set and the ability to assume the role of "the creative person." The results of that study were reported at the 1962 Utah Creativity Conference (Taylor, 1964).

The study of dancers at the Boston Conservatory of Music was initiated by Judy Alter, then a student at Harvard who did her Master's thesis under my direction. This occurred at the same time as the work at Rhode Island School of Design, and later came to include work with dancers at Brandeis University and in 1968 at Mills College.

My research on aesthetic judgment goes back to 1949 and the beginning of my tenure at the Institute of Personality Assessment and Research, but it took a new turn in 1965 when I launched a study of twin resemblances in aesthetic judgment and creativity in a sample of Italian twins in Florence and in Rome, at the Institute for Medical Genetics and the Mendel Institute, respectively. This was followed by a replication of the study at Berkeley. Both studies were supported financially by the Richardson Foundation.

The bulk of the research reported in this volume, however, stems from work accomplished within the past two years at the San Francisco Art Institute, and supported entirely by the United States Office of Education. The faculty and administration of the college of the Art Institute collaborated closely in this work, and without their aid it would manifestly not have been possible.

As director of the research and author of this volume, I salute too my collaborators in psychology who worked as research associates or as occasional consultants for the project. I am especially grateful to Dr. Wallace B. Hall, Associate Director of the Institute of Personality Assessment and Research, for his active participation and assumption of responsibility for data analysis in the San Francisco Art Institute study. He contributed particularly to Chapter 5, in which results obtained with the Turney-Hall Mosaic Construction Test are described. My other collaborators on various occasions or for particular studies included Drs. Robert H. Knapp (Chapter 6), Phebe Cramer (Chapter 9), and Marvin Rosenberg (Chapter 10); and such students or research assistants as Isabel Conti, Diane Denman, Jerrell

Kraus, Cynthia Marlowe, and Judy Alter. My thanks go also to Susan Hopkin, senior statistician at the Institute of Personality Assessment and Research, for her invaluable work in data analysis, and to Florence Cho and Jane Wachsmuth, the secretaries who have kept things together and helped make this manuscript a reality.

Several of these chapters were first prepared as written reports on data analyses carried out by one or more of my collaborators and then revised by me; I have had responsibility for the final form of the whole work. Diane Denman contributed particularly to the psychometric portrait of the artist and to the analysis of the questionnaires filled out by dance students. These questionnaires had been constructed earlier by Judy Alter, and the data collected by her; Jerrell Kraus wrote the part of the chapter on the San Francisco Art Institute which reports the views of its students, basing her report on interviews conducted by herself and Isabel Conti. Cynthia Marlowe analyzed the same interviews for sex differences and wrote a preliminary report for that section of the chapter. Robert H. Knapp, Marvin Rosenberg, and Phebe Cramer have equal responsibility with me for the chapters bearing their names. I am grateful to all these colleagues, without whom the present work would not have been completed.

Finally, my thanks to all the blameless students and their teachers who took part in the research at the San Francisco Art Institute, Rhode Island School of Design, Boston Conservatory of Music, Brandeis University, Mills College, and the University of California.

PART ONE

STUDENTS OF THE VISUAL ARTS COLLEGE OF THE SAN FRANCISCO ART INSTITUTE

Introduction: The School and Its Students

Fred Martin *

By way of introducing the reader to the research undertaken by Frank Barron and his fellow psychologists at the College of the San Francisco Art Institute, I shall try to tell you something of the school itself. I say *the school*—for that is what we go on calling it, out of habit, I guess, and with nostalgia for its days as the California School of Fine Arts. More than habit and nostalgia, though—respect, rather, for the freedom of the fine arts which was established here in those days, and an intention to keep that idea alive, continuing.

The College of the San Francisco Art Institute is the collective fantasy of everyone entangled in it, from students to trustees and including faculty, staff, and animals. Because the fantasy is collective, it cannot be summed up: it is forever flowering in some other head. Because it is fantasy, it can never be defined in a prose whose stylistic purpose is to exclude the emotion-charge which led the writer to participate in the first place. Therefore, in the

* Director, College of the San Francisco Art Institute.

description of the school which you will find below, you must remember that only one member of the community is speaking (me) and only one fantasy is being presented (mine). Yet I can use words I have used before, for the fantasy fits the reality well enough that I continue and so does it.

Our purpose is to be a place of the living edge in art and artists, to be a school in both senses: as a group of creative men and as a teaching organization. Our first care is for culture, for the creation of art. Our second care is for education, the economy of the spirit which naturally arises from the production of art in a community of creative men.

The College's structure consists of two parts. One part is the faculty, the mature but generally younger creative artist who teaches at the Institute and is therefore able to create on an independent basis. In a sense we regard our faculty salaries as patronage, and the $450,000 we will spend next year will make it possible for about 30 of the 50 faculty to pursue their independent creative purpose without any obligation to us or to anyone else beyond two seven-hour teaching days per week for 32 weeks. The second part is the community of students who have come to the Institute to learn, that is, to associate with a creative faculty in the relation of student to master. By coming to the Institute to learn, they form the chief source of economic support for the faculty's own creative endeavor while helping to clarify in the mind of the artist-teacher his own particular creative purpose. And, after clarifying, and becoming clearer and richer in experience themselves, we expect that some of the students will come to fill the teaching ranks of the school as present faculty pass on into other colleges which are more secure and full of academic esteem.

Our educational activity is organized as follows. The studio curriculum consists of what we still call "the fine arts": painting and drawing; sculpture and ceramics as sculpture; printmaking; photography and film making as noncommercial endeavors. (Here is probably the key to all our differences; everything is approached as a noncommercial endeavor, a personal adventure. Here too is the key to whatever success we may have: It is in the strength of the personalities which come to us; and the key to the failures in their development as persons and as artists is also in the fallibility of man.)

The studio teaching is organized entirely around the concept of master/student although many of the masters are physically indistinguishable from the students. There are no syllabi for studio courses. Instead, the courses are established at general levels such as first, second, third, and fourth year; and the content of each course is determined by the artist-teacher out of his own experience in interaction with the students and with the current events of art and the world. The teacher treats each student as an individual, working with him and making demands, offering help, ideas, and insights, acceptance or rejection, as he feels them to be appropriate in each case. The overall curriculum pattern, the range and emphasis of subjects, of media, of ideas, of dreams that we will try to bring to reality, is established by the Director of the College in consultation with the faculty, and is based upon the faculty artists' views as to how best at the present time to teach sculpture, painting, printmaking, photography, or film. Since the studio curriculum is the faculty, and that is creation of art itself, tenure is not possible, and neither is unanimity of purpose, logical rigor, or even, sometimes, pride in our achievement.

And so, in short, the College of the San Francisco Art Institute is as close to the fantasy of artists as we can achieve in the world of the 1970's. But, since it is the fantasy of a particular group of artists at a particular place, it is shaped in part by the situation of that place.

First, it is in a large city, and the students and faculty ordinarily begin by living in the city. Because they are usually poor (the full-time faculty pay is not very far above the nationally defined poverty level, the students' income is mostly below it[1]) they tend to live in the less desirable parts of town, the central city, the ghetto, the slum. They are quickly aware, no matter how sheltered their earlier lives had been, of the actuality of existence on the night side of the American dream. That existence is seen by them as primarily composed of horror, ruin, and despair. They and their friends experience these directly. They are busted for dope; they get jobs in bars as topless waitresses; other friends die of an overdose of this or that; they act in or make pornographic films; they live as laborers and see the very early wearing out of lives. They live by their wits. They find jobs where no one else can; they stick persistently on, until they find some small crevice where they might settle in a city of stone, where they might quietly, secretly, flower. Some die to the school, lured by some *amor fati* or bohemianism on into the alleys of North Beach, where they become minor poets, small-time surrealists, sideshows for tourists. Others die to the school because, quite simply, they cannot take it. The strain of the city is too much. They go home. But some stay at the school. In a few years, they will mark the school with the passion

[1] Although the Institute is a private school, it has a far higher percentage of poor students than the usual private college or university. The reasons seem to be (1) the public college or university cannot ordinarily provide the freedom to develop a personal counterculture that a small art school can and so the students, no matter how poor, will not go to taxpayer-controlled places, (2) the fine arts have little economic utility and so the art student must have already given up dreams of "a good salary and a nice home," must already have assumed close to voluntary poverty in order to expect to survive.

of their fantasy; theirs will be, quite literally, the art of the San Francisco Art Institute.

In recent years, those who have stayed in the school have nonetheless usually left the city. The exodus to the country is very great. Most move to woodsy places near the ocean, the coast south of San Francisco, or the valleys going toward the sea along the Marin coast. They are able to do this because they have begun to be independent, to find just enough money to survive, and to find in their work sufficient independence, sufficient affirmation and expansion of their experience, to be able to begin to live alone, partly apart from "the art world," feeding not so much off the works of other artists as from the ever-renewed pastures of perception and psychic reverberation in their own lives.

Therefore, and partly because of geographic situation, the art and the artists—students and faculty—of the Institute exemplify more strongly than most the tendencies in American art called "coonskinism," private surrealism, and provincialism—all terms used by the capital to denigrate artists or movements distant or independent from it. Converted into "Bay Area Funk" a few years ago, the art world tried it temporarily and unsuccessfully as a new sensation. However, each local artist who lives it continues to see it merely as his own life. And because it is a life of art lived far enough from the pressures of the moment to be able to see the whole landscape of time and the world against which it is played, it is his own life in relation to, evaluated by, the highest, rather than the newest that has been done.

I have spoken of the effect of place on the school. Now I should speak of time. Just as the school is slightly aside from the geographical power centers of art in America today, so it is slightly aside in time. Its peripheral geographic position frees it, for better or worse, from the commands of fashion (their arbiters are so very far away); and in being freed from fashions, it is freed from the tyranny of the present. It need not measure its achievements so much against current exhibitions striving for attention in galleries of undoubted economic clout but very doubtful artistic understanding; its remoteness has given it the stage of world history, not the fashions of upper Madison Avenue, for its reference. Although the main arguments in art criticism today are won by novelty, from Morse Peckham's theory of art as "non-functional stylistic dynamism," and Clement Greenberg's *et al.,* definition of aesthetic value as "modernist," and although the success of these arguments is proven by the undoubted impact on the development of American art by *Artforum* as a medium of fashion, nonetheless the very dominance of this view and the concomitant lessening of its own intrinsic newness has formed indeed a new academy (Rosenberg's "tradition of the new") and has established once more another art, a counterculture, outside, beyond, its province. Because traditional modern art has timeliness at its root, this art seeks timelessness. Because traditional modern art is based in the naturalist to phenomenologist aesthetics of the West, this art seeks the mythical and metaphysical aesthetic of the East. It often establishes itself in one or another of the East–West syntheses which have been developed in recent centuries, as these have been recently expanded and transformed by the drug culture, psychedelics, and the entry of Eastern religion into the consciousness of Western youth. It is subconscious or supraconscious; it is almost never conscious as consciousness has come to be defined in America (i.e., as rational, practical, or realistic). Thus the school is far from the noon and midnight competition of New York and the editorial offices of *Artforum, Art News,* and *Art International*; but it is close to the Haight-Ashbury (it still remembers the "Summer of Love") and to the setting sun.

The school is what its members (faculty and students) dream; it is the collective fantasy of its population. Its population is influenced by its remote setting in time and space from the power centers of American art: that is, it tends to hold those who would march to different drummers, who would be remote. But it is a "professional school." What is the profession, anyway? Is it not itself different?

As a professional school, this is a school for a profession which no longer exists if it ever did. Perhaps, as art lifted itself above the crafts, it overshot, missing the proper and respectable locale of the professions, to land, awkwardly for aspirants to social station, in that curious never-never land of the vocation—the "calling." Vocation and calling are old words, now seldom used in favor of the more modern and more important "profession." Now we call it the profession of the artist; then, they called it the vocation, and the change in terminology in these recent years indicates an accommodation to the passion of current society for climbing. Everyone wants to be better than he was, and what were called jobs are now elevated to positions. The vocation of the artist has been elevated so that even upon his grubby nonentity may rub off some of the importance and gloss of the doctor, the lawyer, and the merchant chief. The professions have associations, codes of ethics, subject matters, and systems of training; their established patterns of purpose and action exist as well in the world of artists. But for the artist, and quite probably not for the professional, these are not the substance of his work. It lies quite elsewhere. The land of his calling (calling to him, and his call to us) is rather beyond this world than in it, rather unknown than known, and rather for his own sake than the sake of others. The doctor, the lawyer, always serve other men first, the artist serves them only later.

Yet the four goals of the artist's vocation are ones which all men believe he achieves for them. These are civilization, salvation, immortality, and peace. These art may give us (maybe not practically or really); it implants the lingering dream that they are, and that we have shared in them. But the selfishness of art comes from the fact that the artist makes them for himself—to civilize himself, to save his soul, to make his own immortality, and to find his own peace. The rest of mankind only trails along, picking up crumbs.

The artist makes civilization; his work marks out for him the boundaries of the stable world. In the words of Morris Graves: "I paint to rest from the phenomena of the world, to mark and to hold in the silence the presences of the inner eye . . .," or, as Martin Heidegger said of Hoelderlin, "to name the gods, that men may come to live in their light." This is a very great high aspiration for the inauspicious daubing and scribbling of a nonprofessional.

The artist makes salvation, too; he saves himself from loss. What is it to be saved, from what are we to be saved? Some 200 million souls live in America today—200 million unique particles as inconceivable as the myriad individual grains of sand which a bird took from the beaches of the world to make eternity. And so, in that windswept beach of humanity that is America, where the sand forever drifts and is pounded by the waves of politics and history and family tragedy, the joy and the births of little children and their deaths as well, the tiny grain of sand that is the individual soul is lost. We have, in our simple culture, a way of finding it: we get our names in the newspapers. Then someone has heard of us; we are, we exist, saved from the drifting dunes of anonymity, the nonbeing of nothing. We establish ourselves in relation to those who will name us, we ask the hospitals to tell the newspapers of our birth, the funeral directors to tell when we die, and we send in pictures of our children's weddings, hoping they are important enough to print. We are saved, we think, by the mass media from the very emptiness of the mass; our name is placed, a somebody for a day, in the mind of 400,000 other nobodies like us. And so art is the salvation, the saving of the artist from the ocean tide of loss in nonbeing, because with it he marks himself, establishes his name (like the "von" in German, the "de" in French, his art names the place he is from, and then he himself has a name—his "from there") and he is saved, held in his own mind aside from the petty, deadly round of endless days and men.

So he establishes the civilization of his work, he builds himself a far kingdom; and he saves himself from eternal loss by giving himself the name of the one who is from that land of his. And in so doing, he becomes immortal, and that is the third thing that the artist's vocation is about. It was popular in the seventeenth century to paint "Fame Conquering Time," wherein bright-winged angels blew fame's shining trumpets across the heavens as the ancient graybeard Time crumbled dimly into the tomb. The artist now is suspicious of fame because it is awarded by newspapers to the spiciest product that is sold by the most sophisticated manufacturer of daily forgettables for the public table. The artist's work lives after him; it is the incarnate frame of his mind and life. As the shell of some long-dead crustacean calls of the sea, so his work echoes the sound and spaciousness of his life. The artist is our civilizer and lawgiver; and the monument of his life, that very special civilization, remains after his death, it is the immortality of his soul. Until the paint flakes, the drawing fades, the paper rots, or the language itself of its framing is finally forgotten—like the thousand-year nonexistence of the art of Greece and Rome in the West, the indecipherability of the living cry of Beowulf, the present fading of the talk of Shakespeare.

But finally for the artist his vocation is for peace—not the peace of nations or of tribes, but the peace of contemplation. (We have been trained now to make the economy run by wanting to have, that is to buy, the object of desire which we might have merely contemplated and so possessed through seeing, through the act of perpetual union.) So the artist is for peace, the peace in the eye of the tiger, which Blake knew when he hymned the tiger burning in night's forest, which the Zen master rode when he laughed amid the roaring.

So the artist's vocation is for civilization, salvation, immortality, and peace. It is not a profession; it is a calling. We may aspire to answer its call, we may fail, and we may also forget.

Herman Hesse's *Journey to the East* is the story of such a forgetting; and there are artists that we know who seem so to have forgotten: the university or college artist one so often meets, whose work has in the end been called upon to build for him a niche of respectability, a position among college professors for his mature, later, forgetful years.

So, then, the school's present may be described as an aspiration toward the fine arts. An aspiration, mind you. Few succeed. But most have in their hearts the gnawing tension which will drive them to the brink where failure or achievement are separated. Henry James remarked that the world brings us all down somehow or other, and surely it will bring down each artist before he is finished. Sex, dope, drink, or responsibility will get him; disease, accident, misfortune, or success will occur; fear, power, pride, or old age will eat out his days. Those he escapes as a student (and they are not many) will get him after he commences and surely before he dies. But for the "good" student at the school, all of these acts of God will be met with the passion that is the fine arts; and for the "bad" or mediocre student, when he meets them (and he will also), at least he will have some old recollection of how one might bear up, nobly.

And how may one predict who will make it? Heavens, but the roads of God are long, labyrinthine, and various. And who is to say that one destination is more holy than another? (Baudelaire said, "Do not despise the sensibility of any man; the sensibility of each man is his genius.")

What of the school's future? The major, immediately visible, unresolved problems before the fine arts in America (and hence before the school) are the impact of technological development on the media and thus on the form and content of expression; the ever more precarious position of the individual vis-à-vis the mass (the false abstraction, "mass," but how to maintain the authenticity of one's own life in the face of the mass-produced mass life offered, force-fed, by the all powerful mass media?); and the rapidly surfacing problem of the apparent irrelevance of the individual artist's work to the desperate need for help of a society in transformation. If we knew the answer to these, they would not be problems because we would be living already in the context of their solution. But we do not, and so we live instead in their rising tension.

Can the psychologist indeed help the artist? I do not know. Perhaps what we do we must do alone. Perhaps it is more likely that the artist may help the psychologist. Whatever the case, in these pages you see the first results of a tentative collaboration. And whatever the results, I expect we will live in the future as we have in the past: hand to mouth, happy with what the day brings us and somehow overcoming the lack of what it does not; as a school, not so great or important or relevant as other places; too fallible, but managing.

CHAPTER ONE

Talks with Students
at the San Francisco Art Institute

Art students mostly do not like to take tests. Who does? Yet they did, to help in this research. And I and my fellow psychologists doing the research mostly do not like to give tests, but we did, because it is the only way we can gain a certain sort of knowledge we consider valuable. It is our hope that the art students who took the tests will eventually find it valuable too. Or at least that someone will. Valuable or interesting.

The situation is not really quite that painful, however. At least some of the students enjoyed the tests, which can be construed less as tests than as occasions to do something interesting and possibly self-instructive. Some of the tests, such as Drawing Completion, call for expression on paper with pencil or pen in a fairly free setting. Others are clearly related to visual abilities important in art, such as the ability to discern a simple figure masked by a more complex one. To free the simple figure embedded in its irrelevant but confounding surround might be one way of describing the task, and surely this is a process important in art. Still other tests presented visual illusions, or problems in accuracy of visual perception. Another group of problems called for perceptual discrimination and imagination in other sensory modalities, such as the olfactory and tactile. Some called for aesthetic judgments or preferences. Others presented ambiguous perceptual fields, as in the case of inkblot forms, and asked for interpretation. Only a very few of the tests got at all personal: one called for the expression of vocational interests through a comparison of preferred activities, and others asked for self-description or for a response of True or False to questions related to personal philosophy and experience.

The bad thing about being asked to take these latter tests, whether in the service of science, art, or the school administration, is the suspicion—True, not False—that they are being scored in some secret or at least generally unknown way by someone who thinks he knows the answers. That is what makes everyone mad at simplistic and dualistic tests, whether they are printed up and called tests or merely are standards of judgment being exercised by someone other than the involuntary subject. Yet life does continually ask us to say True or False, and the scoring key is not always fair or known.

In this research we found over and over again that *critical judgment coming from outside* was resented by both students and faculty. But the sympathetic eye or ear, the non-evaluating but interested viewer or listener, was welcome. For this part of the research we therefore asked two graduate students who are both artists and educational researchers at the University of California in Berkeley to interview the students at the school. Isabel Conti, recently arrived from Rome and engaged in a study of Fellini's "8½," with Fellini's help, teamed up with Jerrell Kraus, recently arrived from Paris by way of Istanbul and engaged in a study of Hundertwasser's painting, with Hundertwasser's help, and the two of them together constructed an interview schedule and interviewed 64 of the beginning students. They found the students lively, interested, a pleasure to talk to. Excerpts from those interviews form the basis for this chapter and the two that follow. Jerrell Kraus wrote the following report, based on her own impressions and those of Isabel Conti.

"The Art Institute gives me a different image of school. I've always hated school, but this is a really pleasant place."

"It would be nice if this school would emphasize the importance of dedication to art rather than just be here to enable people to find themselves."

"This school is a great place. It gives you the time to do your thing. You don't get that in other schools. I can make my own decisions here and find things out for myself."

"I like the free atmosphere, but it is too unstructured. Sometimes it seems aimless."

"This school is a good beginning, but it is too protected—sometimes like a womb."

These are some of the feelings that first-year students interviewed at the San Francisco Art Institute expressed about their school. Of the 64 first-year students interviewed, 42 are male and 22 female. They range in age from 17 to 43, though the majority of students (40) are between 18 and 20 years old. The greatest number (28) are painting majors, followed by 19 who are majoring in photography or film making (or both), 12 in sculpture or ceramics (or both), and 5 in printmaking. The present discussion is based on their feelings about this unique school and about themselves as artists.

Most educational institutions, art schools included, are grounded in the premise that there are important things that must be imparted to the student. The Art Institute is an exception: Its apparent premise is that everything important is already in the student and that his need for instruction is secondary to his need for freedom and encouragement. Thus there is little didactic instruction. The teachers prefer to create an atmosphere of total freedom in which the student is at liberty to attend class or not, to work at his own pace, and to create and solve his own problems. Much of the student's learning experience comes through the choices and decisions that he must therefore make on his own regarding all artistic matters.

The bond that unites students, faculty, and administration is a subtle one. It is not reinforced by meetings and assemblies or put forth in speeches and memoranda. It results from an implicit understanding of the common nature of their needs and of their reasons for coming together. Students teach each other and teachers learn from students. The emphasis is upon each student's recognizing and developing his personal expressive arena—his own forms, his own imagery. Because there is a minimal amount of explicit instruction, the necessity of academic training for an artist is seriously called into question. Art is seen as an experience, and experience cannot be taught. It can, however, be facilitated by an environment that is both free and stimulating, and by people whose sole involvement is with the experience of art.

The Art Institute's educational philosophy works best for students who have previously resisted authoritarian teaching, yet have a high degree of self-motivation:

"I'm very happy here. I feel that everything I'm doing here *I* am doing. Somebody else isn't forcing me to do it. I wanted a school that was completely free and open to see if I could really stand on my own and cope with it. There are a lot of people who can't cope with this school. But then it does help a lot of people."

"I like the way this school is run. The teachers get into your work instead of pushing their own style. I don't think the school is too loose."

"The teachers don't go out of their way for you. You have to turn them on to what you're doing. But that's good because I don't like anyone to tell me what to do."

One student came to the Art Institute after dropping out of a well-known east coast art school where he was on scholarship, because "It was too strict. Everybody had to do the same thing and work in the teacher's style. And everybody worried about grades. Here it's so different. You can do what you like." But for this student, the Art Institute's freedom is too great. He goes on to say, "It's even a little too free here, too loose. There should be more control."

The need for greater "control" was expressed by a number of students, particularly by those who were especially troubled in their personal lives and who sought a high degree of direction and order in school. One such boy stated, "The school is too loose. It needs more organization. A school should have some formality. After all, it is an institution."

Most Art Institute students appreciate the freedom of being able to work on their art at home rather than coming to class. Painters especially prefer to work on their own, since "painting is an individual trip; it's not a communal thing."

"I don't like to work at school because I don't like my paintings to be criticized while they're in transitional stages."

"When I'm developing an idea of my own I prefer to work at home. I don't like someone looking over my shoulder."

Students majoring in photography, printmaking, and sculpture work at school more than do those majoring in painting because of their dependence upon the school's physical equipment. Over half of the painters say they do all their work at home. They come to school only to do life drawings from the model or to attend the regular class critique. The critique is a pivotal part of the student's formal learning experience when each student brings in his recent work for class discussion. For most students it is the most profitable class session, and for those who work at home, it is the only one they attend.

"For learning it's easier to work at school; for doing things it's better at home."

"I like to work at home if I'm sure what I'm involved in. If I'm looking for more stimulation, I'd rather work at school."

"I prefer to work at home. I'm not so sure of what I'm doing so I'd rather be by myself. When something is finished, I take it to school and show it to my teacher."

"I like to be at school. I like the people. But I don't like to work here. I like to be around people for the security, not for communication."

Those students who are beginning in art with little or no previous training are generally least suited to profit from the Art Institute. The most determined among them attempt to get help from their instructors or from other students. The least determined request and receive virtually no guidance at all.

"The teachers leave you too much on your own," said one student. "Maybe they do it because they assume that everybody who comes here has already had previous training. But I wish I could learn more techniques."

Students who have little inner sense of discipline or motivation become very frustrated at the Art Institute. The pressure to produce and achieve that prevails at most academic institutions is absent. Roll is not taken and teachers are often not present during studio classes. Many new students cannot respond well to this lack of outer structure and find themselves doing very little work. A photography major who said that he was no longer doing any art work at all commented:

"If you're going to be an artist, you have to do it every day. You can't have excuses to not do it. This school gives you excuses not to work at art."

But what is for one student an excuse not to work is for another the opportunity to progress at his own speed and in his own direction. For young artists who have a strong inner sense of creative and personal direction, the Art Institute is an ideal atmosphere. One such student is an 18-year-old who said, "I have a hard time *not* painting. I paint about 10 hours a day. Painting is my life." Despite his ability to discipline himself, this boy appreciates his need for a stimulating school. "I'm at this school because I need the people and the environment." The Art Institute is the perfect place for him to fully pursue his own work unburdened by assignments that might be irrelevant to his strongly developed artistic vision. It is also the ideal place for him to test the effect of his work on others. This young painter recently held a seminar session for other students and teachers in which he presented and discussed at length a series of his own paintings—a rare experience for a first-year art student!

The Art Institute's most valuable contribution to students beginning in art is the awareness it gives them of the artist's need to draw upon his own experience, to believe in his own work, and to trust in himself as an artist. The school's essential function is as a place where students can meet and discuss their ideas with people whose main involvement is the same as their own. It is also where they may see the work of others. So its vital function is that of an active community that feeds its members, yet directs them toward totally independent creative efforts.

"This school is like a community," remarked a film-making major. "It's not the academic, Aristotelian school where the teacher leads the students around by the neck. Here, teachers learn from students, too."

"Students criticize each other's work," a girl explained, "so that sometimes you can't tell who's the student and who's the teacher."

A majority of the first-year students like the way the Art Institute is run, but feel that basic technical training in art is conspicuously lacking. They miss the introductory courses that form a substantial part of the curriculum of most art schools:

"I think there should be more regular teaching; so many students don't even know what questions to ask."

"They should offer more substantial courses in techniques, but they should not be compulsory."

"I would like to see this school more structured and organized. I don't relate to teachers here. I wish there was somebody I could talk to about the problems I have in painting."

Several students felt inhibited by what they see as the school's overly exalted view of art. In one girl's words, "This school is too uptight in the sense that there is this intellectual myth and everyone is so involved with himself and his work. Everyone thinks he'll be a great artist."

A printmaking major commented, "Everybody coming into this school is *supposedly* an artist. So everybody has to live with this kind of image. And I think a lot of people are very lost here. They don't really know who they are. And it's a very hard place to find yourself, because there's no structure. And if you don't have your own—or at least an inkling of your own—or any discipline, it's really hard. I think there are a lot of really lonely people. There's nothing they can actually hang onto for a beginning, for a start. There are a lot of really young people here. And they're all trying to live up to this image of an artist. And it's a really hard thing to do. I find myself working sometimes against myself, because I have these high standards. It takes a lot of discipline."

When the students were asked if they thought of themselves as artists, some of their responses were the following.

"An artist is someone who already knows how to organize experience coherently. I wouldn't be here if I were an artist."

"I'd rather say I'm crazy than say I'm an artist. Because 'crazy' means untold vision, infinite vision. Whereas 'artist' means you have a few visions, maybe."

"Yes, I think of myself as an artist. It's something I can identify with."

"Sure. It's a feeling which is becoming more and more involving. The point is that I'm starting to be an artist not only by myself, but with other artists."

Many of the students spoke of their elementary and high school experience as a lonely time when they felt alienated from their peers. The pain experienced because of this loneliness was soothed only through the solace of their art work. But art was not a social experience. It was a very solitary experience that brought a sense of satisfaction, but not a feeling of belonging. Yet it did bring them the approval of others. Their parents often approved of their work, but parents were cited less often as sources of encouragement than were peers and teachers.

Skill in drawing is a talent particularly admired among older children, and in junior high and high school it becomes especially important. In every class there are one or two "good artists" who are asked to do all the school posters and art work. The students who had this experience in school said that the approval of others brought them a sense of self-worth; but at the same time it added an unnatural dimension to what was previously a totally spontaneous and personal creative experience.

For a number of the students interviewed, the Art Institute is the first school where they have felt comfortable. These are the students who were considered odd by their peers in childhood and high school. At the Art Institute, however, they are completely accepted for the first time.

"I hated school," one girl stated. "The dreams I have about it now are filled with monsters. I really had a bad time with other kids. I had long hair and the kids called me a witch."

Another girl spoke of her high school experience, saying, "I felt removed, isolated. I didn't want to, but I did, because I had nothing in common with anybody else. I always did what I wanted and didn't care about pleasing others."

"I really hated school," said another student, "because I can't stand being told what to do."

Several of the boys felt removed from their peers because they were uninterested in sports. And a number of the girls felt they were the only ones at their schools who weren't concerned with conventional feminine subjects. Many students reported feeling older than their peers. And others remembered their high school experience as a time when:

"Other kids looked at me as if I was some kind of a freak."

"I was a lone wolf. And a daydreamer."

"I was really a freak, so lonely."

"The other kids were more dominant, outgoing, and social. I was more interested in being by myself."

"I was quiet and sensitive; I thought a lot. I was alone a lot. People thought I was strange."

Many students found all their high school subjects devoid of interest. They were particularly turned off by the way that art was treated. "In high school, art was just a Mickey Mouse routine," one student sculptor remarked. "Here it's really different."

Though they are no longer freaks within the Art Institute itself, many of these students still experience a strong sense of alienation. One boy said, "I've always felt alienated. I still feel alienated. Everyone at this school does."

Many of the students interviewed place little value in human communication. Some of them felt they relate much more easily to animals and nature than to people.

"I've always felt very detached from people," a 19-year-old boy commented. "Even when I'm talking to someone, I don't feel like I'm really communicating at all."

"As a child, I felt apart," said another student. "I felt closest to the woods and nature—inarticulate things. A tree or my dog seemed to understand me better. People always want to interpret you for themselves."

"Half of my life is my art," stated a student sculptress. "The other half is the outdoors."

Most of the students are more concerned with finding themselves through their art than in communicating with others through it. Their art is, above all, a deeply intimate experience.

"Painting," explained one young girl, "is . . . my most important source of growth."

Most of the students regard art as their only permanent activity—as the necessary and sufficient substance of their lives. As one 19-year-old put it, "Art is the only way I can make it." And an older girl, who had studied other subjects and worked at several jobs before beginning in art, said, "I have to make it in painting or not at all." In none of her previous activities did she feel her identity being tested. Now, in her painting, she has invested herself totally.

Among the other students who felt that their art was their entire reason for being were those who said:

"My sculpture is very important to me. If I wasn't doing it, I'd probably have to cement myself into a wall."

"I couldn't do anything else but paint. Without my painting I don't think I could function. The only thing I could do if I didn't paint would be to undergo some kind of religious discipline. I mean that very seriously. That's the only thing. Anything else would be meaningless."

Few of these students are interested in closing the communication gap between artists and the rest of society:

"The most disturbing thing," said one girl, "is the way nonartists feel about artists. They think that artists have an obligation to make things that are clear and understandable to everybody. That's not true. Artists must work for themselves alone. Nobody asks mathematicians to produce things that are clear to everybody, so why should they ask artists to do it?"

Though many students lamented the fact that most people do not understand artists, even more were glad of it. One of the older students said,

"I used to worry about whether you could make a comfortable place in society and still remain an artist of integrity. I don't care about the comfortable place in society any more. I'm not bothered by what they think. Because I don't want to be in society. It's really a drag. I don't want to go to cocktail parties or any of that stuff. And I don't like running around in a suit and acting important. I don't like explaining my work to a lot of people. The kind of people I'm interested in communicating with are people who really live like I do. A very simple manner. If I ever make any money at what I'm doing, I don't want to live any other way."

The typical first-year student at the Art Institute is giving little thought to the future. His complete involvement in his immediate creative project precludes a preoccupation with the future course of his work or life.

"Right now everything is painting, but in a year from now I don't know what I'll be doing."

"I'd feel like I'd accomplished something by getting my degree, but it's the painting that's most important. Right now painting is a real struggle."

Most of the students interviewed assume that they will stay on four years at the Art Institute and get a degree, though it is something that few of them now dwell upon. Their principal motivation for graduating is to be able to teach art. Nearly half of them hope to teach, as well as to continue working as fine artists.

They seem, though, to be less interested in the satisfaction inherent in the teaching role than in the freedom of an art teacher. As art teachers, they will have a continuing contact with other creative artists. They will also have considerable economic freedom and time for their own work.

"If I have a degree," a ceramics major explained, "then I can teach and be in the art world without having to go get a miserable job."

But among these students are several who do look forward to teaching as a valuable experience in itself:

"I plan to become a teacher," stated one girl. "Art is such an exciting thing that you want to run and call others to participate in it. And teaching is sharing."

Less than a fourth of the students are considering careers other than teaching. Very few are interested in working in commercial art.

Nearly all of them expressed a distaste for regular jobs, which would necessitate routine, working for someone else, and too much time away from their art. Those few who now hold part-time jobs generally dislike the work (usually unrelated to art) that they must do.

The Art Institute curriculum is unique in that it provides training solely in the fine arts. Its graduates are really prepared for just two careers: fine art and teaching fine art. Even in photography, the Art Institute's emphasis is entirely upon photography as an art form, rather than as a salable skill. The small number of students who plan to work in professional careers other than teaching (architecture, advertising, scientific photography, and industrial design) expect to transfer to another school for the bulk of their training.

Several students said they feared the day when they would have to leave the Art Institute:

"I don't want to go out into the world and find a job," said one boy. "I'd be afraid. I don't dig those people and they don't dig me. Here I'm protected—like being in the womb."

Another said, "I have two sides of me that I can't reconcile. One says I should be more active and involved in the future; the other says I couldn't stand it if I were. I don't know which one I believe in."

The Art Institute will not tell this student which side to believe in. It is not an atmosphere of answers, but one of questions. It encourages students to look to their instructors not as authorities but as people more experienced in dealing with the questions of art. The teachers seek to give their students the same freedom that they require for their own creative work. Thus the Art Institute becomes a test of the student's own personal motivation and artistic direction.

The Art Institute's approach toward aesthetic education fails those students who desire a considerable degree of outer control and direction. But for those young artists whose creative potential is realized only in an atmosphere where they can freely pursue their own aesthetic visions, the Art Institute is a rare and satisfying place to study.

CHAPTER TWO

Six Highly Regarded Students in Interview

At the end of their first year at the San Francisco Art Institute, all students were asked to exhibit at least four pieces of work they had completed during that year. These works, chosen by the student artists themselves, were put on display in a single large gallery so that the work of the entire class could be seen at one time. Eight faculty members, many of whom had seen only the work of a few students prior to this occasion, now acted as raters or judges of the work. In brief, they now rated the exhibited work of all first year students relative to one another. They also nominated three students whom they considered to have very high or very low potential for serious work in art.

From among the ten most highly regarded students as determined by the ratings and nominations, three men and three women were selected randomly for inclusion in this chapter. Each had been interviewed during the course of the year, before the year-end exhibition. Their responses to the interview questions are given here without comment. Fictional first names have been assigned them.

I. Sean

Q.   Do you think of yourself as an artist?

A.   I think the ultimate artist is a magician, but there are a lot of stages in between. I live a Bohemian life. Before coming here I cut my hair and my beard to get out of that ego trip; it was a humbling thing. I do it every year, when the sun is in Virgo.

Q.   When did you begin working in art?

A.   September, 1967. I stopped writing poetry, which I did for four years. I did publish things, but I didn't like the public I had. I traveled around for awhile [the South, Boston]. Then came here. I was on the streets for awhile.

Q.   As a child, did you ever sense yourself as different from those around you?

A.   In high school I had access to all social states: athlete, All-American, studious types, beatniks. I wanted to participate in all, but remain aloof from all at the same time.

Q.   Did any experiences or people affect your interest in art?

A.   The main reason for coming to painting was my dissatisfaction with the poetry medium; I couldn't reach enough people, while with painting you can reach lots of people.

Q.   What effect have art classes had on your work?

A.   This place is really loose, not structured. That's why we don't have a revolution here. Classes give me a structure and a discipline which I need. Otherwise I wouldn't be doing anything.

Q.   Do you work best in class or at home? Or other environment?

A.   Where I have more space: my paintings are big, so I need studio space and there isn't much room here. I'll be moving to a new place and then I will do most of my painting alone. See, here painting is an individual trip; it's not a communal thing.

Q.   Do you admire the work of any artists in particular? Who? Why?

A.   Magritte. Van Gogh. Max Ernst. Aries artists—astrological sun sign.

Q.   Are you consciously influenced by their work?

A.   I use the works of others as a reference. My work is different so I have to think by myself. I might be unconsciously influenced, but not consciously.

Q.   Do you think about others' possible reactions to something while working on it? How do you feel about opinions of others (instructors, students, friends)?

A.   I try to do things that the man in the streets can dig, respond to. But if I don't get response, that's cool, too. Mostly I paint because I've things to say, otherwise I wouldn't be here.

The method of instruction that leaves you free to do what you like is the one I prefer.

As instructor I like F.; he's also my friend. He's very loose. This is the opposite and I try to balance my teachers, so I get the best from each one. W. is good too.

Q. Do you like to talk about your work?

A. Not so much. I prefer to let my work stand by itself.

Q. To what extent do materials or techniques affect your work?

A. Depends on particular paintings. There is a great variance. Sometimes I've very technical, sometimes not. The content regulates the form. It's not the opposite. My techniques have to respond with what I have to say.

Q. Do you ever experience an artist's block (inability to work)?

A. When I can't work I consult the stars. They tell me in what direction I should go or on what I should focus in order not to have troubles. It's usually divided into periods.

Q. Are there aspects of your work which you dislike?

A. When I'm not happy with the finished products. Particularly when techniques lack and so my ideas don't come through the way I would like them to.

Q. What changes do you anticipate in your work?

A. I'm now going backward toward the womb: in the direction of the child's awareness. Through the womb and then out.

Q. Are there moods in which you work best?

A. Maybe in the past, not any more. But I have to be pretty well together physically.

Q. What feelings do you experience when beginning work?

A. I start with a drawing, then I paint. Mostly I'm excited. I usually get ideas when I'm working.

Q. What do you feel like doing with something once it's finished?

A. Hanging it up, and look at it, for a couple of months. See if I like it. If I don't, I take it down and use the canvas again.

Q. How important is your art work to your life as a whole?

A. That's what's happening now to me. All my life right now is centered around it. It's what's happening now.

Q. Have you ever tried to work through hang-ups by translating them visually?

A. Whatever comes to my head I put it down in my paintings. I have to get it out.

Q. Has your work ever been a mystical experience?

A. Sure. Not induced by drugs, just by what happens to me, or by my feelings. I've had blinding white lights. When I paint I'm happy, I really enjoy it—but not mystical.

Q.   Would you want to paint if the results did not endure after the making of them?

A.   No. I paint to have the painting. I don't believe in painting as a therapeutic means.

Q.   What aspects of the total work or life of an artist bother you?

A.   To some degree, having to be in touch with other artists. You are forced to listen to their particular painting trip. You listen because you think you can get ideas, but it rarely works.

Q.   To what extent can art be taught?

A.   They can show you what colors to mix, techniques. They cannot teach you concepts or ideas. These either you have or you don't.

Q.   What changes will occur in visual art in the future?

A.   Films will be the happening, particularly because of their possibility as media. Especially animated films. Paintings will continue but more of an elite thing.

Q.   What plans do you have for the future?

A.   I would like to go into animated films, but not for a while.

Q.   Have you ever considered careers or major activities other than art?

A.   I was a poet, as I said, and I also wrote short stories. I would like to play the shenai. Music is very important and can express everything. Sounds are the real thing for the future.

II. Richard

Q.   Do you think of yourself as an artist?

A.   No I don't. Wow! What a question! I don't like to think about it.

Q.   When did you begin working in art?

A.   I've been working in ceramics for two years. I never drew before I came here. Now I'm drawing and painting for the first time. In the 12th grade I had a student-teacher who turned me on to my cousin, whom I'd never met. Then I met him.

Q.   Did any experiences or people affect your interest in art?

A.   My cousin. He's teaching painting now. He's a top artist. He's insane, but everyone appreciates his work. His work is excellent. My student-teacher is the one who got me interested in art. Actually, it was my sister who got me to take a ceramics class. Before that I was really into math.

Q. What effect have art classes had on your work?

A. I went to a junior college and didn't have any art classes. I just worked in art on my own. I've never drawn or painted before. But it's mostly me, because you can't show stuff to teachers until you do it.

Q. Do you work best in class or at home? Or other environment?

A. At school. I don't have the facilities at home or the money to set up a studio. If I had the money, I'd set up my own studio, but I'd still come here to talk to the teachers and show them my work, and to see what was going on.

Q. Do you admire the work of any artists in particular? Who? Why?

A. I like my cousin's work.

Q. Do you think about others' possible reactions to something while working on it? How do you feel about opinions of others (instructors, students, friends)?

A. Sometimes. But if I'm doing something I really like, I won't care. I work for myself.

As to the opinions of others, I like most of the teachers here. It's the students' responsibility to get what they want. I like the way the school's set up. But most of the instructors don't know what I want. They can't answer my questions. But I have to go through my own growth anyway.

Q. Do you like to talk about your work?

A. Yeah. It's helpful.

Q. In comparison to the work of others at the Institute, is your work particularly unique or good?

A. It's different. But I don't see much of the others' work, so I really can't say. Some of my stuff I think is good.

Q. Are there aspects of your work which you dislike?

A. Yeah, there are a lot of things about my work I don't like.

Q. What changes do you anticipate in your work?

A. I want to combine painting, drawing, sculpture, and music. (I play the flute.) I want to paint on sculpture. I want to get into a big environmental thing. Well, I don't know. I'm stuck.

Q. Are there moods in which you work best?

A. I can't always work.

Q. What inhibits your work?

A. Living in the city. So many things hit me, distract me, so I just want to split.

Q. What do you feel like doing with something once it's finished?

A. Throw it away. Except for some things I keep. But there's not too much that I really like after I've finished.

Q. How important is your art work to your life as a whole?

A. That's all there is. Art's going to be my life.

Q. Have you ever tried to work through hang-ups by translating them visually?

A. Yeah—about a year ago I was really mad at people and I made this big huge thing, and it shows my state.

Q. Can you relate your sexuality to your art?

A. Yeah. I made a sex pot—a big, huge pot that you can put flowers in. I think I made some other things.

Q. Have you ever gotten high on working?

A. Oh, yeah.

Q. Would you want to paint if the results did not endure after the making of them?

A. I want some of my stuff. My best work should be kept in the family—somewhere where I'll always have it if I want.

Q. What aspects of the total work or life of an artist bother you?

A. None.

Q. What changes will occur in visual art in the future?

A. For me it's going to be this environmental thing. More people will get into environmental things. But there will still be people doing piecework for galleries.

Q. What plans do you have for the future?

A. I want to just work on my art all my life, and for money. Now I'm a longshoreman. I guess I want to sell my work. I don't know.

I want to go to Japan. But my parents don't want me to. I'll go if I can get a medical deferment—then my parents will let me. I want to work with a Japanese potter.

Q. Have you done any creative writing, composing, performed as a dancer, or played a musical instrument?

A. I used to play the flute. I want to get hold of a Moog synthesizer. There are too many things I'm interested in. I don't know what's going to happen. I'm trying to keep up with sculpture, ceramics, drawing, and painting. But I want to do it all with an environment—with electronics, light, music, and people being part of it.

Q. Is there something that we haven't talked about which affects your work?

A. This school should be more of a community.

I used to make pottery and sell it. It was just crap—but I sold it in a store in Hollywood. One Christmas I made $600. I could have made $1200 if I wanted to.

It's weird. You're talking to me like I'm supposed to be an artist, asking me all these direct questions, and I don't have everything all down.

III. Larry

Q.   Do you think of yourself as an artist?

A.   I suppose so. You have to think of yourself as something.

Q.   When did you begin working in art?

A.   I've been taking pictures since I was 14 or 15. But I hadn't done much art photography before art school. I'd done drawing and painting on my own. As soon as I got into Art and Design in New York, I began with photography.

Q.   As a child, did you ever sense yourself as different from those around you?

A.   My mother thought so. She sent me to a psychiatrist. I thought it was a drag. It was when I was 8 to 11 years old. I didn't care about school. I wasn't interested in getting good grades. I could have if I'd wanted to, but I didn't want to. I didn't get along with things in school.

Q.   How important is your art work to your life as a whole?

A.   It's had a big effect on me—in my whole way of looking at and thinking about things. My photography is just about the most important thing in my life.

Q.   Do your dreams influence or relate to your work?

A.   I always forget my dreams.

Q.   Do you like to talk about your work?

A.   It depends on who you're talking to. I don't like to have to answer questions about anything.

Q.   How would you describe yourself as an artist?

A.   I do a lot of series of photographs. I'm interested in documentation. I think about what they will look like 15 years from now.

Q.   What aspects of the total work or life of an artist bother you?

A.   None, except there's no money in it.

Q.   Do you work best in class or at home? Or other environment?

A.   I work at school mostly. I like to come here at night and work all night. During the day there are too many people.

Q.   Do you think about others' possible reactions to something while working on it? How do you feel about opinions of others (instructors, students, friends)?

A.   Photography can't be just for yourself.

I like this school because of the people. Everything is so loose. I went to a commercial art school before: Art and Design in New York. All the teachers here have their own trip. You can pick out one that's similar to yours.

Q.   What plans do you have for the future?

A.   I'll come back here next year if I can afford it. Last summer I worked making photographs of New York actors for publicity pictures. It wasn't art, though. I'll work in some field of art. Maybe a combination of photography and something else, like painting.

Q.   Have you ever considered careers or major activities other than in art? What?

A.   I almost went into architecture. My mother took me to aptitude tests at N.Y.U. They thought I should be an architect. I went to the class for two days and then dropped out.

Q.   Have you done any creative writing, composing, performed as a dancer, acted, or played a musical instrument?

A.   I've played guitar in groups and gone through the whole rock 'n' roll bit.

Q.   Is there something that we haven't talked about which affects your work?

A.   My mother pays my tuition. And I took out a loan, too.

IV. Polly

Q.   Do you think of yourself as an artist?

A.   In a way, not really. I know that if I weren't in an art school I wouldn't be painting that much.

Q.   When did you begin working in art?

A.   When I was in kindergarten. My mother is an artist so I was encouraged. I did about 10 paintings when I was 13. My mother started an art school a few years ago, and there I was free to paint as much as I liked.

Q.   As a child, did you ever sense yourself as different from those around you?

A.   In a way. I was quiet and sensitive. Also in school I was "the artist." Always had A's in art. But I went along with other children, except when I started to go to a regular high school.

Q.   Did any experiences or people affect your interest in art?

A.   My mother and this experimental high school where I did mostly painting.

Q.   What effect have art classes had on your work?

A. They help me work more. I really like the classes here. It's hard for me to keep up with the humanities classes, because I didn't have those in this experimental high I went to.

Q. Do you work best in class or at home? Or other environment?

A. I don't paint at home, I don't have room. I like to paint here. Although classes are too crowded.

Q. Do you admire the work of any artists in particular? Who? Why?

A. Van Gogh, Dali, Magritte, Blake.

Q. Are you consciously influenced by their work?

A. In a way. I go to the library and study their work and compare it with mine. I went through different stylistic periods (surrealistic, abstract).

Q. Do you think about others' possible reactions to something while working on it? How do you feel about opinions of others (instructors, students, friends)?

A. I would like people to react more, but I don't know many people. But really I don't care that much.

Q. Do you like to talk about your work?

A. Yes, I do.

Q. In comparison to the work of others at the Institute, is your work particularly unique or good?

A. My work is good, but I cannot compare it to that of others. I'm perfecting my style. Also I would like to try different styles, explore them.

Q. Are there aspects of your work which you dislike?

A. Yes. Recently I found that my work is becoming too hard-edged. I want to go into something more flowing. Also my paintings look too flat. I don't like that.

Q. Are there moods in which you work best?

A. When I'm feeling good. If I feel bad, you can tell that from my paintings and that makes me mad.

Q. What inhibits your work?

A. I can feel what's going on in the class, people talking, that disturbs my work.

Q. What feelings do you experience when beginning a work?

A. Scared, because I don't know what I'm going to do.

Q. What feelings do you experience when finishing a work?

A. I feel good. I feel like it's finished. Definitely.

Q. What do you feel like doing with something once it's finished?

A. Showing it to somebody and having their opinions. I really like to have people looking over my work.

Q. How important is your art work to your life as a whole?

A.   Pretty important. If I didn't have it, I wouldn't know what to do. I might be a straight girl and look for a job, or else I'd be a bum.

Q.   Have you ever tried to work through hang-ups by translating them visually?

A.   I used to. Just take pieces of chalk and express my anger. I don't do it any more.

Q.   Do your dreams influence or relate to your work?

A.   Yes, I dream a lot and I would like to be able to paint them. I try to, but it doesn't work out very well. My paintings are dreams anyway.

Q.   Have you ever had a mystical experience or vision?

A.   Yes, when I am on some drug. I took mescaline when I was 15, it was really a powerful experience.

Q.   Would you want to paint if the results did not endure after the making of them?

A.   Yes. I used to give away my paintings and throw my drawings away anyway.

Q.   What aspects of the total work or life of an artist bother you?

A.   Well, the fact that people look down on you as if you were a bum. But I don't mind it too much, because I know I'm doing something creative at least. Also artists make little money, but I couldn't get any other job anyway.

Q.   Can art be taught?

A.   Yes, to a certain extent. You can teach techniques, but people have to learn by themselves how to paint. They can learn something from teachers, particularly colors and shadings, no more. That's why I like the loose type of classes here.

Q.   What plans do you have for the future?

A.   I wish I could get a scholarship here. If not, I might go to another school.

Q.   Have you ever considered careers or major activities other than in art? What?

A.   I really liked biology when I was in school. I might go back to it later on.

Q.   Have you done any creative writing, composing, performed as a dancer, acted, or played a musical instrument?

A.   I've done a lot with encounter groups, etc., bioenergetics. I think I could lead an encounter group. The only other thing I've tried is sculpture.

Q.   Is there something that we haven't talked about which affects your work?

A.   I wish they had here some sort of seminar or encounter group so that students can get together and get to know each other better, also express their ideas and feelings.

V. Virginia

Q. Do you think of yourself as an artist?

A. I consider myself a drama major. But I am into so many things, I couldn't tell. I consider myself quite a good actress.

Q. When did you begin working in art?

A. I was born with a talent for acting.

Q. As a child, did you ever sense yourself as different from those around you?

A. I like to think that I did. Well, I really felt isolated in that all-girl school I went to: I had a strong Southern accent. I thought that all the girls were snobs.

Q. Did any experiences or people affect your interest in art?

A. My parents were both artists. My mother is a painter—my father a photographer and an actor, movies and theater, also TV.

Q. Do you work best in class or at home? Or other environment?

A. Here, particularly when there are people and a lot of noise.

Q. Do you think about others' possible reactions to something while working on it? How do you feel about opinions of others (instructors, students, friends)?

A. I guess I'm not sure of myself enough and I need others' opinions.

Q. Are there aspects of your work which you dislike?

A. I'm pleased with what I'm doing. The results may not be that good, though.

Q. Are there moods in which you work best?

A. I'm happy only when I am busy. Moods (particularly when I am angry) affect the result of my painting.

Q. What do you feel like doing with something once it's finished?

A. I save them.

Q. What plans do you have for the future?

A. Maybe teaching. The theater is a hard and unfair life. It's hard just to keep your head above the water. I can always go back to acting, but I've decided I wanted first to get a good look at art. Then I might want to go to college where I can get those courses, like psychology or geology, that I cannot get here.

Q. Have you done any creative writing, composing, performed as a dancer, acted, or played a musical instrument? If so, how do these experiences relate to your art (now)?

A. Acting, dancing—creative writing. I had two years of piano—had a singing class. All my art work has to do with people, all my photographs are of people. I guess that this is the connection with the theater.

VI. Amy

Q. Do you think of yourself as an artist?

A. No. I'm beginning to now, though. I think I'm afraid to be an artist.

Q. When did you begin working in art?

A. When I was about 9 or 10. Lots of people in my family are artists: my brother, my father, my grandmother. Everyone criticized my work. So when I left home, I wanted to get away from art. So I didn't paint again until I came here.

Q. As a child, did you ever sense yourself as different from those around you?

A. Oh, yeah. I thought I was an artist then.

Q. Did any experiences or people affect your interest in art?

A. I took a photography class at the high school I was going to. The teacher was really great. As far as art is concerned, I really did have it in me, but I'd been holding it back. And it just came out—like madness—when I picked up a camera. Everything happened. Photography is a social art. I like to take pictures of people.

Q. What effect have art classes had on your work?

A. I hadn't painted for two years before I came here, and then I started again. I'm not sure yet whether photography is more important to me than painting. Photography is more usable.

I like the freedom here at this school. There should be more technique courses, though. You're more stimulated by the people than by the work here. There's not much basic work that you have to do. You just do what you want—you do your own thing. They should offer more substantial courses in techniques. Not compulsory, but if you want to, you can take them.

Q. Do you work best in class or at home? Or other environment?

A. I like to work at home if I'm sure about what I'm involved in. If I'm looking for more stimulation, I'd rather work here.

Q. Are your best ideas arrived at in solitude or company?

A. I like to take pictures of people in relationships.

Q. Do you admire the work of any artists in particular? Who? Why?

A. Magritte, Cartier-Bresson.

Q. Are you consciously influenced by their work?

A. Right now I'm influenced by everyone. I don't really have a style yet of my own. I'm just a beginner.

Q. Do your think about others' possible reactions to something while working on it? How do you feel about opinions of others (instructors, students, friends)?

A. Photography is more for communicating with people than the other arts. I want people to look at things and think. If it doesn't mean anything to them, then it's not really art.

Q. Do you like to talk about your work?

A. Not really. I'd rather do it. Maybe when I've done it more, I will.

Q. In comparison to the work of others at the Institute, is your work particularly unique or good?

A. Mine is different from a lot of people here. But I can't think about levels. Everyone is an individual.

Q. What changes do you anticipate in your work?

A. I'm really just beginning here. A lot more is going to happen while I'm here.

Q. Are there moods in which you work best?

A. If I'm feeling violent and angry, my work comes out violent and angry.

Q. What do you feel like doing with something once it's finished?

A. Throwing it away. I did do one painting that I'd like to keep though. My photographs are more personal than my paintings.

Q. How important is your art work to your life as a whole?

A. It used to be really important. I just don't know any more. Now I'm not sure any more.

Q. Have you ever tried to work through hang-ups by translating them visually?

A. Yes. I haven't done enough of that. I should do more of it.

Q. Would you want to paint if the results did not endure after the making of them?

A. I enjoy the process more than the result. Keeping things sometimes inhibits me. I prefer to throw things away.

Q. What aspects of the total work or life of an artist bother you?

A. You have to look at everything deeper down than most people. Sometimes for me it's hard to face what I see.

Q. What plans do you have for the future?

A. This school has given me so many channels that I don't know which one I will pursue yet. When I was working on my own I was sure of my direction. Now I'm not.

I have no idea at all. Oh, I do have some ideas for series of photographs. I don't think I want to continue here for four years. I want to try other areas besides art. Like marine biology. I think I'll always work in photography. But I don't have any plans.

I've always been interested in biology. It's really interesting to me. I'm not sure what I'll do with it. I've thought about being a reporter. I wish I were brave enough to be a reporter. I wanted to be a veterinarian, an architect, and to work in electronics.

I've done architectural drafting.

Q. Have you done any creative writing, composing, performed as a dancer, acted, or played a musical instrument?

A. I was going to be a writer. I always wrote a lot. I've written songs. Music is really personal to me.

CHAPTER THREE

Sex Differences in Self-Definition and Motivation

One of the things we had hoped to find from the interviews presented in the two preceding chapters was whether or not one could predict which of these students would be most likely to continue their work in art. Could we find some signs that would tell us which ones would pass through their student days and develop later on into artists with a lifetime commitment to their career?

As we looked closely at the interviews to try to answer this question, another question of great interest was generated. Were there differences between the men and women students that might relate to their potential as artists? Did they differ in consistent and noticeable ways? We knew from work already done on creativity that those personality correlates generally ascribed to one sex or the other are much less pronounced in creative people (Barron, 1968). Creative women have fewer "feminine" traits and more "masculine" interests than noncreative control groups. Sex-specific interests and traits that are descriptive of men and women in general seem to break down when we examine creative people.

However, looking at the interviews of the students at the Art Institute, one can find striking differences in intensity and in practicality being expressed by the students. Such differences do not show up on a more general personality test, as we shall see in the next chapter. There may be many reasons why they escape detection, but one is that psychological tests rarely reflect intensity of motivation. In any case, based on these interviews, one can state unequivocally that the men are far more passionate than the women about their commitment to their art work.

We see immediately a dramatic difference when we look at the answers to the question *Do you think of yourself as an artist?* Of those who answered, most of the women said *no* (67%), but most of the men said *yes* (66%). The men already think of themselves as artists. The women are not nearly so ready to view themselves as artists—student artists, perhaps, but not artists, not yet.

When the students were asked, *In comparison to the work of others at the Institute, is your work particularly unique or good?,* another sex difference in answers was noticed. Forty percent of the men but only 17% of the women felt their work was of superior quality. (Perhaps in answering this question in this way the girls are more realistic, but the difference in self-image as an artist is our main concern.) And in fact, 36% of the women but only 14% of the men felt that their work was inferior *in comparison to others at the Institute.* Thus the percentages are almost reversed; 40% of the men felt their work was superior, only 14% that it was inferior; whereas almost 40% of the women felt their work was inferior, only 17% that it was superior.

None of the differences we find between the men's and the women's evaluations of their work would be startling if, in fact, the men did produce better art work. But this is not the case. When all the students' art was rated by a large and varied number of judges, the women's work ranked as highly as the men's did. There were no discrepancies in ability or quality of work based on sex differences. The quality of the women's art work was equally high.

The quality of the women's intensity and commitment to art, however, is not nearly as strong. The men in their interviews make statements like "If I couldn't paint, I would rather die," or "If I couldn't sculpt, I would cement myself into a wall."

Nowhere in any part of the interview do any of the women make such statements. When the question was asked, *How important is your art work to your life as a whole?,* the men answered with "...It *is* my life"; "...I believe art is the only thing I was born for"; or "...I couldn't do anything else. Without painting I couldn't function."

These are not isolated or dramatic responses, but rather the typical response of the men. They stand in great contrast to the kinds of answers the women gave. None of the women said anything nearly approximating the kind of dedication expressed by the men's intense statements. Only one woman said her work was "essential" to her life. The rest answered like this:

". . . It's pretty important."

". . . It's half my life, the other half is my future family."

". . . I'm not sure yet, but I like it."

". . . It's helpful but not an absolute."

". . . It's most important right now, maybe when I have my baby that will be another source of growth."

Only one of the men said his art took second place (after his "wife and kids") but even he said "third, I put clothing and food." Of those who answered this question, fewer than 40% of the women considered their work in art to be very important. Almost 70% of the men felt that their art work was very important to their life as a whole.

Nowhere in the women's interviews could we find any indication of the passion with which the men approach their work. Some of the men speak of the canvas, colors, and cameras as if they were alive. "My photography isn't separated from my life. The two things aren't separated at all. They can't be." Some see their work as themselves. "I am my work." And for some, their work is an encounter with a lover or a deity.

". . . My painting is the only thing that gives me a real happiness, real ectasy."

". . . Painting is a love for me. I cannot live if I don't love my old lady [girlfriend] and my painting."

". . . I've passed out painting sometimes, I get so stoned with my work."

". . . Painting to me is like praying."

Such statements reveal a very high degree of motivation and dedication in the men students, a dedication that is just not expressed by women art students. But there are, besides the abstract quality of dedication, some very real, concrete demands made on all artists. An artist must be able to deal in a realistic way with the requirements of making a living in a society that does not often appreciate or understand his work. How a young art student prepares himself to face such concrete challenges must have some bearing on his ability to pursue his art work in the future. There is a curious difference in answers to one question, which attempted to learn something about the psychodynamics of the creative outlook but which may instead, or in addition, be tapping into a quality of concreteness or perhaps even realism.

The question is *Would you want to paint (etc.) if the results did not endure after the making of them?* All the women who answered this question said they would still want to paint. Only half the men, however, said they would still want to paint. Maybe the women are more interested in "art for art's sake" or maybe the men are more practical. (The psychodynamic interpretation might be that for the man the works of art are his children, whereas women can have their own real children.) Be that as it may, answers to other questions definitely show that not only are men more intense in their expression of commitment to art, they are also more realistic in their responses to society's demands on them. The men are far more concerned with the financial difficulties of an artist's life. For example, in response to the question *What aspects of the total work or life of an artist bother you?,* the women expressed a greater diversity of dissatisfaction. They were concerned about such things as:

". . . conflicts with being a conscientious mother";

". . . artists limit themselves to relations with other artists":

". . . It's so unstable if you have other people to take care of";

". . . People don't like dirty, grubby artists";

". . . You have to look at everything deeper than most people. Sometimes it's hard for me to face what I see."

Some of the women did mention the financial difficulties, but in general their concerns were more social or intellectual than economic: how they would relate to their families and friends; what other people thought of them; how introspective one had to be; and so on. In general, the concerns of the men were far less subtle. A few men worried about society's view of artists, but most of the men said things like:

". . . it's almost impossible to make a living out of it";

". . . being dependent on other people to buy my work to keep [myself] alive;

". . . having to work other than on your painting";

". . . the probability that I will not be able to eat";

". . . the lack of money."

The men are thus more concerned with the financial difficulties that may await them. And, as if in response to that concern, the men are more interested in getting a degree than are the women. To be sure, not all the men want a degree or even have plans for the future. Of the men, 15% said they have no future plans, whereas 30% of the women said the same. And in general the women are less clear about what they want to do with their art work. Of those who do say what they want to do, most express a desire to teach children. Most of the men want to teach also, but none of them mentioned teaching children. If they talk of an institution at all, it is likely to be a place similar to the Art Institute.

Supporting the general impression that the male students see their art as a career commitment and are more practical about it, the men are more ready to undertake commercial work: 60% of the women and 70% of the men hope to use their training at the Institute to prepare themselves for a career in art. But the men again are considerably clearer about what they will do. They are more often specific about the kind of activity in which they will engage themselves for pay.

It was clear from these interviews that the men students, although they are no more gifted than the women, seem much more likely to pursue their work in art. The men are more intense in their motivation to be an artist and they have a more realistic sense of the role of an artist. The women are less likely to display singlemindedness in their commitment to art. Their concerns are more diffuse, involving a variety of considerations and covering broader areas of life. Even those women who recognize their own talents mention other considerations:

". . . I'm looking for communication in my work";

". . . I wish they had some sort of seminar or encounter group here so that students can get together to know each other better";

". . . All my art work has to do with people."

These last three statements, which were made by the three women students who are considered to be among the most talented and to have the greatest potential as artists by the faculty at the Institute, are not incongruous with the rest of the interviews with women. These statements reveal concerns that the men do not express.

What becomes of these students? Who will continue? Perhaps it is not surprising that in recent years none of the women graduates of the Art Institute has gone on to have a one-person show. We are still a long way from giving any definitive answers that might explain why the women seem to be less intense in their motivation to become an artist. A contributing reason might be that in this society artistic pursuits are considered feminine. These men have had to overcome the negative associations and the financial strains of being an artist. After all, what could be further from the American ideal than a son who wants to be a painter—unless it is a son who wants to be a ballet dancer? Then, too, many of the women probably will marry and have children, making their creative energies unavailable for work as an artist.

CHAPTER FOUR

A Psychometric Portrait of the Student Artist

We have heard these students speak of themselves and their goals in life. Their own words tell the story better than our words can. Still, it is interesting to compare what they will say, not in their own words but in selected standard phrases, with the responses of people who are not artists.

Selected standard phrases are what a psychological questionnaire consists of. "I would rather walk than run in a rainstorm"—True or False? The shortcomings of questionnaires are so obvious that they are hardly worth discussing. Psychologists continue to use them, however, for a good reason: the standard phrase can be presented to thousands of persons of known age, sex, education, socioeconomic class, occupation, or whatever, and their responses tallied to yield a picture of a given group as a whole compared with other groups. Moreover, when the phrases are assembled into sets, or psychological scales, on the basis of their known relationship, either to one another or to some external characteristic of persons or groups, a profile of scores on such scales may be interpreted configurationally to give a complex picture of an individual's way of being.

In the present research, two groups of student artists were given two standardized questionnaires that attempt to measure personality patterns. The two tests, administered variously to students at the San Francisco Art Institute and the Rhode Island School of Design, were (1) the Minnesota Multiphasic Personality Inventory (MMPI); and (2) the California Psychological Inventory (CPI). The San Francisco Art Institute students took the second of these; the Rhode Island School of Design students took the first.

The numerical results are presented in tabular form in the Appendix, a policy we shall follow in general throughout this book; in the text itself, the results will be presented discursively and will be discussed in general rather than technical terms as far as possible.

I. The Tests

A. THE MINNESOTA MULTIPHASIC PERSONALITY INVENTORY (MMPI)[1]

The Minnesota Multiphasic is completely objective in its scoring and is explicit in its use of the normative approach to psychological measurement. It consists of 550 simple declarative sentences, which the respondent is asked to consider one at a time and to say *true* or *false* to. The "normality" of the response is then appraised in terms of its agreement with the consensus of normal adults. One of the sentences, for example, is "I believe there is a God," to which most people say *true.* Another is "I am a special agent of God," to which most people say *false.* Without giving away any trade secrets, we can probably suggest that saying *true* to the latter sentence is more likely to be associated with a serious form of pathology, whatever the actual truth of the matter may be. Leaving the particular example aside, the point is that the test itself is based upon a method of *interpreting responses to a specially designed situation,* and the *mode of responding* rather than the *actual truth or falsity* of the 550 statements as they apply to the respondent is what interests the psychologist.

The scoring, then, is carried out according to certain hard-and-fast rules. Let us consider a fictional example for the development of a scale to measure hypochondriasis, which is in fact one of the variables measured by the MMPI.

---

[1] The following description of the MMPI is virtually identical with a description of the test and its rationale published earlier in the technical appendix, pp. 278–280, of *Creativity and Psychological Health* (Barron, 1963). So too is a later description of the Rorschach.

A hypochondriac is a person who is continually complaining about his health when there does not really seem to be very much wrong with him. Suppose that 100 hypochondriacs are asked to say *true* or *false* to the statement "I have had a backache within the past month," and that 65 of them say *true.* Then the same statement is presented to 100 normal adults in good health, and 12 of them say *true.* This 53% difference based on a comparison of groups of this size would rarely occur just by chance; that is, if we could compare *all* hypochondriacs with *all* normal adults, we would very probably find that the observed difference is a real one. We shall have occasion frequently in reporting research results to refer to "statistical significance" or "level of confidence," and generally this is what we mean: that an observed difference has only a slight likelihood (one chance in 20, or one chance in 100, or one chance in 1000) of being an error of observation, and that on statistical grounds we can specify our degree of confidence that the observed difference is a real one.

But let us return to the development of our scale to measure a person's similarity to hypochondriacs. We now have one sentence or "item" to include in such a scale. By looking at the percentage differences for another 549 items, we might find several dozen items that meet our standards for confidence that hypochondriacs differ from normal adults in their responses. We would now include all such items in a scale, and for each item that the test respondent answers in the same way as a hypochondriac does, he would get a score of 1. The total number of items for which he received a score on our Hypochondriasis scale would now constitute his "scale score."

A difficulty arises, however, if we have more than one scale in our test and if the number of items and the average scores differ for each scale. This difficulty can be solved by using *standard scores,* which in the case of the MMPI is accomplished by making the average score for each scale arbitrarily equal to 50. Dispersion of scores around the average can also be taken into account; in the particular test we are considering, about 68% of all scale scores will fall between 40 and 60, and about 95% between 30 and 70. This provides an immense convenience for the interpreter of the test results, since he can now plot a psychograph of scores on many scales (hence, *multiphasic*), all of which have the same average and the same metric for describing variation.

The actual clinical scales of the MMPI are Hypochondriasis (*Hs*); Depression (*D*); Hysteria (*Hy*); Psychopathic deviation (*Pd*); Masculinity-femininity (*Mf*); Paranoia (*Pa*); Psychasthenia (*Pt*); Schizophrenia (*Sc*); and Hypomania (*Ma*). In work with normal subjects and especially with creative individuals, we have found that these scale names have to be taken with a grain of salt, even when the score is quite high, such as in the top one-tenth of 1% of the general population. Any single score must always be interpreted in terms of the context of scores, as well as in terms of the situational context and the emotional meaning of test taking to the subject. The test itself does have certain built-in "validity indicators" as well, designed to measure aspects of test-taking attitude, and recently there has been much research into the whole question of the influence upon scores of the very human wish to impute to oneself only those traits that are considered socially desirable.

The Minnesota Multiphasic Personality Inventory was developed by S. R. Hathaway and J. C. McKinley at the University of Minnesota in the late 1930's. An early publication describing its development appeared in the *Journal of Psychology* in 1940 under the title, "A Multiphasic Personality Schedule: I. Construction of the Schedule," with Hathaway and McKinley as authors.

The reader who wishes to acquaint himself in a reasonably technical fashion with the problem of statistical inference and the establishment of confidence limits should see *Psychological Statistics* by McNemar (1962), for an especially lucid and useful discussion of these topics. Chapters 4 and 5, titled, respectively, "The Normal Curve and Probability" and "Sampling Errors and Statistical Inference," are most relevant.

B. The California Psychological Inventory (CPI)

A comprehensive attempt to provide inventory-type measures of the positive aspect of personal function has been made by Harrison G. Gough. He has incorporated measures developed over a period of some 10 years into a single test, the California Psychological Inventory (CPI). Like the MMPI, it is based on item analysis of simple declarative sentences answered *true* or *false* (in fact, many of the items are drawn from the MMPI item pool) by groups of persons possessed of known attributes in terms of socially observable behavior. The Socialization (*So*) scale, for example, is based on a comparison of civil prisoners, juvenile delinquents, school disciplinary problems, and the like, with normal adults and with persons selected for their exemplary social behavior. Again, as with the MMPI, one must be cautious about accepting the scale names at face value, especially when extremely high or extremely low scores are earned. One scale, for example, is named "Self-acceptance" (*Sa*), but very high scores seem to be associated with a lack of the ordinary amount of self-criticality, so that the high-scoring subjects appear not so much self-accepting as self-satisfied, in the negative sense of the latter term. Gough himself has been careful in qualifying interpretations based on CPI scales, pointing to the necessity to consider patterns of scores as well as changing implications of scores in certain ranges.

In addition to Socialization and Self-acceptance, the CPI provides measures of these dimensions: Sense of Well-being (*Wb*); Responsibility (*Re*); Tolerance (*To*); Flexibility (*Fx*); Capacity for Status (*Cs*), Dominance (*Do*); Social Participation (*Sp*); Intellectual Efficiency (*Ie*); Motivation to Achieve via Conformance (*Ac*); Motivation to Achieve via Independence (*Ai*); Self-control (*Sc*); Psychological-mindedness (*Py*); Desire to Make a Good Impression (*Gi*); and, finally, Femininity (*Fe*). In addition, there are scales to measure tendencies toward carelessness or falsification in responding and to identify persons who exaggerate their problems or overstate complaints.

The method employed in this chapter for interpreting the CPI results is configural analysis (Gough, 1965). The meaning of each scale varies, depending on the height of other scales and the differential elevation of clusters of scales. For example, an elevation of both Achievement via Conformance and Achievement via Independence scales indicates a different pattern of traits than elevation on one or the other alone. Configural analysis takes into account such factors as the overall profile elevation, clusters of scales, unique contradictions between scales, and the internal variability of the profile. Profile analysis necessarily involves higher-level inference than consideration of each scale separately. Further information about scale interpretation can be found in the CPI *Manual* (Gough, 1965) and the CPI interpreter's syllabus (Gough, 1968). Means and standard deviations for CPI scales in the present study are presented in Table 1 in the Appendix.

The picture of the student artist that emerges from the questionnaire results is consistent from test to test.

II. Results

A. THE CALIFORNIA PSYCHOLOGICAL INVENTORY

The student artists as a group stand out most in terms of broad attitudes toward themselves and others, notably high Flexibility and Psychological-mindedness, and in terms of their deviation from the usual cultural goals of social responsibility, dependability, and self-control. They are less well "socialized," more impulsive, and less interested in "making a good impression" than most people are. At the same time, however, they are poised, confident, and self-accepting. They show little interest in achievement within an ordered structure that demands much social conformance, such as a typical high school might, or a business; yet they do show an above-average desire to achieve and to be successful on their own, through independent effort. Despite their greater independence, flexibility, and insight, they report less of a sense of well-being than others; their typical mood is certainly not blithe or cheerful.

The CPI, then, gives an overall picture of an individualistic, original, energetic person with flexible controls, socially aware but uninterested in timetables and heavy responsiblity, attuned to his own experience and seeking self-actualization while having his share, or more than his share, of the miseries.

It is of special interest, in view of apparent sex differences in motivation and life goals, that the female pattern on the CPI is almost identical to the male as regards high and low scores. One finds the expected difference on Femininity, with the females scoring much higher; otherwise, however, there is a significant difference only on Tolerance, again with the females scoring higher.

B. The Minnesota Multiphasic Personality Inventory

The MMPI profiles for each sex separately are presented in Table 2. One of the most noticeable features of both male and female profiles is that *all* of the scales are elevated above the mean of 50. In addition, there is considerable evidence of what is usually considered pathology in the profile, with the higher scores occurring on the "psychotic" end of the profile, including schizophrenia (*Sc*) and hypomania (*Ma*); and the *F* scale, usually taken as an indicator of bizarre thought, is elevated above 60. At the same time, however, there is no evidence for the usual personality rigidity and symptom formation of truly bizarre types. It is noteworthy that the Ego-strength (*Es*) scale mean score is well above the average of clinic samples. The *K* scale occurs in a range showing realistic behavior, flexibility, and adaptability. The psychopathic deviation score at this level of elevation and in this context can be taken to indicate breadth of interest and spontaneity as well as a certain amount of churlishness. Hysteria (*Hy*) and paranoia (*Pa*) scores are moderate and show a balanced control of aggression without suppression; the mean-average score on social introversion (*Si*) indicates a normal interest in friends and company. In this context, the high *F, Sc,* and *Pt* scores betoken openness, unconventionality, and originality, not unaccompanied by anxiety. The overall profile for both men and women suggests a flexible, energetic personality unusually open to experience, suffering some distress, and yet well equipped to handle its own complexity and uniqueness.

The male artists as a group present on the MMPI a portrait that might be called the "gentleman pirate" motif. They show an independence of thought and unconventionality that leads them to unusual conclusions and experiences. They are flexible, creative, and spontaneous, and there is a certain flair to their personal style. They move toward life with vigor, seeking experience with a restlessness, expansiveness, and enthusiasm that may shade into irritability or quick flashes of anger (*F, Pd, Ma*). This slight swagger to their walk, however, is tempered by a civilized sensitivity to nuance. They see themselves as polite, sensitive, rational, empathic, and fair, with some detachment and capacity for reserve (*K, Hy, Mf*). There is an awareness of the basic requirements of social living, with a sense of individuality and freedom within these broad outlines (high *Es*). This apparent balance between spontaneity and restraint, structure and chaos, is achieved at some cost. Both verve and sensitivity seem to depend on an openness to experience, including heightened sensitivity to one's own physical and mental operations, which brings in its wake intrapsychic struggle and complexity (*F, Hs, Sc*). Feelings of anxiety, perplexity, and isolation are experienced, not repressed (*Sc, Pt*). The group profile of these students seems to indicate an evolving structure; nothing is settled, conflict must be solved, not denied. In the process, the usual aggressive go-getter male role is left behind, its place taken by an emphasis on internal complexity, sensitivity, and a differentiated response to life (high *Mf*).

The female pattern on the MMPI is quite similar to that of the male. For standard scores, the mean difference between the male and female scores is 2.08, with a range of from 1 to 4 points. The profile configuration for the standard scores is essentially the same. The female art student shows a similar set of traits relative to her own sex as the male does relative to his.

The female student of design, like the male, is independent in thought, unconventional, flexible, creative, open. She approaches life with the same vigor, tempering spontaneity with an awareness of social necessities and a sensitivity to nuance. She also is complex, open to experience, and capable of dealing with the feelings of doubt such openness may bring. The main difference between the two profiles seems to be that the female pattern is rather a slightly less flamboyant, more naive, more introverted version of the male. She describes herself as somewhat calmer and less anxious than the male (*Pt, Sc*). She shows a slightly more introverted attitude and may spend more time with fantasy and imagination than he does (*Sc*). When she approaches the outside world, however, she may be less sophisticated than the male, more naively enthusiastic than he, and at the same time, more innocently blunt and forthright in her opinions (*Hy, D*). Compared to other women, however, she would appear strong-minded, extremely independent, and adventurous (*Pd, Ma*). Her vigor, flexibility, and complexity would decidedly set her apart from her more conservative feminine peers.

III. Some Additional Test Results

A. THE STRONG VOCATIONAL INTEREST BLANK (SVIB)

Based on national sample of members of some 51 occupations, the SVIB permits description of any given individual in terms of the *similarity of his interests* to those of these 51 occupational groups.

The results for the class of 1972, San Francisco Art Institute, are presented in Table 3. As the table shows, the interests of these students most closely resembled, in order of decreasing similarity, the following occupations: Musician; Artist; Author-journalist; Advertising Man; and Architect. Scores on all these occupational scales were in the *A* range on the test for the average student; in the usual counseling situation, this would be interpreted as meaning that all the indicated professions were very good bets for the individual in choosing a career. In the *B+* range we find Physician, Psychologist, and Lawyer. Most, if not all, of these occupations call for creativity and the ability to communicate with other people.

Very low scores (all in the *C* range) were obtained by the average art student on the following scales (in order from lowest on up): Army Officer, Accountant, Purchasing Agent, Industrial Arts Teacher, Banker, Office Worker, Policeman, Credit Manager, Farmer, Production Manager, Vocational Agriculture Teacher, Business Education Teacher, School Superintendent, YMCA Physical Director, and Veterinarian. What are rejected are occupations calling for the management (or sometimes coercion) of people and things, or relationships emphasizing the physical, practical, and economic rather than the intellectual or creative.

B. PERSONAL PHILOSOPHY

Two scales of the Inventory of Personal Philosophy (Barron, 1968) were administered: the Independence of Judgment scale, and the Artistic Values scale (originally called Preference for Complexity).

The Independence of Judgment scale was developed by correlating item responses on the inventory with actual behavior in the Asch "independence of judgment" experiment (Asch, 1952; Barron, 1953a). The basic experimental technique employed by Asch was to place an individual in radical conflict of judgment with all the other members of a group and to express quantitatively certain aspects of his mode of resolution of the conflict. Pressure was exerted upon the individual to agree with what was in fact a false consensus of the group. The Independence of Judgment scale is highly correlated with maintenance of independent and correct judgment in such circumstances. This inventory scale has been shown (Barron, 1953a, 1955; Helson, 1965) to be significantly predictive of creativity. In recent studies by Child (1962, 1964), the Independence of Judgment scale has been shown to be significantly positively correlated with Child's test of aesthetic judgment (to be described later) in both American and Japanese samples.

The verbal scale to measure similarity to artists in philosophic values (the Artistic Values scale) was developed by correlating true–false inventory items of the Inventory of Personal Philosophy with scores on the Barron–Welsh Art Scale in several samples of college students and medical school students. In a sample of 180 college students it correlated .67 with scores on the Figure Preference Art scale. Among the significant items in the scale that buttress the interpretation of it as reflecting similarity to the philosophy of life of artists are the following.

I think I take primarily an aesthetic view of experience.   (True)

The unfinished and the imperfect often have greater appeal for me than the completed and the polished.   (True)

I could cut my moorings—quit my home, my parents, and my friends—without suffering great regrets.   (True)

Many of my friends would probably be considered unconventional by other people.   (True)

Some of my friends think that my ideas are impractical, if not a bit wild.   (True)

I don't like modern art.   (False)

Perfect balance is the essence of all good composition.   (False)

I much prefer symmetry to asymmetry.   (False)

I would rather be a steady and dependable worker than a brilliant but unstable one.   (False)

Straightforward reasoning appeals to me more than than metaphors and the search for analogies.   (False)

This scale, too, has shown impressive validities for the prediction of creativity, not only in architecture and creative writing but in science and mathematics as well (Barron, 1963; MacKinnon, 1962; Helson, 1965; Hall & MacKinnon, 1965).

Results for the Art Institute students are presented in Table 4, together with some comparable statistics for other groups. As Table 4 shows, the student artists earn markedly high scores on both scales. The findings are certainly consistent with the general picture we obtain from the personality and interest inventories.

These students were also asked to rate a set of 12 statements relevant to their actual work, using a 10-point scale. Inspection of the average ratings assigned these statements revealed five that received strong endorsement and two that received noticeably low ratings. The highly endorsed statements were:

1. I have definite feelings about most art work I see.
2. I prefer working on my own rather than in class.
3. I completely lose myself while working, forgetting all personal matters.
4. I like my own work.
5. I can bring my emotional life into visual imagery.

Uncharacteristic or low-rated statements were:

1. I do better work in class than out of class.
2. I am influenced by the work of the other students.

Once again, these self-descriptions are consistent with other results and bespeak a high degree of independence and dedication.

C. THE BARRON-WELSH ART SCALE

This test reflects the opinion of artists themselves as to the aesthetic appeal of certain figure drawings. It was developed by comparing the preferences of artists with those of nonartists, using a set of 400 figures as the initial item pool. The final scale consists of 62 items, 38 of which are preferred consistently more often by artists. It is scored in such a fashion that a higher score indicates greater similarity to artists in one's preferences.

Since its development in 1950, the Barron–Welsh Art Scale has been used extensively in research relevant to the topics of perceptual preferences, aesthetic discrimination, and creativity. It has repeatedly been found to have significant validities against criteria of originality and creativity, even in highly selected samples of artists, research scientists, writers, and architects.

Personality correlates of the scale have been reported in detail elsewhere (Barron, 1953b) and need only be summed up here. The following relationships were noted.

1. Preference for figures liked by artists is related positively to rapid personal tempo, verbal fluency, impulsiveness, and expansiveness.

2. It is related negatively to rigidity, control of impulse by repression, social conformity, ethnocentrism, and political-economic conservatism.

3. It is related positively to independence of judgment, originality, and breadth of interest.

We shall not be concerned primarily with validities, but with reporting descriptive statistics and giving some idea of the range of sampling. Table 5 shows means and standard deviations on the Barron–Welsh Art Scale for various samples of subjects studied at the Institute of Personality Assessment and Research from 1950 to the present, as well as the statistics for the Art Institute students. The latter score slightly lower than the original sample of outstanding artists, but are quite high by comparison with other groups.

IV. Summary

The psychometric results presented in this chapter confirm the expectations one might have formed from the interviews with students and from the description of the school given both by students and by its director.

In personality, the students are notably independent and unconventional, vivid in gesture and expression, rather complex psychodynamically but with an emphasis upon openness, spontaneity, and whimsicality rather than neurotic complicatedness. They are very much like other artists—including musicians and writers—in their interest patterns and in their aesthetic preferences.

Their pattern of interests is appropriate to some extent to any profession calling for intellectual creativity. The distinction between profession and vocation does seem apt, however; these students most strongly *value* art and the independent way of life, and this has determined their vocational choice.

In brief, they choose to do what they value most, and this itself sets them apart from many apparently better adjusted people who are doing what they would rather not.

CHAPTER FIVE

Comparative Performances of the
San Francisco Art Institute Students on Tests

The aim of this chapter is to supply the interested reader with further information about tests used in the San Francisco Art Institute study. Tests that have not already been fully described in the text are described here. The Appendix provides a detailed listing of all the tests, with means and standard deviations given both for the total sample and for each sex separately. In the text itself we have not attempted to be exhaustive in mining the information in the Appendix, which in any event needs statistical reduction as well as replication before it can be safely interpreted.

The nature of the sample itself should make us cautious about interpreting the observed correlations. Its homogeneous character may result in serious underestimation of the degree of relationship among variables in the general population. Scores on the Artist key of the Strong Vocational Interest Blank, to give a pertinent example, are quite restricted in range compared with the general population. Of the 91 freshmen tested, 89 scored in the A range on this scale. In groups of nonartists, in which normally only 15% score in the A range, scores on the scale have a significant positive relationship with ratings of professional creativity (MacKinnon, 1965; Barron, 1969). In this particular sample, however, the relationship is close to zero, while scales such as Carpenter and Production Manager, on which artists as a group score low, do correlate with faculty ratings of creativity based on portfolios. The extreme restriction of range on the Artist scale, it may reasonably be presumed, has wiped out its valid covariance with creativity; where everyone has strong artistic interests, those who have a bit of the carpenter in them may be favored so far as productivity is concerned. (This is not to say that the faculty has been reduced to rating the frames instead of the paintings, we hasten to add. There is carpentry in novel writing too.)

The restriction of range on this sort of measure of artistic vocational interests is easy enough to see, given the broadly based norms of the SVIB, and easy also to understand. Some of the other measures we have employed are less easy to evaluate, however, and eventually we must have recourse to a comparison of correlations in this sample with correlations in the general population. We have not yet tested such a sample, though we plan to do so. This chapter, then, presents such information as we have at this stage of the research. Whatever the lacks, the fact remains that for many of the tests in the battery the information given here is the most comprehensive available.

I. Further Descriptions of Tests

A. THE PERCEPTUAL ACUITY TEST

A preliminary version of this test was first described by McGurk (McGurk, 1965). The correct version (Gough & McGurk, 1967) consists of 30 problems, each of which presents several geometrical forms or figures in combination. There are 25 illusion and 5 nonillusion problems. The former include many of the classical illusions, such as the vertical-horizontal parallelogram, the Müller-Lyer, the Poggendorff, Sander's, Ponzo's, and Delbouf's illusions, and Titchener's circle. The problems are presented on slides by means of a 35-mm slide projector, for a period of 30 seconds. The test respondent is asked to make judgments of such characteristics of the figures as their relative size, their shape, the width or length of various lines, and so on. An answer sheet with a multiple-choice test format is used, with five options offered the respondent for each problem. A weighted scoring system based on closeness to the correct judgment is employed.

Normative information has been gathered by administering the test to two samples: 205 college students and 727 grade school children (Gough &

McGurk, 1967). Protocols were scored for number of illusion items correct, number of nonillusion items correct, and total weighted score.

For both college students and grade school children, the number of illusion items perceived correctly is low: 6.26 and 4.68, respectively, out of 25. The nonillusion items, as would be expected, were much easier, with the college students responding correctly to 2.05 out of 5, and the grade school children to 1.80.

The San Francisco Art Institute students scored approximately at the collegiate level on this. They earned an average score of 18.2, standard deviation 5.34, compared with the college norms of 18.50 and 5.40, respectively, for total weighted score (which includes credit for near-misses). Correlates of total score on the test are shown in Table 6.

B. The Barron "*M*-Threshold" Inkblot Test

This is a measure of readiness to perceive human movement in inkblots. The tendency to interpret an inkblot as a human being in motion was hypothesized by Rorschach to reflect inner creativity in the perceiver. It clearly involves "doing more" with the blot than seeing it in its static formal aspect. The readiness to see the dynamic form as human suggests that greater importance is attached to the human form, and perhaps, by extension, to humanness in general.

The present measure was developed to overcome some of the difficulties involved in the use of Rorschach's ten blots (Barron, 1955). The model adopted for the construction of a measure of threshold for perception of human movement was the conventional stimulus series used to determine response thresholds in such sense modalities as the auditory, olfactory, and tactile. Although stimulus strength or intensity is not determined from physical properties of the stimulus in the case of inkblots, this is no great loss so long as relative frequencies of response can be established in large samples and with some stability. By arranging inkblots of known relative frequency in a regularly graduated series, with p values ranging from .00 to 1.00, a measure analogous to the usual perceptual stimulus series is made. The subject's threshold for human movement is then the ordinal position of that blot in the series at which he first gives a human movement response.

One hundred and fifty achromatic inkblots were constructed, using 4- by 6-inch sheets of white paper, which were then mounted on stiff cardboard of the same dimensions. Twenty-six blots were selected from the 150, on the basis of observed frequencies, in such a manner as to make a series with graduations of approximately .04. The stability of the final ordering of the blots is indicated by the rank-difference correlation between a rank order based on observed frequencies in the first 50 cases of 100 adult males tested, and a rank order based on observed frequencies in the final 50 cases: rho is .99. The *M*-evocative power of the inkblot series is remarkably stable.

The possible range of scores for individual subjects is, of course, from 1 to 27 (the score of 27 being assigned to subjects who do not see *M* in any one of the 26 blots). The expected range, considering the method of construction of the measure, is from 2 (since no subject should see *M* on the first blot) to 26. The actual observed range was from 2 to 25, with the mean at 13.

In the Art Institute sample, the average threshold score is 7.92, with a standard deviation of 5.35. In other words, the average art student first sees human movement at about the seventh or eighth inkblot in the series of 26. This compares quite favorably with the average performance of military officers, who see human movement first on the thirteenth blot. Unfortunately, we do not have other data available yet for comparison purposes, but the indication from what we do have is that art students have more of what Rorschach termed "inner creativity." Correlates of the "*M*-threshold" Inkblot Form Test are given in Table 7.

C. THE GOTTSCHALDT FIGURES TEST, CRUTCHFIELD REVISION

This test, developed by R. S. Crutchfield, measures the ability of the individual to locate simple geometrical figures that are embedded and camouflaged in more complex figures. Some of the figures used are borrowed from the experimental research of Gottschaldt (Gottschaldt, 1929), while others were newly constructed by Crutchfield. The test is one of several variants of the Gottschaldt Figures Test; others that might be mentioned are those of Thurstone (1938) and Witkin (1954).

The test may be presumed to measure facility in breaking apart a strong perceptual organization in order to isolate a required part. A considerable spatial factor is obviously involved. We interpret it as being a measure of accuracy of visual perception, reflecting particularly analytical functions in which the breaking down of visual displays into their component parts are involved.

The test is group administered. There are two parts to it. Each part consists of 10 complex figures, in each of which one or the other of two simple geometrical figures is to be found and traced. The time limit is 2 minutes 15 seconds per part.

In scoring, one point is given for each correct answer. No credit is given for partially correct answers. Part scores are obtained for the first 10 and the second 10 figures; the total score may therefore vary from 0 to 20. Obtained scores in a sample of 100 military officers varied over the entire range, with a mean of 9.69, S.D. of 4.90, and a fairly symmetrical normal curve distribution. The split-half reliability of the test is greater than .90.

Perhaps surprisingly, art students, although they do score higher than military officers on the average, do not score significantly higher. Their mean score is 11.2, with a standard deviation of 5.05. As we mentioned earlier, in a factor-analytic study by Guilford *et al.* (reported in Barron, 1969), the Gottschaldt test was found to have the highest loading of any test on a factor that was interpreted as Adaptive Flexibility. This is defined as the ability to rearrange elements in an adaptive way to solve a problem, and is distinguished from Spontaneous Flexibility, which is the tendency or ability to change set rapidly. In Guilford's terms, the former is probably best classified as a convergent thinking ability, and the latter as divergent thinking. Our other findings, taken in conjunction with this one, do seem to suggest that student artists are better at divergence than convergence.

D. THE CHILD AESTHETIC JUDGMENT TEST

The Child Aesthetic Judgment Test, developed by Irvin L. Child (1962), consists of pairs of slides showing works of art. The two pictures in a pair are similar in kind or in subject matter, but one is superior aesthetically in the opinion of expert judges. This is a variant on the method employed in the Meier Art Tests (Meier, 1940), in which each pair actually consists of two versions of the same painting, one the original and the other an alteration of the original to make it aesthetically inferior in the opinion of expert judges.

Seven sets of such slides were assembled, each containing 130 pairs. Child has presented evidence showing that the test does measure what in this research we have called aesthetic judgment. Used in a different way (by calling not for a judgment of "better" or "worse," but for comments on the slides, scored for relevance and variety), it appears to be more closely related to what we here have called aesthetic sensitivity (Rochmas, 1965).

Child developed two tests from his large initial set of slides, one consisting of 120 pairs on which his 14 expert judges were unanimous or nearly so, the other of 120 pairs on which the expert judges were more in disagreement. He called the former set the Easier Test of Aesthetic Judgment, the latter the Difficult Test of Aesthetic Judgment. The two tests proved to correlate highly with one another (*r* of .75) in a sample of 138 Yale undergraduates. The Easier Test was more reliable, with a split-half reliability coefficient of .87. The difficulty level of the items in the Easier Test ranged from approximately .36 to .87, with a mean of .60.

In the present research, 100 pairs of slides from the Difficult Test were chosen on the basis of item difficulty while retaining the high level of reliability.

Professor Child himself supplied additional information on ease of recognition of the artifacts and recommended the exclusion of the more readily recognized.

The test as used in the current research is a test of preference rather than judgment, and the score it yields, with a possible range from 0 to 100, expresses the degree of agreement between the respondents' *preferences* and expert *judgments*.

The Art Institute students attained an average score of 57.4, with a standard deviation of 14.65. We have no comparison data for this set of 100 slides as yet, although from the distribution of item difficulties in the Yale undergraduate sample for 96 of these items we can say that the Art Institute sample scores well above the college sample.

In the Art Institute sample, as the correlation matrix shows, the Child test does correlate significantly with 23 other variables, 17 of which are scales of the Strong Vocational Interest Blank and 4 of which are California Psychological Inventory scales. Its other two correlates are with the Mosaic Judgment Test (Originality, and total score). Its positive correlations with SVIB Artist, Author-Journalist, and Mathematician, as well as with such CPI scales as Femininity, Responsibility, Flexibility, and Achievement via Independence, lend credence to an interpretation of the test as a valid measure of aesthetic judgment.

E. HALL MOSAIC CONSTRUCTION TEST

This test arose from the effort of William H. Turney, carried to completion by Wallace B. Hall, at the Institute of Personality Assessment and Research, to assess the aesthetic productive capacities of individuals by providing them with the opportunity to construct a visual display within a standardized framework and using standardized materials.

Subjects are tested individually. Each is presented with a white card and a large selection of 1-inch squares cut from 22 different colors of posterboard. He is asked to construct within a half-hour period an 8- by 10-inch solidly filled-in rectangle that will be pleasing to him. He is, in brief, asked to make something he would like. No explanation of the purpose is given, nor are any color or design suggestions made. In order to facilitate judgment of the productions and to eliminate the necessity of any artistic ability and influence of any previous artistic training, severe restrictions are imposed on the medium to be used. Thus the instructions permit no curving lines, no partial filling in of the space, no variations of the size or shape of the total production, and no three-dimensionality *per se.*

In an early study reported on this test (Hall, 1958), 146 such mosaic productions were appraised. These were made mostly by research scientists, honor students in engineering, student playwrights, successful well-known writers, and upper-division and graduate students in a course in personality assessment. Although there are a number of different possible ways of scoring or judging the resulting mosaics, to date they have been objectively scored only for actual number of colors used. However, they have been subjectively judged by five persons independently, persons professionally qualified in art and theory of design and color; some of the judges, in addition, are practicing artists or designers. Judgments were made on the overall artistic merit of each mosaic, its good use of color, good use of form, originality, the total warmth or vitality, and finally its pleasingness. Ratings were made individually by the five judges on a nine-point scale and then were composited for each variable. A total composite was also made, combining all the judgments for all the ratings on each mosaic.

A quite satisfactory degree of interjudge reliability was found for this rating procedure. The average interrater r, corrected for number of raters, is .61 for overall artistic merit, .71 for good use of color, .77 for good use of form, .78 for originality, .65 for warmth, and .69 for pleasingness. These correlations have not been corrected for attenuation and are surprisingly high when one considers the anticipated lack of agreement among judges of such complex variables, with no absolute standards. Although there is considerable agreement on most mosaics for most of these ratings, a rather curious phenomenon occurs in the lack of agreement on many of the top-rated mosaics. This is quite analogous to judging of art shows by a panel of experts, where often the most original productions do not receive first prize, which is awarded rather to an entry less unusual on which all the panel can agree. That there is some core of basic artistic principles and preferences to which all judges adhere, however, is attested to by the correlations cited above.

Hall's findings of high interjudge agreement are supported in Child's 1962 study of ratings by "connoisseurs," a connoisseur being defined as "one aesthetically versed in a subject and competent to act as a critical judge of an art or in matters of taste." Indeed, an earlier study by Gordon (1923) would have led to the same conclusion had the data been analyzed in terms of intercorrelation of groups of judges, as Child (1969) recently pointed out. Average intercorrelations of consensuses of *groups* of experts are .83, .92, and .96 for groups of 20, 50, and 100 experts, respectively.

These findings are important to future measurement efforts in that they give reason to believe that stable and highly discriminating measures of aesthetic judgment can be constructed in still other media than those used in the studies we have cited.

In Hall's work with mosaic construction, the various ratings of the aesthetic qualities of the mosaics were found to have many significant correlates with dimensions of personality related to effective functioning and to originality. There were also some interesting failures of expected correlations to appear. For instance, there were no significant correlations with verbal intelligence measures, such as the Terman Concept Mastery Test, the General Information Survey, or the Minnesota Engineering Analogies Test. Nor did the available measures of originality, depending mainly upon verbal skills, correlate with the mosaic ratings. The only significant *r* with any of the tests of the Guilford Creativity Battery was with ideational fluency.

As might be predicted, however, ratings of the good use of form did correlate significantly with scores on the Barron–Welsh Art Scale, which, as we have noted, rewards preferences for complexity and asymmetry of design. Similarly there was a significant correlation with the Crutchfield revision of the Gottschaldt Figures Test, which involves a substantial spatial relations factor. Mosaic originality ratings also correlated with the specialization level scale of the Strong Vocational Interest Blank, a scale known to be a useful index of ability, drive, and motivation.

An interesting relationship is indicated in the correlations with a test battery for social acuity. Persons rating high on ability to perceive the subtleties and nuances in the behavior of others are also able to exhibit similar ability in relation to original and effective organization of form and color. Correlations significant at the .01 level with the MMPI *Mf* scale, purportedly a measure of femininity of interest patterns but usually interpreted for college-trained populations as being indicative of sensitivity and breadth of interest, were also found.

Additional relationships indicate that persons who constructed the more original, more artistic mosaics were more self-accepting and independent. They are seen by psychological assessors as thinking and behaving somewhat differently from others, but effective in their intellectual functioning, sound and adequate as persons, and tending to be dominant and self-assertive. They are also somewhat impulsive, and rejecting of sociocultural conventions. They were rated by the assessment staff as being more likable as persons than subjects low on originality of mosaic design.

The Hall Mosaic Construction Test used in this manner is of course a sample of expressive behavior. The mosaics thus produced, however, can readily be used to obtain estimates of a person's judgment, or ability to weigh his impressions. Since the ratings assigned by expert judges are available, it is a simple matter to construct a measure of aesthetic judgment by pairing mosaics so that one highly rated may be compared with one having a low rating. The respondent's score then is the number of times he prefers the more highly rated of the pair.

Hall carried through just such a selection of mosaics for the rating dimensions described earlier: Overall Artistic Merit, Good Use of Color, Good Use of Form, Originality, Warmth, and Pleasingness. By summing standard scores for each variable, he also was able to obtain an overall score reflecting the respondent's agreement with expert judgment in all dimensions.

The various subscales as well as total score on the Hall Mosaic Judgment Test produced a host of significant correlations, as Table 8 shows. Good judgment of the use of color, for example, is related to independence, flexibility, and complexity of outlook, as well as to complexity and expansiveness in drawing completions. Good judgment of the use of form goes along with CPI Communality. Judgment of originality is most strongly related to the Child Aesthetic Preference Test, but also to Perceptual Acuity, SVIB: Mathematician, and originality in nonhuman responses on the M-threshold inkblots. Total score shows substantial correlation with the Child test, CPI Femininity and Flexibility, and preference for complexity.

Since no other samples are available, we cannot evaluate average level of performance on this test in this sample.

F. THE BARRON SYMBOL EQUIVALENTS TEST

Since measurement of individual differences in symbolic scope was one aim of the research, we decided to begin with an inquiry that would lend itself readily to one of the usual psychological test formats. Two possibilities suggested themselves:

1. A sort of "analogies" test in which the respondent is given a choice of several alternative images, one of which bears a more apt relationship to the terms of the analogy than do the others:

Example: A rose is to a woman as a tower is to: (1) a geyser; (2) a king; (3) a tree; (4) the sun.

By constructing many such items and administering them to many respondents, one could obtain consensual validation of hypotheses concerning symbolic equivalences.

2. A free response test, in which a stimulus image is provided and the respondent is asked simply to produce a symbolically equivalent image.

> *Example:* Stimulus image: *Leaves being blown by the wind.*
> Suggested equivalent: *A civilian population fleeing chaotically before armed aggression.*

This latter method offers a way of studying the spontaneous production of a variety of equivalences by many individuals, and thus is less constrained by the imagination of the experimenter. By studying a set of responses to a given stimulus image, one might discover the processes of generation of symbolic equivalences.

We decided for the time being to concentrate on the second method, without foreclosing the possibility of returning to the first format after having accumulated a mass of spontaneously produced equivalences that could serve as the basis for the alternative test format.

The test was made to yield four scores: (1) number of common responses; (2) number of unusual responses; (3) number of acceptable responses (sum of 1 and 2); and (4) total weighted score, giving twice as much weight to unusual as to common responses.

As we should expect, Common Responses correlate highly with Acceptable Responses (.96) and Total Score (.86). Other significant (.01 level) correlations are with Common and Acceptable Responses on the Consequences Test. Apart from these, the yield is slight: Gottschaldt Figures Test, Complexity of Outlook, and several SVIB scores, such as Author-Journalist, Advertising Man, Life Insurance Salesman, and Real Estate Salesman. Commonplace realism does seem indicated.

For *unusual* responses, however, the picture is quite different. There are 34 significant correlations, notably Originality on the Franck Drawing Completion Test and on Consequences, SVIB Physicist, Psychologist, Chemist, and Engineer, grades in Photography, Independence of Judgment, Preference for Complexity, choice of human movement responses in Part II of the inkblot form test, Gottschaldt Figures Test, and Perceptual Acuity. These results are encouraging, in that they do suggest that the test is one of original imagination in the visual sphere, even though the problem is presented verbally and verbal responses are called for.

A new wrinkle in the measurement of originality was introduced in our research at the San Francisco Art Institute by the construction of a test for recognition of originality, based on free responses of earlier subjects who had taken the symbol equivalence and consequences tests under standard conditions. From a pool of such responses already scored for originality, pairs were selected, one highly original and one quite banal. The task now given the respondent was to choose the more original.

An example for the consequences test item *What would happen if the world's supply of coal and oil were suddenly exhausted?* is:

A. There would be serious disruptions in the transportation system. (Banal)

B. Shoes would wear out faster. (Original)

For the test item *What would happen if a way were discovered by which everyone could read everyone else's mind?* an example is:

A. People would learn to think only good thoughts. (Banal)

B. "Thought-screens" would be invented. (Original)

The Barron M-threshold inkblots were also adapted in this fashion to a multiple-choice format in which the respondent is asked to choose from among alternatives in which are represented both original and banal responses, sometimes in human movement and sometimes in pure form. Thus a comparison of the correlates of originality in pure form with originality in M may be made, in addition to discovering the correlates of M-choice under such conditions.

Recognition of Originality in Consequences proved to be correlated significantly with the Barron–Welsh Art Scale (and Welsh Revised Art Scale, itself correlating .90 with the former), and with the Child Aesthetic Judgment Test. It is positively correlated also with CPI Achievement via Independence and with the Barron Independence of Judgment scale; also with CPI Flexibility and Responsibility; and IPP Complexity of Outlook.

Recognition of Originality in symbol equivalences is positively correlated with the Barron–Welsh Art Scale and with Preference for Complexity, as well as with SVIB: Author-journalist and the self-description "My work is unique." Its negative correlates are SVIB Army Officer, Printer, Aviator, Accountant, and CPA, and the self-description "I do better work in class than out." It is also negatively correlated with the Hardyck Stick Figures, which is essentially a measure of conformance in visual perception.

Originality in Human Movement was highly correlated with the general tendency to choose human movement (of which it is a part score), and also with unusual responses in Consequences I. It had an interesting pattern of relationship to Perceptual Acuity, producing a significant negative relationship to number of illusions items correct but a significant positive relationship to number of nonillusions correct. It is as though to see M in the blots one must be susceptible to illusion to some extent, while yet discriminating accurately where no illusion is present. The variable is also negatively related to CPI Achievement via Conformance and to SVIB Specialization level, while being positively related to SVIB Architect and to the self-description "There is something in my work which escapes explanation."

Originality in purely formal responses is most strongly positively correlated with Originality in mosaic judgment and with a number of SVIB scales: Mathematician, Engineer, Physicist, Dentist, and Architect. Its negative relationships are with total score on symbol equivalents and total M on both Parts I and II of the inkblot form test.

Many of these findings are interesting in that they suggest hypotheses for future work, even though nothing conclusive can be drawn from results in the present sample. Several new ideas in testing have been incorporated in the battery used in this study, and the future direction of work will be to refine the measures, state definite hypotheses and their rationale, and test again in a sample more representative of the general population.

CHAPTER SIX

Correlates of Forms of Expression in the Visual Arts

I. Introduction

The point of departure for the study to be reported in this chapter may be found in earlier research by Barron (1952). The Barron–Welsh Art Scale was interpreted there as a measure of a bipolar dimension characterized by "simple symmetry" at one end and "complex asymmetry" at the other. By comparing the painting preferences (on a set of 100 famous paintings) of subjects high and low on this dimension, and obtaining personality descriptions of them as well, Barron discovered relationships between aesthetic preferences and expressive personal characteristics that suggested a formal stylistic link between what one likes and what one does.

In that same study, a hitherto unpublished result was also discovered. The Franck Drawing Completion Test was scored for complexity–simplicity and asymmetry–symmetry, and subjects were then classified into four groups on the basis of these coordinates. Scores on the Barron–Welsh Art Scale showed a substantial positive relationship with this classification. The highest *preference* scores for complexity–asymmetry occurred in those subjects whose drawing completions were both complex and asymmetrical, whereas the lowest occurred in those whose drawings were simple and symmetrical. Middle scores characterized the two middle categories.

This way of approaching the relationship between personal style of expression and aesthetic preferences is not without a history, of course. Notable landmarks have been the extensive investigations in the late 1920's and early 1930's by Cyril Burt and his students, the derivative studies of Eysenck (1940, 1941a, b, 1942), the two-volume work *Painting and Personality* by Alsculer and Hattwick (1969), and the researches of Morris (1956) and Cardinet (1958).

The first of these lines of investigation [summarized by Burt (1939)] was centered on the discovery and description of factors in personality. Burt distinguished four temperamental types: (1) the unstable extrovert; (2) the stable extrovert; (3) the unstable introvert; (4) the stable introvert. Tendencies toward these types, when measured by a regression equation or some similar device, prove to be approximately normally distributed; Burt therefore selected the extreme 10% of the distributions as more or less "pure" representatives of the type. In samples thus selected, he found these characteristic aesthetic preferences:

1. The unstable extrovert likes dramatic and romantic art, and prefers color to form and line in drawing. In music he likes chromatic rather than diatonic harmony, and prefers rhythm to melody. His penchant is for dramatic events, emotionally or even sensationally treated. Pictures in which a human figure is conspicuous are preferred to landscapes, interiors, or still lifes. The unstable extrovert likes vivid colors, strong contrasts, and vigorous and flowing curves. There is strong empathy for "restless movement" in art and architecture.

2. The stable extrovert differs in emphasizing the cognitive rather than the emotional aspects of external reality. He is strongly representational and practical, and sets more store by solidity and mass than by decoration and flowing curves. He likes historical subject matter, realistically treated.

3. The unstable introvert prefers impressionistic art, with emphasis on the supernatural and the mystical—a sort of romanticism, but without the element of adventure in the real world that characterizes the unstable extrovert. The unstable introvert prefers landscapes, especially if "mystically" treated, to portraits; he likes the work of such artists as El Greco, Blake, Corot, Dürer, Monet, Botticelli, and Rossetti. In literature, his preferences are for Spenser, Shelley, Yeats, Coleridge, and De Quincey.

4. The stable introvert has a strongly intellectual attitude, and attends to the picture as an object in itself. The chief appeal is in "the significant form." Pattern rather than content is important. Good drawing, clean lines, and chiaroscuro appeal more than colors. There is a strong repugnance for the sentimental and the theatrical. Tranquil landscapes and formal, closed-in scenes are preferred. The stable introvert has little interest in portraiture, except that of Rembrandt and Van Eyck. He prefers unity and repetition to diversity and variegation, likes economy rather than exuberance, and prefers the conventional to the obtrusively original.

The second line of investigation, deriving historically from the first but conceptually somewhat different, is that carried out by Eysenck. Rather than working from personality factors to their correlates in aesthetic preferences, he began by establishing factors in the latter realm of behavior, and then sought their correlates in personality.

Eysenck demonstrated for a number of stimulus classes (colors, odors, paintings, polygons, poetry, etc.) the existence of a general factor of aesthetic appreciation, and showed that when the influence of this factor is eliminated, a secondary bipolar factor can be found (Eysenck, 1940, 1941b). This factor, which he named K, generally has positive and negative saturations in about equal numbers in the populations studied. One of its poles seems to be represented by preference for the simple polygon; the strong, obvious odor; the poem with the obvious rhyming scheme and definite, unvarying, simple rhythm; and the simple, highly unified picture. At the other pole is preference for the more complex polygon; the more subtle odors; the poem with a less obvious rhythm and a more variable and loose rhyming scheme; and the complex, more diversified picture.

Eysenck then showed that the K factor (as measured anew by a "K test" consisting of 100 pairs of pictures) correlated significantly with both extroversion–introversion and radicalism–conservatism. Subjects who preferred the modern, impressionistic painting were extroverted and radical, whereas those who preferred the older, more conventional paintings were introverted and conservative.

The Alsculer and Hattwick work with creative expression in children is more clinical and case oriented than the Burt and Eysenck approaches, and their results do not lend themselves to easy summary. The case studies themselves are convincing in their clinical detail, however, and support the generalization that personality style and personal problems find expression in creative, artistic activity.

Morris approached the problem of aesthetic preferences in the more general context of "philosophy of life" or "ways of life." He found that when people were asked to rate their reactions to a number of ways of life defined in various religious and ethical traditions in both Western and Eastern society, factor analysis of these ratings consistently yielded three dimensions. An inspection of the content of the most characteristic ways of life marking these factors strongly suggested the characteristics, respectively, of detachment, dominance or mastery, and passivity or dependence. Morris subsequently found that reactions to paintings yielded three factors that could plausibly be interpreted in these same terms. Cardinet's work supports that of Morris in identifying three similar clusters of painting preferences.

The question has been advanced somewhat in the present study, which provides a direct link between style of expression by painters themselves and the painter's own preferences and aesthetic judgments.

II. Background of the Present Investigation

The research with students at the San Francisco Art Institute provided an opportunity to study the relationship between a painter's style of expression in his serious work and various characteristics, such as aesthetic preferences and judgment, vocational interests outside of art, dispositional tendencies in perception, and the like. The tests listed in the Appendix or described in earlier chapters had been administered to entering freshmen in 1968. Included were (1) the Child Aesthetic Preference Test; (2) the Barron–Welsh Art Scale; (3) the Hall Mosaic Judgment Test; (4) the Perceptual Acuity Test; (5) the Gottschaldt Figures Test; (6) the Barron M-Threshold Inkblot Form Test; (7) the Franck Drawing Completion Test; (8) the Barron Symbol Equivalents Test; (9) Part II of the Barron Inventory of Personal Philosophy; (10) the Strong Vocational Interest Blank; and (11) the California Psychological Inventory. Also available for analysis were portfolio ratings at time of admission, grades, and ratings of student work at the end of the first year, not only by faculty members but also by the research staff.

The occasion for the latter ratings, which were focused on creative potential, provided also the occasion for systematic description of the work of the painters in terms of a schema developed by one of the present authors (Knapp). It is to a description of this schema that we now turn.

III. The Psychophysical Scaling Problem

Any painting may be described in terms of the source of imagery incorporated in its content. Three main sources are representational, geometrical, and expressive. (There are others, of course, not dealt with here.)

By *representational* is implied the degree to which *identifiable* objects in the material world are incorporated. By *geometrical* is meant the inclusion of images drawn from the world of rational mathematics, linear or curvilinear. *Expressive* refers to that category characterized by inchoate abstract art devoid of either representational or geometrical features and notably exemplified by contemporary abstract expressionism.

In order to make these categories amenable to research, one must determine the degree to which judges can with consistency rate a body of paintings on a series of psychophysical scales. A group of seven judges was therefore constituted, only one of whom claimed by any professional artistic experience and most of whom were relatively naive, both in matters of psychological rating and in the varieties of modern art, though all were perceptive and intelligent persons.

In developing these psychological scales, Knapp (1962) employed 40 paintings representative of 20th-century art, including examples of the three types discussed earlier as well as intermediate varieties.

He also included some further, secondary, scales. The first dimension involves essentially the qualities of *blitheness* versus *melancholy*. The second dimension involves *configurational dynamism,* as represented at one end by asymmetry, curvilinearity, dynamic imbalance, and other features suggesting contained energy and turbulence; and at the other end by static, balanced, and stable configurations. The third variable, *chromatic dynamism,* is defined as the employment of saturated, contrasted colors and brightness as opposed to the contrary. The fourth scale, *diffusion,* characterizes work in which it is difficult to discern a central focus of interest or where there is none.

A question naturally arises concerning the reliability of ratings on the primary and secondary scales. As Knapp has shown elsewhere (Knapp, 1969), the reliability in judging the primary variables of imagery source is impressively high. The reliability on the secondary variables is somewhat less, the weakest being that for configurational dynamism.

A second question from a psychophysical point of view is whether these primary and secondary variables are independent of each other. In Table 9 are shown the intercorrelations between the three primary and four secondary ratings, averaged for the seven judges. That the three primary variables are negatively correlated is to be expected in view of the requirement of the rating procedure that their sum be 9. On the null hypothesis, the average intercorrelation should be $-.50$, and none depart significantly from this expectation. It is clear, therefore, that the primary variables represent independent parameters of the stimulus. Among the secondary variables one would expect on the null hypothesis that the correlations would be zero. There is a single exception, namely, the correlation of $-.70$ between diffusional and representational. This is not a serious embarrassment, since the depiction of objects against ground necessarily involves a denial of the impulse of the eye to wander.

After originating this rating schema, Knapp applied it in a study of the significance of form in the stylistic evolutions of Picasso and Cézanne (Knapp, 1969). In the present study, test data already collected in the study of student painters (by Barron) were correlated with the ratings (by Knapp) of the work of the artists. These results are the subject of this chapter.

The group of painters numbered 16, 9 males and 7 females. All were first-year studio workers at the San Francisco Art Institute. Their work was rated at the end of the first year, while the test data were obtained at the beginning of the year. Their average age was 23 when the year began.

Results are presented for each variable individually. Only those correlations statistically significant at the .05 level of confidence are discussed. The actual statistical values are given in the appropriate tables in the Appendix.

A. Representational

It should be noted first that the representational component in this set of ratings is correlated −.80 with the expressive. This is higher than previous experience with the schema had led us to expect. Inspection by other staff members of slides of the paintings Knapp had rated served to confirm the implication of the correlation. These students were clearly of one school or the other, and in terms of history of the Art Institute during the past two decades it would appear that students now were choosing to be clearly of the abstract expressionist camp or were clearly representational; figurative expressionism had few followers.

In view of this high negative correlation, the findings with regard to the abstract expressive component will be considered in conjunction with representational. First, however, let us look at the correlates of the latter, which are presented in Table 10.

From the correlations in Table 10, the following general picture of the painter whose work is highly representational and low on abstract expression emerges.

1. His work is focused, but not dynamic in configuration.

2. He is very poor at judging the quality of mosaics (none of which is representational, it might be added).

3. He shows little originality in his choice of human movement possibilities in inkblots.

4. In spite of this, his expression of vocational interests is similar to that of individuals of *high verbal* originality [see Barron (1969)].

5. He is intellectually efficient and has a high capacity for social status.

6. He does well in school and his work is highly rated by the faculty and by research psychologists.

Before leaving this hypothetical individual and going on to consider the correlations with the abstract expressive component, we might note that the distinction between "inner-creative originality" as presumably measured in the inkblot human-movement response, and "external verbal behavior originality," toward which the SVIB measure is directed, may be important here. The interested reader should consult the writings of Stark (1968a,b), who has been most vigorous in pressing this distinction in his theoretical analyses of originality.

B. ABSTRACT EXPRESSIVE

From the correlations for this component (presented in Table 11), the following general picture of the painter whose work is highly expressive and nonrepresentational may be drawn.

1. His painting is quite dynamic configurationally, though not in the use of color; it tends toward diffusion, lack of central focus; it is dysphoric in tone.

2. He prefers complexity and asymmetry, and probably in personality is emotionally expressive, vivid, whimsical.

3. He is good at judging value in mosaics, but he is not good at figural reasoning (are these contradictory?).

4. He dislikes whatever is involved in being a psychologist or a psychiatrist, but he likes whatever is involved in being a banker.

5. Psychologists rate him low on originality, whether in drawing or in making up images through the use of words.

6. The drawing instructor of the art faculty, however, gives him very good grades in drawing, though the faculty raters as a whole do not think highly of his potential as judged from his paintings.

7. He appears well socialized and is like most people in his general attitudes.

C. GEOMETRICAL

The geometrical component in the Knapp rating scheme does not correlate significantly with any other component in this particular set of ratings. It does, however, produce many significant correlations with the earlier test data, as Table 12 shows. These may be summarized as follows.

1. The highly geometrical painter is excellent in aesthetic judgment, on both the Child test and the mosaic judgment test.

2. His entering portfolio is highly rated by the research staff, and so is his work of the first year.

3. He does poorly in school, especially in English composition, but also in drawing.

4. He says he does his best work outside of class and he thinks it is something rather special.

5. His attitudes are uncommon; however, he makes a good impression.

6. In terms of vocational interests, he is most unlike a sales manager and a production manager.

In general, the painter who puts many geometrical aspects into his work appears low in verbal facility, high in autonomy and independence, and of good judgment aesthetically.

D. BLITHENESS

This variable produced no correlations significant at the .05 level with any of the other variables, whether of the Knapp schema or the IPAR tests. Correlations at the .10 level yield no consistent picture.

E. CHROMATIC DYNAMISM

This component, too, is independent of the other components of the Knapp schema. However, it has significant relationships with many of the IPAR test scores. These may be summarized as follows (see Table 13).

1. The painter whose use of color is dynamic describes himself as spontaneous in his work, and he feels that he can bring emotional life to his painting.

2. He is notably poor at resisting illusions, and in general does poorly on the Perceptual Acuity Test.

3. In interest pattern, he is most unlike a chemist or a mathematician, and is more like a mortician and a real estate salesman (!).

4. In mosaic judgments, he is good at discerning good use of color, but poor at discerning good use of form.

5. He is independent in judgment, yet scores high on "good impression."

6. On several measures of originality, both verbal and nonverbal, he scores low.

F. CONFIGURATIONAL DYNAMISM

As we have already seen, configurational dynamism is highly correlated positively with the expressive component. It is, however, negatively related to almost everything else when there is any probably nonchance relationship at all. Among the negative correlates are the following (see Table 14).

1. In vocational interests: psychologist, psychiatrist, public administrator, school superintendent, minister, and music teacher. Professional specialization is most highly negatively related to configurational dynamism.

2. Verbal originality and verbally expressed imagination.

Configurational dynamism is positively associated only with the Barron–Welsh Art Scale, which rewards a preference for complex, dynamically balanced figures.

Once again, we see that what the person does, he likes; or, what he likes, he does.

G. DIFFUSION

The diffusion component bears a strong negative relationship to the representational, as might be expected, and a positive relationship to abstract expressiveness.

In terms of external correlates, this component of the Knapp schema is most strongly associated with grades in sculpture. It also is strongly positively correlated with total score on the mosaic judgment test. It shows no relationship at all with anything having to do with personality, values, or vocational interests, but is positively correlated with grade point average (see Table 15).

IV. Discussion

At this stage of development of the research with painters, these results must be considered merely as suggestive of possible leads for better-controlled observations with a suitably large number of individuals. What the results do suggest, however, may be very important. We interpret them as indicating the importance of seeking different sets of predictors for work in the visual arts, depending upon the expressive style of the individual artist. Different kinds of abilities may be involved in determining quality of work in someone who chooses primarily a geometrical mode of expression as distinct from those who choose the representational or the abstract expressive. If so, then psychological testing in the arts may be of value in counseling as well as in selection. Moreover, more differentiated prediction for selection purposes alone should result if this sort of refinement of the goals of prediction is borne out in further research.

Another implication of the findings is that the student artist's characteristic mode should emerge from his actual work in the first one or two years, and that the major research effort should be directed at prediction of performance in an established, self-chosen mode.

PART TWO

STUDENT ACTORS, DANCERS, WRITERS

CHAPTER SEVEN

Students in the Theater Arts

Twenty students in dramatic arts at the University of California in Berkeley were interviewed in person. The interview was unstructured as to sequence of questions, though the interviewer did attempt to get the same comprehensive coverage of basic questions for all interviewees. The results are not always readily reduced to numerical statements, and in what follows we have attempted to abstract the representative views of the group as a whole and to illustrate the views by statements from the students.

I. Origin of Choice of Theater as a Profession

1. How did your interest in the theater begin?

For most of the students, interest in the theater began during adolescence. They had participated in high school drama, had enjoyed it, and had pursued their interest through college. For others, interest in drama began later in life, after college, through chance encounters with the theater stemming from other interests, "My first interest was in music . . . then I had one role singing a song in a play. . . ." The theater interest then became paramount, and the person continued to participate in plays whenever the opportunity arose. For those who thus stumbled across acting in later life, earlier interests had been in the liberal arts.

2. Do you intend to make the theater a career? If not, do you think it will continue to be an important lifetime interest? Do you think your experience in it will affect whatever other career you choose?

Almost all those interviewed said that they intended to continue with their interest in theater, in some capacity. Almost half mentioned that their interests were mainly in directing and writing and they intended to base their career on efforts in that direction, "Directing and writing primarily; though I enjoy acting, but I'm not as talented as that." Some expressed excitement with the world of theater and said they intended to participate in the field, for example, in community theater or the like, but mentioned the difficulties in trying to make a living in drama, "Would like to and intend to, but it's a hard road." Others felt they would continue to perform in some way, but did not feel their dedication to theater was sufficiently strong enough to "tromp all over" with a professional company.

Most students made clear distinctions between academic and commercial theater. Typically, they had serious misgivings about academic theater and preferred to work on "the real thing," although one, a woman, enjoyed the protection the university afforded.

3. How do you picture yourself ten years from now?

Ten years in the future they could see themselves as either associated with a repertory company or a troupe of directors and writers performing original work; or performing individually in plays of special interest, "I'd like to be in or around any troupe or group of playwrights like the Berliner Ensemble . . ."; ". . . driving trucks or gardening . . . but continuing to do artistic work of various sorts in theater. . . ." The emphasis was on regular performance and productivity outside of the academic setting, "Perhaps in a rep company, a stable sort of thing." One-fourth expected to be associated with a university with outlets to professional theater, "In 10 years, ideally I would be in a combination directing-acting role in a rep company linked to a university."

All of the students, then, had definite plans to continue in theater, preferably in a nonacademic setting.

II. Significance of Acting in the Individual's Life

Of the 20 students, 10 were interviewed in connection with the student production of *King Lear* described later, in Chapter 11. Some of the questions dealt with acting in general, while others were specific to the production. The sample is very small, yet some of the exchanges are thought-provoking and will be reported for that possible value.

1. Do you ever consciously "play a role" in your everyday life?

More than half of the student actors said that they never consciously played a role in everyday life. The students who felt they did not play roles mentioned that they were conscious of the possibility that they might role-play and tried hard to avoid it; they disliked situations where role playing was necessary, or did so only when "clowning around": "Very rarely, though sometimes, I pose, but it's obvious to everyone when I do . . ."; "I don't like to get into any situation where I have to play a role." For the others, role playing was more extensive, whether in acting out roles when alone, adopting habits of people around them, or consciously mocking another. "It's rather extensive with me . . . I'm susceptible to speech patterns . . ."; ". . . usually out of a conscious viciousness or with contempt."

2. Have you ever impersonated anyone?

Eight of the nine students responding said they had often "impersonated" others in daily life, most often to mimic or play a joke on others, as opposed to "playing a role" in the preceding question. Six of the students mentioned that they might imitate another or pretend to be someone else at a party when bored, or to deflate pompous people: for example, "Whenever I'm in Greece I always pretend not to understand Greek"; "I'll imitate people a lot"; ". . . I do it when I'm bored or at a party where I don't know anyone." Most of the students, then, tended to imitate others in daily life, either as a form of play or when ill at ease.

3. Have you ever been hypnotized?

Regarding hypnosis, only one of the nine had ever been hypnotized. Of the eight remaining, five felt they would like to try it, whereas three did not. Comments included that it would be interesting to experience a different state of mind, or that the person would "try anything once"; and the three who were not interested in hypnosis definitely rejected the idea of loss of self, "I think I would fight it all the way"; "I reject that sort of thing"; ". . . wouldn't want to lose myself."

4. Are you happier when in the process of creating a role in a play?

Eight out of the nine answering stated that they felt much happier when involved in a play than when not. This change in mood was expressed as exhilaration, absorption, "Yes, I feel much more exhilarated, have much more energy, need less sleep . . ."; "Much happier because 'thoroughly engrossed.' "

For some, the exhiliration was not always entirely a positive experience, but included extreme mood swings, indicating the extent of their emotional involvement in the play, ". . . absolute exhilaration, but more swings of mood . . . great anxiety, despair." Only one felt that at present she was happier when not in a play, because the work was so demanding, though satisfying.

5. How do you feel when the final performance of a play you are in is over?

The exhilaration of performing in a play, however, was matched by concomitant depression and emptiness when the play was over. When asked to describe their feelings, 11 out of 13 different responses mentioned sadness, a sense of void, letdown, depression. "Very let down . . you get to like the play and the people"; "I feel very lost for a week or two."

Though some mentioned also a sense of relief, relief alternated with sadness. "I was immensely relieved at first, for one day, then an immense depression set in, sort of a void. . . ." Of the two who felt glad when performance was ended, both women, one took a philosophical stance, ". . . it's part of theater . . . when it's over, you tear down the set . . .," while the other was not satisfied with her performance in this particular play and was glad to have an uncomfortable situation brought to an end.

For most, then, involvement in a play was accompanied by an emotional uplift, and sense of exhilaration, whereas the close of the play brought corresponding depression. The process of role creation apparently was an intense emotional endeavor having much meaning for most of the students, influencing their emotions accordingly. The process of emotional uplift during the creative release of energy and consequent "postpartum blues" is a sequence often encountered among those who participate in any creative experience.

6. In the play just finished (*King Lear*), did your conception of the role change in any way from first tryout to final performance?

For almost all the student actors, the conception of the character changed considerably from first tryout to final performance. Two major reasons were given for such change: a change in understanding through "getting to know" the character better; and change in performance for technical reasons.

Most of those whose conceptions changed gave the former reason. It seems that performing the role often gave the actor a better understanding of what kind of person would do what the character did. In the process, the actor's original impressions of the character were strengthened, modified, or reversed, "... at first I saw him as being both a person of action and also introspective, but eventually I felt the latter wasn't true, he doesn't think much at all ..."; "my initial impression was constructed charitably ... I felt he was dignified ... but in point of fact, as I discovered, he was thin-skinned, coarse. ..." This process of modification often took place in the interaction of the character with other characters during rehearsal, as the actor assuming the role sensed his own emotional reactions to the action of the play. "I found that I was getting really mad at Lear, it was a pretty ratty thing he did at the beginning, and in the final rejection scene I realized that that was exactly what *I* wanted to do"; "... details were in relation to the acting of the other characters, to establish and experience the 'reality of the moment' ... this colored how I changed some of the lines." The assumption of the role was not simply putting on a facade, but was more like the establishment of empathy for a fictional character, so that the actor came to feel and think as the character would in the situation he faced, and so "understood" the character better.

7. Did your personal life during rehearsals and performance come to reflect or be affected by the role itself?

The personal lives of the actors and actresses were for the most part definitely influenced by the process of growing into a role. Six out of nine said they were emotionally affected by playing their roles, while only three said they were influenced purely on a physical level (fatigue and lack of time) or not at all. The emotional effects of the role went in two directions: either the person had to draw on himself, stirring up old fears and memories, to create the character; or the character carried over into daily life, so the person acted and felt like the character.

In the first group, students mentioned becoming more aware of aspects of their own relationships to important others, or drawing on real emotions of their own to understand the character's feelings: "Real guilts of my own had to be drawn on, the grubbier aspects of sex had to be riled up out of the muck." For others, the character began to assume an autonomous role in the actor's personality, strengthening or weakening him: "Yes ... I became quite cocky, extreme sureness, and it's held over, I'm much stronger as a result of playing it." "This always happens with me, that's one reason I didn't want to act it ... I became bitter and laconic in my relations to other people." For the remaining three, the role affected them only in terms of physical fatigue and lack of time, while one girl felt that she had learned to keep herself and the character separate.

For the most part, then, role playing was not an emotionally simple task for the students: it demanded a strong personal response. The difference in the direction of effect is interesting and deserves stress. For some, the character was created from parts of their personality, and the character never became more than a part of them. For others, the character seemed to be helping the actor to create himself, rather than the other way around, and temporarily took over the personality of the actor. Both procedures give considerably more clarity to the process of role selection by a performer, a process that appears to involve, at least sometimes, very deep levels of the personality. In both cases, where either the actor must become aware of parts of himself that create the character, or where the role is identified with, becomes autonomous, and is eventually assimilated by the actor, the effect is the same. Parts of the self are temporarily emphasized, objectified, and made conscious. It would seem likely that strong unconscious motives direct the choice of role toward those parts of the self that the actor needs to experience consciously, or that he can at least tolerate experiencing, in himself.

8. Did you have any dreams related to your role, or to the play as a whole?

Given the heavy involvement of the person with the character he played, it is interesting that most of the dreams experienced by the students during rehearsals involved seemingly more trivial aspects of the production. First, only four out of the seven who answered could remember having dreams about the play. Of these four, one had an anxiety dream about forgetting his lines; two dreamt of another character or person involved in the production; and only one dreamt about the character he played. For those who had no dreams about the play, two stated that they usually have dreams about forgetting lines but did not this time; whereas one remembered no dreams at all during plays. The most typical dream, across productions, then, was *anxiety about poor performance.* The next most frequent grouping were dreams about interpersonal problems: Two had dreams about getting angry at the director, while another actor dreamed of playing the lead role, which actually he had wanted to play.

Only one actor had a dream relating to the personal meaning of his role. In this dream, someone—first a man, then a woman—was trying to kill one of two interdependent characters (Lear and the Fool). Which character would die was in the balance. The two characters together made a whole personality; and it is interesting that the dreamer felt in his own personality the conflict expressed by the dual roles.

In general, then, these students did not dream much about the production. Nor, surprisingly, did the dreams reported seem very significant; one might expect more frequent and more vivid dreams. Possibly much of the psychological work of relating the self to the role takes place consciously, during rehearsals. At any rate, the relations of dreams to intense role-playing experience is a question that deserves further study.

9. To what extent do you feel that you "became" the character?

Answers here ranged from "considerably" to "not at all." For those who felt they had successfully become the character, answers described "feeling right" about the role and comfortable with it; being aware of thinking like the character; or being deeply emotionally involved with the character. Others felt they had only moderate success, that "putting on the character" was difficult. Two felt that they did not become the character at all, and they never identified with the character. The two who rejected the concept drew clear boundaries between themselves and the character: "You never really become the character . . . you forget yourself, it's true, but it's still parts of yourself that you're draining into the role . . ."; "Whatever life the character has, I give it."

Some did not react strongly to the idea of "becoming" another, whereas others objected strongly to the idea and emphasized that the character was always part of themselves. The question of identity seems much involved in the answers. Those who did not identify themselves with the characters at all did not feel close to or become the character in any way. Others identified partially with the character, insisting on the boundaries between themselves as a whole and parts of themselves that made up the character; still others did not maintain such distinctions but rather seemed to identify entirely with the character, at least temporarily for the duration of the play, so that a part came to assume the whole.

10. Did the director's conception of the role affect your conception of it and the way you played it?

The director influenced the production in terms of both technical advice and character conception; his influence, for most, was considerable. This influence worked both ways, either positively or negatively. Among nine answering, five felt the director had considerably influenced them in a positive direction, helping to improve their performance. Two felt he had influenced them negatively, interfering with their conception of role, and hence with their ability to perform. Another two felt his influence was minimal, because they felt as he did.

The director's role in the production was most heavily exercised in the understanding and development of the personalities of the stage characters. Seven out of the nine students, independent of direction or extent of influence, mentioned the director's attempts to interpret and clarify the characters and their relation to one another. Some felt his interpretations were helpful and illumining, ". . . [his] interpretation, which he gave fully, included the negative aspects of the character as well as the positive." A few, however, did not agree with his interpretations, and they felt unable to get into the role because of the disagreements, "It worked negatively . . . couldn't relate it to the general picture." "I would have been more simply bestial . . . she's a hellion at heart." Those who felt his influence on characterization was minimal either agreed with his interpretation entirely or ignored it and followed their own preferences.

A second role of the director was that of critic, improving the dramatic impact of the scenes, and advising students on the timing of lines. Two out of the nine students mentioned the director's influence in this connection, ". . . he pointed out a crucial thing in the timing . . ."; ". . . at times he clarified things. . . ."

The director's role, then, was of considerable importance in the production. The relation between director, actor, and play seemed to be one of mutual influence, with the final decisions in the hands of the director. He presented his interpretations of the play, which were accepted or rejected in varying degrees by the actors, who must understand the role within the lights of their own character. In the course of playing out the roles vis-à-vis one another, the actors came to clearer understanding of the personalities they played, aided also by the director, with the action further shaped in the process. Given the importance of the director in imaginatively interpreting character and shaping the action as drama, it is not surprising that many of the students sought future careers in writing and directing.

III. Summary

The process of assuming a role was a task, for most, that deeply involved the personal resources of the actor or actress. The conception of character changed throughout the performance, as the actor responded to other characters and came to empathize with the character's thoughts and emotions. Other changes in the role were due to technical reasons, for dramatic emphasis and making the action plausible. The director heavily influenced this process, both in his interpretation of the characters and in his control over the artistic and dramatic necessities of the production. His influence on the characters heightened their understanding or interfered with their conception of the role, hence aiding or hindering the excellence of the final performance. The process of role development most often deeply involved the performer, asking him to draw on his own fears and emotions, or bringing about such a degree of identification with the character that the actor temporarily became the character offstage and on. Dream life on the whole was intensified during rehearsals for only one or two, and remembered dreams did not seem to have much effect on the performer. The performers themselves felt that they had successfully or unsuccessfully become the character, depending on their degree of identification with the role, while some rejected the idea of becoming the character, according to the preferred mode of role development. The process of creating the characters on stage seemed a complex interaction among director, actor, and character, mutually influencing each other to produce the whole, demanding intense personal involvement on the part of the actors.

CHAPTER EIGHT

Dancers Write of Themselves and Dance Education

The informal conversation and the directed interview both have great value in producing information and impressions about the way a student is experiencing his schooling and his work in his art. The give-and-take of the interview, and its flexibility, are its most desirable features.

The open-ended questionnaire, however, has unique merit if subjects are willing to express themselves fully in writing. It lends itself better to codification and the development of some simple statistics to summarize the information obtained. This chapter, and the one following it, employed just such a questionnaire. In the present chapter, the written responses of student dancers to questions about themselves and about dance education are presented. So too are their self-descriptions obtained from them through their responses to the Gough Adjective Check List (Gough, 1960).

The group of dancers included 32 students, 26 females and 6 males, studying at the Boston Conservatory of Music and Brandeis University.

The questions asked the students were designed to elicit information about various facets of their lives. First, we needed some idea of the extent of the student's commitment to the artist role, to find out just how important his field was to him as an individual. A second focus was education: how did the student feel about the necessity for training in the arts and about this own training? A third general category had to do with emotion, motivation, and artistic production. How did the student's moods and feelings vary with the success of his artistic endeavors and his opportunity to perform? A fourth issue of concern was the relation between personality traits and choice of field. Did the students seem to show propensities inclining them to their mode of expression? And fifth, what was involved in the process of creating? Did the students see themselves as creative, and what elements of personality were important in the process of creativity itself?

These questions were put to the students in the form of a questionnaire to be completed in writing. The data were handled by categorizing the responses into groups of answers that seemed to express the same theme, then tabulating the number of responses that fell into each group. Where answers required a simple yes or no, the total number for the frequency count equals the number of respondents. In other cases, where answers required some thought, most of the students gave more than one response. Each ideational unit was taken separately for arriving at the frequency count; and responses, not people, were categorized. Hence the total number of responses usually exceeds the number of respondents.

An ideational unit was defined simply as a complete thought expressing one idea. If the subject spent two or three sentences elaborating upon the same idea, this was tallied only once in the appropriate category. If in one sentence he gave two reasons or expressed two identifiably different thoughts, each was tallied separately. The categories and frequency counts are described for each question.

The questions have been divided into five sections: (1) commitment, (2) education, (3) dance and motivation, (4) dance and personality, and (5) dance as an art form. For each section, the questions are listed, then answers described in a free-flowing manner, with quotes from the students, in order to summarize effectively what was initially a large bulk of material. More precise information is given in the frequency tables for each section in the Appendix (Tables 16A–16E).

I. Commitment

The first two questions were designed to get some idea of the extent of the student dancer's commitment to and identification with dance. Not all students are seriously interested in the subject matter that they pursue, and the student's commitment very much affects our understanding of their answers. The questions were the following: (1) Do you consider yourself a dancer? Why or why not? (2) Do you plan to continue dancing? As a professional?

The group of 32 students was on the whole highly committed to their field, identified themselves as dancers, and planned professional careers for the future. Of the 32 students, 31 considered themselves to be "dancers," either unequivocally or to a degree. Those 8 students who felt ambivalent about applying the label "dancer" to themselves hesitated because they had not yet attained the high standards they set for themselves. Similarly, 31 of the 32 students planned to continue to dance either professionally or on their own. The majority, 27 students, planned professional careers. Only one student, a female, did not think her interest in dance was serious and did not intend to continue.

Those accepting the title of dancer did so almost exclusively on the basis of long years spent in formal training or intense motivation to dance and to succeed in the field. Surprisingly, claims to innate talent or expressive gifts were mentioned infrequently. One became a dancer just as one became a carpenter, lawyer, or banker: through training and effort. Students called themselves dancers because they had been studying dance for long years, and met standards set for themselves, or knew how to use the body effectively as an instrument: "Because of my knowledge of the body and how it moves as an instrument of expression." "Because I have studied dance for nine years ... it's my life profession." Others gave themselves the title because of their intense love for and devotion to the field, independent of the standards achieved. These students felt they had drive and endurance; they enjoyed dance intrinsically and were interested in the elements of dance: "Because I love to dance and am very much interested in line and form in movements."

Those who were ambivalent about calling themselves dancers felt equally motivated, but did not feel they had sufficiently mastered their technique: "This is what I've chosen to study but as yet I would not consider myself an artistic dancer." Others felt they could call themselves dancers only when they had attained professional status: "Not yet ... I am still a student, no matter how perfected my technique may be I am still not dancing professionally." On the whole, even for those students hesitant about calling themselves dancers, the group was intent on mastering their art and becoming expert in the field (see Table 16A).

II. Education

The second group of questions concerned the education of dancers. Given the personalities of the dancers—flexible, individualistic, spontaneous—one might expect that they would have special needs in their training for individual attention, or room for creative expression, that other kinds of persons might not want or expect. This expectation was verified in some ways but not others, as the dancers, surprisingly enough, while disliking overconventional or rigid dance methods, nonetheless laid heavy emphasis on discipline and rigor in their training. There appeared to be a rather complex, interesting set of relationships between discipline and freedom expressed in their answers to the following questions.

The questions in the section were the following: (1) Are there any aspects of dance you dislike? (2) List the most important qualification a dance teacher should have. (3) What is a good dance class? (4) What is a good dance student? (5) Are you one? The response to each is described in the same order.

Answers to the first question of the set seemed quite consistent with the expressive, individualistic nature of the dancers. The most common complaint was that too often dance involved technique without content. The demand, above all, was for meaning. Dance should be expressive and should avoid movement for movement's sake, or contrived movement that is merely original, "being merely a tuned-up machine." Dance should also be more emotional: ". . . why use it as an art form if it shouldn't express what one feels?" Commercial forms of dance cheapen the art form and communicate nothing. In addition, a few students felt that too often they were made into carbon copies of one style, while their individual talents for expression went unnoticed. These students disliked set views in dance and felt the need for greater innovation. The focus of all of the foregoing comments was in general the need for more flexibility and meaning in a field whose purpose was to express meaning.

A few of the student dancers disliked the ardors of physical training in dance: the necessity to work every day, and the occasional fatigue connected with strenuous exercise. Yet a good-sized fourth group of students replied that there was nothing they disliked about dance: they felt completely satisfied with the field. Interestingly, all of the males who answered the question fell into this category.

A. THE GOOD TEACHER

While setting high standards for themselves, students set equally high standards for their teachers. They wanted the same warmth, flexibility, and enthusiasm from their teachers that characterize themselves, as well as a capacity for discipline and order. The picture of the teacher put together from the adjectives supplied by the students resembles a very enlightened sort of person, an ideal teacher in any field.

The most frequently mentioned requirement for a teacher was a solid background of knowledge and experience. The teacher should have an understanding of what technique is in its most perfected state. He should have a thorough knowledge of different forms of dance; and he should be able to perform with proficiency the techniques he was teaching: "Knowledge of the technique of the types of dance, including a knowledge of the means of achieving this technique." Some mentioned that his background should be rounded, covering the fine arts in general. He should also have a knowledge of, and sense for, music and rhythm. Of great importance, he should have a thorough knowledge of the body, anatomy, and principles of movement. A good teacher must know how to help students build their bodies, and he should be in good physical condition himself: ". . . he should know exactly what is beneficial and what not for the body." In addition, he should have an up-to-date knowledge of the dance world, either being a performer himself or having connection within the professional world. Students, then, expected to be taught a solid body of knowledge about physique, movement, and dance forms, and expected their teachers to be able to supply this knowledge.

Second, a good teacher loves his work. His attitude toward his profession should be characterized by enthusiasm, delight. He should take pleasure in teaching and believe in the merit of what he is doing. The good teacher seeks to inspire, to communicate his love of his work to his students: "The teacher should have interest and delight in his own work. This will naturally radiate to the student." In his respect for his profession, the teacher maintains the stance of the student. He is sincere, humble, generous, and open to what his profession has yet to teach him: "good humor, generosity . . . willingness to keep learning." Related to enthusiasm and devotion is another quality, "energy" or drive. Some students felt that vitality, a certain dynamism and impulsion in the classroom, was motivating and attractive.

A third set of characteristics listed involved the teacher's attitudes toward his pupils. The good teacher is interested in his students, appreciates their feelings, and relates to them with consideration: "An understanding of people and their feelings. . . ." He is observative and insightful, able to see the individuality of each student and help him develop himself in his own unique way: "He knows how to open the minds of dancers and find out each individual's personality." Along with an understanding, insightful nature, students expected an impartial, objective attitude on the part of teachers, showing no favoritism, seeking to develop each student according to his own lights.

The teacher's manner of training students, however, should be strict. He should have the ability to correct and discipline the students in their efforts.

Students wanted and expected a teacher to be a perfectionist—demanding, firm, but not punitive: "severity, but not the drill sergeant type." While expecting to be disciplined and prodded to achieve, they also emphasized the need for patience and tact in a teacher: "patience, firmness . . . tactful, calm, but strict." In a study as demanding of oneself and the body as dance, they expected a teacher who was purposeful in carrying out the order of the lessons. In this connection, they also expected a certain businesslike attitude from the instructor, expecting him (or her) to be reliable, prompt, neat, and efficient. The teacher should also be able to communicate ideas efficiently in class, to teach verbally as well as through performance. He should show clarity, order, and precision in thought and speech. And last and in many ways least, some few asked in addition that the teacher be creative, inventive, imaginative; that he be able to innovate and bring that vital spark of creative energy to their classes.

In general, then, students expected to learn a solid body of knowledge of dance. They hoped for a warm, humane, involved, and inspiring human being as their teacher, able to relate to them as individuals flexibly and insightfully, as well as to help them discipline themselves and demand the best from them. They expected a capacity for order and clarity that were not strong points with the dance students themselves. The creativity of the teacher was not stressed; rather his ability to help the student discipline himself and to teach a knowledge of dance and the body, within the context of each student's unique personal needs, seemed to be the combination students most desired in a teacher.

B. THE GOOD CLASS

A good class was defined mainly by its effects on the students. Almost all of the student dancers agreed that the class should be demanding, arduous, and challenging, leaving them with a feeling of satisfaction and accomplishment. They did not expect routine work; rather, they wanted to be stimulated and inspired.

The most frequently mentioned requirement of a good class was that it be inspiring, stimulating, challenging, enjoyable. Students felt that it was important to learn something new, an exciting or difficult movement; to work on hard, technical material, or to be taught one point thoroughly in detail. Others mentioned a preference for variety in the class, meaning the use of the body in both slow, sustained movement and fast rhythmic movement, maintaining interest through a series of interesting combinations. A good class is a challenge; the class feels moved and inspired, and the individual student is encouraged to search for more knowledge about movement: "One which inspires the student . . . one that excites the dancer's mind as well as his body . . . and that makes the dancer search. . . ." Connected with the sense of inspiration was the sense of accomplishment. A good class makes the dancer feel that he is developing new skills, that he has accomplished some task and has done his best: "One which brings the student at least one step closer to perfection in at least one step or exercise."

In addition, a good class gives the body itself a thorough workout, increasing one's physical strength and skill, loosening the body, and helping to mold it into an instrument. Several students mentioned in particular the importance of a good set of warm-up exercises that relaxed the body and prepared it for the lesson. The arduous use of the body also included the satisfying feeling of exhaustion after the class, the sense of having been cleansed: "One that strives to mold the body into the most perfect instrument that it could be . . . a feeling of cleansing out body and mind."

Some students also mentioned the organization of the class, its coherence and group atmosphere. The class should be homogeneous, so that all could follow and all dancers feel part of the group. Classes should be small and well organized, with a purposeful, but light, atmosphere. And again, some few mentioned that the good class should be creative, combining technique with expressiveness, or allowing the student free rein to create his own expressions.

As in their opinions of a good teacher, students then expected a good class to be both inspiring, challenging, and interesting, as well as arduous, difficult, and aiding the student's development toward mastery of the body. Despite the focus on creative expression in the first question of the series, creativity was mentioned least of all regarding the teacher and the dance class itself. Students apparently feel that class should be mainly a training ground for learning use of the medium, mastery of the body, and technique.

C. The Good Student

Dance students were next asked to turn their critical eye to themselves, and describe a good dance student. Consistent with the emphasis on discipline and learning in the answers to the previous questions, the most frequently mentioned quality of a good student was the ability to work hard, practice regularly, and devote one's full energies to the discipline and perfection of the body. The focus is again less on creative potential and much more on the discipline required to make the body into an effective instrument. Personal traits, native talent, or physical strength are mentioned infrequently, less than one might expect from those involved in a creative field.

Hard work and practice itself were the most frequently mentioned attributes of a good dance student. The good student is persistent and constant in his efforts. He practices regularly, and uses his class learning outside of class: "One who applies himself constantly . . . practices to a good extent on his [or her] own." The emphasis is on a willingness to work hard, seriously, and conscientiously in developing one's technique. Second, the good student has a perfectionist attitude toward himself. He is driving, motivated, constantly seeking improvement in technique, and asks the most from himself and his body: "One . . . who strives for the greatest perfection he is physically capable of." Third, the good student works to the utmost in class. He attends regularly, pays attention, and tries to learn the most he can from his teachers: "A good dance student is a person who goes into class with nothing on his mind but dance, and who wants to get everything that he possibly can from the class and teacher."

In terms of personal traits, the good student is receptive, alert, attentive, and understands quickly. He is cooperative, open-minded, and desires knowledge of dance concepts. He seeks a good technical foundation in dance. Above all, he is patient with his faults, willing to learn from criticism, and does not let himself become discouraged: ". . . he doesn't get discouraged over technical failings but will continue to work with a knowledge that there is an area in which he is weak." In addition, he has a real love of dance, a joy in movement; he is eager and devoted to the field.

Beyond these attitudes of the student, some mentioned traits that might be considered more "innate" dispositions of the potential dancer. Physically, the dance student should have or be interested in attaining a flexible, strong, coordinated body. He should show endurance and his body should be capable of development. Some mentioned talent: a feeling for line, dynamics, and rhythm, or a natural sense of spontaneous, unaffected movement. Again, the most infrequently mentioned category was creativity. A few students felt a creative nature was necessary, that a dancer should be able to dance with feeling, to relate dancing to the wider life of the dancer, but these were the only three comments out of 61 total responses.

Given such an ideal picture, how many of the students felt they qualified as good dance students? Among 25 women answering, 11 felt they qualified; 8 said they sought improvement; and 2 stated flatly, "No." From the males, two felt they were good students; two sought improvement. The remainder of the students declined to answer. (See Table 16B.)

III. Dance, Emotion, Motivation

The purpose of the questions in this section was to get some idea of the role of dancing in the lives of students, how dance fits into their emotional life and needs, and what kinds of things attracted them to dance, as opposed to other art forms. One of the simplest approaches was just to ask the dancers why they danced, and this was the first question of the series. The next four questions sought to explore more deliberately the relationships between dance and feelings, moods, tensions, fatigues. The questions were the following: (1) Why do you dance? (2) Do you enjoy dancing more when you are in certain moods, and if so, which ones? (3) Does being tired affect your dancing? (4) Does being tense affect your dancing? (5) How does dancing affect your moods, fatigue, tension?

A. WHY DANCE?

For the first question, the most frequent answers focused on the feelings of joy experienced by the dancer while dancing. This sense of joy, uplift, or release was sometimes difficult for the dancers to explain. Some simply replied that they liked to dance better than anything else, it gave them pleasure, they liked to move: "I feel a great deal of pleasure and feel an inexpressible joy when I dance. . . ." "Because I love to, this is the most difficult question for me to answer." Others elaborated more on the sense of joy, which for them included love of movement itself, love of music and rhythm, and delight in the feeling of free movement through space, "I dance because I enjoy the freedom of being able to move through space." Dancing seemed to provide intrinsic reward through the kinesthetic sensation of unhindered movement.

The use of the body as a tool for self-expression was another important feature of dance. Many students felt that dancing was their best skill, their proper medium, for expressing feelings and thoughts that might not otherwise find outlet: "I get great joy from knowing that I can say something with my body that no one else can duplicate." In particular, dance allowed emotional expression: the dancer can portray what he feels; he can simultaneously release and express the joys and unhappinesses he experiences in life: "Because I want to portray what I feel . . . emotional expression and release." Needs of the intellect were not mentioned and were seldom central in the dancer's response to his art. In addition, in this grouping, too, though self-expression was the focus, the particularly self-satisfying nature of dance as a medium was emphasized: "To me it gives life more meaning to be able to clearly express through your own body your feeling about your existence." Dance, then, provided a uniquely satisfying means of self-expression for these students, particularly the expression of feelings and emotions.

Another motif was the pleasure felt by the dancer in being able to entertain and give joy to others. Some students felt as though they were giving a gift to others; they liked to make people happy, to create beauty for others, and to please. A fourth set of answers concentrated on the discipline of the body itself. For these few, the ability to master the body, improve it, and achieve physical well-being were the most intrinsically rewarding features of dance: "To master my body, know it, discipline it, improve it . . . feel at ease with it."

The fifth grouping consisted only of two responses, both from males, who mentioned the need for a profession and felt that dancing was the best way for them both to meet their own needs and to earn a living. A few additional responses that could not be grouped included one dancer who stated she had always naturally turned to dance since childhood and another who felt dancing was compensation for a childhood illness requiring confinement to bed.

For the most part, then, students stressed intrinsic rewards of dance—movement itself, self-expression, pleasure in entertaining or in discipline and physical coordination. Dancing seemed to meet needs for unhampered, coordinated movement, which was self-expressive, allowed emotional outlet, and also related the self to others through performance, with different students emphasizing one or another phase of the interaction.

B. MOODS AND DANCE

The close connection between emotion and dance was further emphasized in responses to the second question. Of the 32 respondents, 25 stated that moods—happiness, excitement, anger, sadness, depression—did affect dancing, whereas only 7 replied that there was no connection. Surprisingly, the particular mood that most inspired the dancer varied from student to student. Whatever mood was experienced, it seemed to carry over into the dance, expressing, relieving, or changing the dancer's original state of mind, making dance more enjoyable.

The feeling state most frequently mentioned as affecting dance was happiness or joy. Many dancers found dancing most enjoyable when they felt happy, light, carefree: "When I'm happy, I want to thank God for something." This sense of joy was also expressed as a feeling of excitement or inspiration: "Sometimes I get greatly inspired and have huge drive." Others answered that they found dancing most enjoyable when they were *either* happy or depressed, or even angry, as long as the mood was extreme. Dancing provided outlet for the intense emotion, be it positive or negative: "Sometimes when I'm very happy, sometimes when very sad, . . . always when I have difficulties with men." "Elated, happy, angry; usually when depressed I don't feel like dancing but once I start it cheers me up." Others felt that they did their best work *particularly* when they were depressed, sad, or hurt. Dancing helped to get one out of the depression, to relieve fatigue and tension associated with the unhappy state: "Many times if I'm sad or have been hurt, I will let my emotions out by dancing." On the other hand, six of the answers were just the opposite: the person felt best dancing only when they were *not* depressed or sad but rather felt energetic, in a "working" mood: "As long as I am in any but a greatly depressed or worried mood, I can enjoy dancing." "When in an energetic mood and just wish to move for the joy of moving."

Seven of the answers said that particular moods did not affect dancing at all. Of these, four students stated that dancing was always enjoyable, no matter what mood one began with. Three indicated more of an intellectual rather than an emotional interest: dancing was most enjoyable when one felt stimulated by and interested in the class: "When the class interests me. My moods change so often that I would never enjoy dance if I had to wait for certain ones."

On the whole, then, mood definitely affected the dancer's enjoyment of dance. For the majority, the relationship was a positive one: any extreme emotion, whether joy, anger, or sadness, could be carried over into and expressed through dance, relieving the emotional state. For some, the relationship was negative, with depression interfering with dance; while others felt that their love of movement overrode the influence of any particular mood, and a few felt that intellectual interests most influenced them.

C. Physical Factors

Fatigue, however, affected dancing for the most part quite differently than did emotion. Though some dancers felt that fatigue disappeared during dance, most felt their performance greatly impaired when they were weary.

The most frequently mentioned deficit was that of alertness and responsiveness. When tired, most felt lethargic, slow. The muscles were less responsive; one was careless and apt to lose control of one's movement: "You are not as alert and you don't react quickly; also your body is tired and may seem heavy or sluggish." "I am slower in everything I do and it is painful."

Another deficit was loss of strength and endurance. Coordination, sustained movement requiring strength became more difficult: "My technique is more careless, extensions lower, because the muscles lose strength and control." Others feel unable to concentrate on what they are doing: "I find it hard to pick up combinations and remember them." Students mentioned that such loss of coordination and smoothness is frustrating: it takes more of an effort to do one's best, and one does not really much feel in the mood for dancing. The end result is an overall loss in creativity, bounce, and eagerness, which can be very unpleasant: "Spirit willing but not the flesh, causes frustration." Some also mentioned the possibility of injury through exertion when tired.

Another group of answers emphasized some of the positive aspects of fatigue in dancing. Some felt that they pushed themselves harder to compensate and thus ended up surpassing their best efforts. For some, dancing itself revived the person and he "snapped out of" his weariness. Only one person, however, said that fatigue had no effect on her dancing.

In general, then, fatigue has detrimental effects on the dance performance and on the dancer's feeling of satisfaction.

D. TENSION

Tension, unlike emotion, affected dancing in much the same way as fatigue, leading to deficits in control and concentration, while occasionally leading to better performance for some. The main difference between the effects of fatigue and tension was that while fatigue seemed to slow the dancer down, making him feel lethargic and uncoordinated, tension led rather to a lack of fluidity, grace, and flow, and to a sense of constraint.

Out of the 35 responses to the question, 17 mentioned the lack of fluidity in dance brought about by tension. Dancers complained of a sense of tightness, an inability to let go, a restriction of the free flow of movement. Movements may become smaller, breathing irregular, and balance is lost. The dancer finds it difficult to project feeling through his body: "Being tense must jam the muscles ... I almost freeze." "It restricts the free flow of movement ... you don't give enough in your movement."

Other related complaints were the loss of control and coordination, and the need to use excessive strength to accomplish movements. It is more difficult to keep control of the body and takes more energy to keep going. As with fatigue, there is also an inability to concentrate or attend to the dance. Technical sections fall apart; the dancer may feel confused, unable to think: "I tighten up, can't work or think about what I'm doing."

On the other hand, as with fatigue, a few mentioned the occasional positive effects of tension on dance. Sometimes tension gives additional energy, which, if it can be released through the dance, makes the dance more vital: "It either gives me energy I need or tightens my body so that it will not work for me." "Sometimes it shoots adrenaline into my system, makes me more alive." Or, for some, tension may gradually dissipate through the dance.

A few of the dancers stated that tension had no effect, either because the person never got tense or made it a point not to bring tensions to class. On the whole, however, the effects of tension, like fatigue, were detrimental to performance, and the extra energy it might bring to the dance could not be released and used as effectively as that provided by emotion and mood.

E. Moods Produced by Dancing

Independent of the effects of movement itself, the dancer's judgment of how good or bad his performance was in class definitely affected his later moods. If class performance was good, many felt elated, happy, sociable; but a bad class performance could send the dancer into a bleak depression. Dance students felt that often class work made them aware of their faults and the need for improvement. They could become dissatisfied with their work, and feel that they were accomplishing nothing: "Sometimes a good class makes me feel wonderful no matter how tired or depressed I was; bad classes make me cry or make me indifferent or stubborn." Dance is an integral part of the lives of students, and deeply involved with their emotional response to life: "Dance is so much a part of my life . . . if things go well for me dance-wise, I am generally more happy and if I am upset dance-wise, I am that way in every mood."

A few said that dancing mainly affected them in terms of causing fatigue. Often they felt weary, exhausted from too much work, though it could be a happy, satisfied sort of weariness. Only two stated that dancing did not affect their moods.

In summary, then, students were attracted to dance for the intrinsic rewards of unhindered movement, self-expression, and pleasure in entertaining or in self-discipline. There was, in addition, a reciprocal relationship between emotion and dance. Dance for the most part provided outlet for any strong emotion, negative or positive, leaving the dancer with a feeling of renewal, strength, self-confidence, and happiness. On the other hand, an unsuccessful dance workout could cause depression, resentment, and irritability in the dancers, affecting the feeling–tone of their whole day. Fatigue and tension, though largely detrimental to performance, could also be dispelled through dance, though emotion was more closely connected to and released through dance than were the former.

The student dancers' comments on what attracts them to dance and on the relationship between mood and dance correspond very well with the personality descriptions obtained on the Adjective Check List (see p. 111). Emotional, impulsive, spontaneous, and unconventional, the students have chosen a field that both allows outlet for and channels emotional expression into appropriate forms. The dancers' emphasis on the feeling of joy in unhampered, free, coordinated movement itself, is interesting in this connection. The mode of expression—movement—has a specific attraction in and for itself. Motility and rhythm are very basic ways of patterning, integrating, and releasing impulse and emphasize the emotional nature of the dance students. They are not intellectuals; and their need to move under the impact of their impulse life, rather than resist it or find other modes of expression, is predominant.

Second, dance is not only an outlet for impulse and emotion, but also a channeled, disciplined outlet. Students may need to move with their impulses, but such movement must also be coordinated, graceful, expressive, rather than random. The students showed in their earlier test data a spontaneity and openness to themselves that can have both positive and negative aspects: more joyful and enthusiastic, they may also be more irritable, chaotic, hostile, or depressed. Dance seems to provide a constructive means for organizing what otherwise could be a too impulsive, too chaotic, too motile sort of person: they are learning the discipline and self-control that allow them to utilize creatively an impulse life that they do not choose to suppress in themselves. (See Table 16C.)

IV. Dance and Personality

In addition to emotional outlet, dance can also be considered in relationship to other aspects of the personality: the need to create and express oneself, and the need to relate to the wider culture in a meaningful way. As mentioned earlier, it is not necessarily true that all those engaged in artistic fields are creative. Do student dancers consider themselves creative, and if so, how do they define the term? The next two questions of the series dealt with the relationship of the dancer to the wider population. If the dance students were expressive in dance, they might also be equally expressive and motile in other spheres, such as the use of gestures when speaking. The third and fourth questions, then, asked the dancers if and when they "talked with their hands." The fifth question asked the students if they felt they were normal, and the sixth asked how they defined the term. The last questions in the section, concerned primarily with the male dancer, asked the students what they thought about male dancers and why there were not more of them. (Responses are summarized in Table 16D.)

In answer to the first question, 18 out of the 30 respondents felt that they were creative. An additional 6 said they were creative "sometimes;" while 6 either answered negatively or rejected the question. The basis for response fell into three general groups: results and achievements of past work; the need to express oneself and one's feelings; and personal traits, such as receptivity to the new.

The most frequently mentioned answers had to do with achievements. Many dancers considered the ability to choreograph, compose, and plan dance movements to be an indication of creativity. Some answered that they enjoyed improvising, had been able to develop their own dances well, and saw no reason to perform another's dance movements when they could just as well innovate on their own: "Why do the same thing all the time that someone else thought up? I can think something up just as good and maybe better." Others mentioned that in the past they had always been considered creative, that others looked to them to design and plan dramatic or dance productions: "I derive a great deal of satisfaction from choreographing and believe some of my efforts to be pretty good."

A second grouping defined creativity as the ability to express oneself through dance. These students felt they were creative because they tried to use dance to communicate their feelings to others: "Yes, I try to use dance as expression of how I feel." They were not afraid to express themselves, enjoyed composing, and saw dance as an extension of themselves and their self expression.

Other criteria were personal traits the individual felt to be indicative of creativity. The most frequently mentioned aptitude was receptivity to the new and original: "Because I find my mind susceptible to a variety of ideas that can be expressed in an art form in an interesting manner." These students felt they had new ideas that seemed to work, liked to try new ways of communicating their feelings to others, and were individualistic in their personal style. A miscellaneous set of traits included the sense of having a creative mind; being sensitive to the environment, and being daring and adventurous.

The answers of those students who felt they were "somewhat" creative grouped themselves into the same sets. The difference was that these students did not feel that they had lived up to their own standards. Some felt that their achievements were not yet up to par: "I seem to get good ideas and start along a good track . . . material rolls out, and then I get stuck." One might feel the need to express oneself, but be unable to realize one's idea: "Sometimes I am inspired to do something but it may or may not be exceptionally creative." In terms of personal traits, some felt they were not daring or original enough to warrant the label. They might like the new and different, but feel they could not produce enough original material: "I like the new and different, but often I can't get the ideas to bring out what I want to create."

For those answering the question negatively, the most common response was lack of sufficient background and training. These felt that they had not sufficiently mastered dance to be able to use it as an expressive tool. A few simply felt they were not original enough: ". . . creating of dance does not come especially easily, nor do originality and inspiration come regularly." "I enjoy being told what to do rather than finding my own way."

For the majority of students, then, dance was meeting needs to create something new and express the self, at least to an extent. For most, they either had been creative and productive in the past; felt the need to express themselves through dance; or felt they had the personality traits to do so; though some did not judge their results as particularly creative, and for others the need appeared infrequently. Creativity was defined most often in concrete ways, as the ability to choreograph with originality. Meaning and self-expression were more in the background, with the predominant emphasis on original and effective use of the tools of the trade, as the dancer participated in his professional world.

A. THE EXPRESSIVE GESTURE

The student dancers, true to their colors, were gesturally expressive and exuberant. Of 31 respondents, the majority (22) gave an emphatic "Yes" to the question, with an additional 4 stating that they sometimes talked with their hands. Only 5 said they seldom or never did so.

The most frequent reason given for using the hands in expression was to communicate the emotional intensity of the message. Nearly all mentioned that they spoke with their hands when they were "excited." This included either an intense desire to communicate "Excited . . . especially when I'm anxious to get an idea across," or an excitement over the subject matter discussed: "When excited over the subject I'm talking about . . . exact words escape me momentarily."

Others used gesture for descriptive purposes: "When I am trying to explain something or can make a better picture by doing so." "Usually when I'm making a nonspatial statement and translating it into spatial terms." These students found that gesture helped them to dramatize a situation or emphasize a point, in order to more effectively communicate what they wanted to say.

B. AM I NORMAL?

The next question concerned the relationship between being a dancer and "abnormality," as defined by the students. The pursuit of any art requires a life style usually at odds with the dominant themes of the culture. Moreover, motivation and endurance in the pursuit of goals must be intense and constant. Did the dancers consider themselves "abnormal" in their choice of career and mode of expression?

Of the 32 respondents, over half considered themselves normal. Five students redefined the question, saying that in some ways they were normal and in others not normal. Five rejected the question, and another 5 answered flatly, "No."

There were only 30 responses to this question, as 5 of the subjects answered only "Yes" or "No" and did not elaborate. Of these 30, 7 rejected the question at least partially, and some refused to answer at all. Objections included the usual points, that normality is difficult to define; that we are all individuals; and even that calling oneself abnormal was pretentious: "I don't know what normal is, so I can't say." "Not too many people are, completely, and if I said I was abnormal it would be because I was trying to be so."

Those who did accept the question varied considerably in their definitions of normality. Some considered normality to be a question of emotional balance. They felt that their emotions and attitudes were not extreme; that few problems seriously upset them; and that they were capable of maintaining their own equilibrium and solving their own problems: "Yes, I never get extremely tense or too apathetic, and in most things I have a healthy, balanced attitude."

The second and most frequent criterion was adjustment, the ability to get along with others. Those answering in this category felt that their interests and inclinations were not very different from others. They have little trouble fitting in with others, desire a normal family life, and are not considered strange by others: "Yes, because I enjoy people and doing things; I am not in the habit of doing things people consider weird." These students felt that they could adjust to new situations confronting them and to their own problems: "Yes, normal for every person is different, it's adjusting to your environment and problems."

A few set very high standards for "normality" and felt they were meeting those standards. Normality is finding meaning in life and developing one's potential, it is not the ability to be average. These few felt they were doing what they wanted to do, life had meaning, and that was good: "Normal for my own potential, but not average."

Those who answered that they were "somewhat" normal, also considered themselves normal but not average. They saw themselves as capable and adjusted relative to others, but drew lines between the kind of person they were, contrasted with others. The most frequent distinction made was that of being an artist itself. These felt that an artist can never really be considered normal. The intense devotion to and love of one's work, the willingness to put up with vocational insecurity, the confrontation with the deeper issues of life, and the energy required to sustain oneself set the artist apart from others. "Normal in comparison to others ... but since normal connotes average, I and other artists are not normal because of our intense devotion, love, and work in an insecure, rigorous, often disappointing vocation." Related to this distinction, another group considered themselves different because they were emotional. Though considering themselves normal, they did not see themselves as particularly emotionally balanced. They felt they were more moody, changeable, and intense than others: "I have more anxieties than the normal, more changes of mood, get more excited, and moved more easily."

Those answering that they were not normal based their answers on much the same distinctions as the foregoing. Many felt they could not consider themselves normal because they were dancers: "A normal person does not want dance as a career and wouldn't give up as many social activities, and an artist has a different outlook—perhaps enjoys it better—on life." The dancer has more feeling, "passion," than others and can not consider himself normal. Of the three men who did not consider themselves normal, two of them fell into this grouping, automatically excluding themselves from "normality," not without a trace of bitterness, simply because they were dancers, with no further explanation: "No, because I am a male dancer." Only one person, a male, excluded himself from normality on the grounds of pathology, "Just confused, I guess."

Dance students, then, on the whole, did not see themselves as disturbed, pathological, or eccentric. Many considered themselves like others in their social life and in emotional equilibrium, while others saw themselves as an intensification of the "normal" person, responding more deeply to life, asking more from it, and willing to take more risks.

C. THE SITUATION OF THE MALE DANCER

The male dancer, however, is in a much more difficult position than is the female dancer, socially. As was brought out in the test data, he is more personally conflicted than the female; also, the social negativism he must face is much greater than that for the female. How did other students react to the male dancer?

The most frequent answers focused on the need for men in the profession and the role of masculinity in dance. Many of the answers stressed how necessary men were to the art. Women students felt that dance could not do without men dancers and wished there were more of them: "They are essential to the art." "We need them." A slightly different version of the same theme concerned the nature of masculinity in dance. The opinion among female students was that there was a distinctly masculine form of dance, equally as important as the feminine, which should be emphasized and developed. Men should not be expected or taught to dance like women but should be allowed to use their exclusively masculine attributes—strength, agility, strong rhythms—in dance: "When a man dancer is truly masculine, he surpasses the woman and is far more exciting to watch." "Some of them are strong and dance as men should. . . ."

The second most frequent set of answers had to do with the dancer as an individual. These students felt that male dancers were the same as female dancers—they were all dancers, and they were all individuals. One theme was that being a dancer took precedence over one's sexual identification; there were more similarities among dancers of both sexes than there were differences: "I have no particular feelings: I judge them by the same criteria as female dancers." "To me in the dance world there are only other dancers." Another related stance was to insist on the individuality of each: "They are people like anyone else . . . all individuals."

The third group of answers were value judgments or feeling reactions, all of them approving. Among women, the consensus was that male dancers were "fine people." Answers included admiration for a man daring to go against social mores and continue his profession, and sympathy for the ridicule he must often face from others.

Other students concentrated on the masculinity–femininity dimension itself. Five of the answers in this category stated that men encountered within the dance world were too effeminate, lacking in masculinity; or that they tended to dance effeminately, which was felt as a disappointment. Needless to say, none of the male dancers answered in this category.

Among the six men answering, three replied that male dancers were to be taken as individuals, that they were the same as other men. One reacted in terms of professional identification, saying that men were necessary to the profession and there should be more of them. Two gave a value judgment, approving the male dancer and showing sympathy for his plight vis-à-vis the society.

The second part of the question asked why there are not more male dancers. There was an overwhelming consensus in response to this question. All of the answers mentioned social pressure as having some relationship to the scanty number of male dancers.

Regarding social prejudice, most of the dancers agreed that the social label of effeminate scared most men away from dance as an occupation. Some mentioned that men feel it is sissyish to dance: "The reason there aren't more is because men think dance is feminine." Men who might be interested in dance are discouraged by attitudes toward them, "Family objects, friends laugh, desire not strong enough." Parents steer their sons away from dance as a physical activity into sports or in other ways discourage the child, "There aren't more of them because parents make their boys feel that to be a dancer is to be a sissy." The society does not consider dancing to be part of the masculine role. Americans have made the mistake of confusing sensitive, emotional men with feminine men and condemn masculine interests in the arts. The history of dance, stemming from ballet, contributes to the aura of femininity surrounding dance. The consensus was that society frowns on male dancers, labeling them effeminate, so that the dance world loses much potential talent in this way.

Other answers followed from the social prejudice against male dancers. Two of the women students mentioned that because of social attitudes, the man who wants to dance must face isolation and ridicule from the community, particularly the community of other men. Others felt that sex-linked traits brought about a lack of interest in dance from men. Men in general do not have the prerequisites for dance. They may be uninterested in movement, not talented, or may consider the field too impractical. "They don't join simply because they're not interested in movement."

All of the men who answered mentioned the social prejudice against dancers. "Ask the populace."

In general, then, student dancers felt a great need for more men in the profession and for a distinctly masculine performance in dance. Male students were either taken as individuals or on the whole were liked by female dancers, though some felt they were too effeminate. The consensus among the students was that social prejudice caused the scarcity of men in the profession.

The majority of the student dancers, then, considered themselves to be creative, which they defined by concrete achievement in the past, by the need to express themselves, or by a capacity for originality in thought. As a group, they were gesturally expressive when speaking, corresponding to their needs for motility and expression in dance. Dance for most was a means of self-expression occurring within the confines of a discipline that provides also a means by which the individual relates to life. In this relation to the wider culture, dance students saw themselves as quite normal, able to solve their own problems, interacting freely with others, and seeking to realize their potential, though they were perhaps more emotional, active, and intense than others. Male dancers were socially in a more difficult position than females, and the students commented on the immense social negativism the male dancer had to fight as well as the isolation he might experience as a result of his career choice. Some women students felt he was too effeminate, whereas others stressed the possibilities for uniquely masculine expression in dance.

V. Dance as Art

The need for self-expression and the channeling of emotional reaction were dominant themes throughout most of the questionnaire material. As with any art requiring a mastery of a medium, however, there is a fine line to be drawn between expression and control. Where discipline and formalism become too rigid, they are a means of suppression of impulse; where they are moderate and flexible, they become a means of channeling and a tool for expression of the personality. There has been, for example, a constant subtheme running through the responses to the questionnaire: there are those few students who appreciate most the discipline and mastery of the body; who like most the long hours of training; and who would rather be a part of a performance than create their own forms. Dance is a form, a way of analyzing movement into elements and building meaningful patterns from them. How do the majority of the students approach the formal aspects of dance as art? The students' response to dance as art may give more information about the balance of expression and control, impulse and channeling, in his personality makeup. The following set of questions was designed to explore further the dancer's reactions to and use of the formal properties of his art. (Responses are summarized in Table 16E.)

The purpose of the first question in the series was to elicit the students' attitudes toward art in general, its social purposes, or its functions in human nature. The question was simply, "Why is there art?" The second and third questions asked about dance in particular: Did students consider dance to be an art, as music, painting, and poetry are arts? The fourth question dealt more specifically with the students' use of form in dance and asked if there were any elements they felt all dances should have. The last question of the series asked about dance in the future. Did students see their profession as vital, dynamic, and expanding; or removed from the rest of the culture, static, losing its impetus? The attitude the students expressed toward the future of dance might well indicate their attitudes toward their own use of and future in dance.

Responses to the first question, "Why is there art?" fall into four large groups. The most frequent basis for response was self-expression. Art exists because the need to express oneself is a very basic, inherent part of man's nature: "Because man is creative and he has to express himself." Art is like any other natural outgrowth of man's activity, such as science or technology; it is part of his makeup: "Because it is inherent in human nature, movement being the first of human expressions." Art serves as expression not only of oneself, one's individuality, but of the wider life principles working through one. Art is an expression of life, an outlet for emotions, and a path for the spirit: "Art exists as a means whereby man's spirit can find outlet and expression." The central focus for all the foregoing answers was the outgoing flow of feeling and idea in the attempt to express oneself, life, feelings, or spirituality.

Other students felt the purpose of art was to capture in form the beauty of life. There is beauty in the mundane, which can be reflected through art: "it is to life what the desert flower is to an Arab ... there is beauty in all life, why not emphasize it?" For these students, art was the expression of beauty itself; and perfection in art meant the fulfillment of an aesthetic ideal.

Another function of art was to provide the basis for a universal means of communication, in order to share some of the most basic and meaningful experiences of human life: "The purpose of art is to refine the feelings and emotions so that they may be shared with mankind." Moreover, art can entertain, give joy to, and please others: "To entertain, give joy." The interaction between audience and artist was the central focus of all these answers.

Fourth, art was also seen as a means of revealing truth, increasing awareness of the human condition. These responses were more psychological and philosophical than the others. Art can help people to learn about themselves, through the portrayal of their emotions and needs. It can uplift the mind, make people think about life, or bring greater awareness of man's relations to himself, to others, and to the cosmos. As one of the male students said, the purpose of art can be "to show life as it is, without a lot of gluck covering up the truth."

In general, then, students saw art forms as the natural outgrowth of man's inherent need to express his own nature, bring harmony and aesthetic grace to the irregular, share and communicate with others, and explore his own nature.

Without exception, all dancers considered dance to be an art, though some also pointed out differences between it and the other arts. The most frequent basis for response was, as in the foregoing answers, expressiveness. All of the arts, including dance, are creative means of self-expression, despite their differing modes. The crux of the artistic process is the ability to express meaning through form. Through movement and rhythm, one can express as much as through words or colors. A person can even tell stories with dance, as with other arts: "The talent of expression is in the body, painting the hand, poetry the mind." Moreover, movement is a very basic, primary means of expression and is actually the first of the arts: "people move first, long before they experiment with other arts." Dance, like all art, gives expression also to universal principles of life, mind, spirit: ". . . it is an individual expression of life; creative, personal, yet universal." Others emphasized the expression of emotion, while a few felt that dance, like other arts, gives expression to an ideal of beauty: "It is the transcription of beauty just as any of the other arts."

In addition, dance, like all art forms, is a creative means of communication between audience and artist. Dance is a distinct communicative medium; it is creative; and it is appreciated by its audience: "It is a means of communication which is inspiring, creative."

A third set of responses mentioned that dance shares the same basic elements of expression with the other arts. All are skills, requiring the perfection of technique: "Dance has a technique, like the other arts." Moreover, all depend on the same units, "Form, color, outline, tone, rhythm are all formed in these arts, but expressed according to their medium." Dance, like all arts, is a specialized skill, using standard tools of the trade.

A fourth group of answers seemed to be based on the criterion of success or survival. The argument seemed to be simply that dancing exists and has survived the centuries, therefore it must have the same reason for existing as the other arts: "Because dance has come just as far as any other art in the world." Dance has succeeded, so it must have meaning to others, as do the other arts.

Though all students agreed that dance had much in common with all of the arts, some of the differences drawn among them were as interesting as the similarities. Out of the 45 responses, 10 included mention of differences, in addition to similarities, between dance and other arts. Of these, the majority concerned themselves with the formal differences among the arts, stressing the use of the body and movement in dance. Dance is a "living" art. Performed once in time, it exists momentarily, offers its gift of meaning, and disappears into memory again. Unlike arts that can be retained as monuments of meaning, such as a sculpture, a painting, a printed poem, the dance is perhaps more closely a parallel to the fleeting, enigmatic nature of life itself. Once performed, the scene can never happen again in just that way, in all its living particulars: ". . . it is something created in time and space and may never be the same as painting or poetry . . ."; "I call art like drama and dance impure because they use life as their medium." The act of creation in dance does not require that the artist detach himself from life to capture and still one of its moments; rather, ongoing life is the medium.

All of the dancers, then, definitely considered dance to be an art form like other arts, because it is a means of creative expression, communicates with a receptive audience, requires skill in developing technique, and has survived the centuries. The differences between dance and other arts were in the emphasis on the body as the primary tool of expression and on the immediate, "living" nature of the medium. Dance was considered both a form and a tool for self-expression by the students.

The student dancer's use of form in his own compositions was in general flexible and individualistic. Although 28 out of the 33 responses to the fourth question indicated that there were some elements all dances should have, the meaning of the term "element" was expanded beyond the sense of a unit of dance to include meaning, creative spirit, and the like.

The most frequently mentioned "element," in fact, was that of meaning. Dance should be expressive, it should say something, leave a message, create an atmosphere, draw a conclusion, or reflect life in some meaningful way: "Dance should have a definite message, that is what dance is, a means of communication through movement." Dance should also project emotion and feeling: "All dances should be danced with feeling, project an emotion, and say something. . . ." Responses in this first grouping deplored pure body mechanics and asked that whatever elements were used, dance be meaningful.

The second most frequent response stated that dance should use all of the elements of composition and use them well. No particular element was more important than any other. Rather, all elements integral to the medium—space, time, form, dynamics—should be included: "There are many basic elements . . . dance composition should include the basic constructs of composition . . . style, form, rhythm, dynamics." The focus of all of these answers was that the dancer should be aware of all the basic elements of composition and use them appropriately.

The third group of answers emphasized variety and creativity in composing. The most important feature of dance is that it be interesting, vital, unique. A dance composition should have a characteristic distinction or spark of originality that only the creator of it can give. The creator should understand dance so well that it becomes a creative extension of himself: "I feel it is very necessary for the dancer to improvise without thinking of technique and to fully understand what he is trying to express." The dancer should have a clear idea of what he wants and should implement his conceptions with variety and originality.

A few felt that dance compositions should above all be unified, harmonious, and beautiful: "Unity . . . otherwise there is nothing but scraps." "Continuity, beautiful movement." Aesthetic grace appeared to be the dominant concern of these students.

Five of the students felt the composition should be left entirely free and up to the individual. These students felt that all people are different and will utilize different elements according to what they want so say: "I would not specify one criterion for all dance compositions, for each one conveys what the choreographer wishes and communicates it in the best way he or she can, whether sacrificing even beauty of movement." Further, if the elements of dance were to be fixed and specified, dancing would become boring and there would be no experimentation: "No, how can you know an element should be there if you have not tried creating without it?"

The approach of the students to the use of form in dance was hence on the whole flexible. The emphasis was mainly on the creator's effective and educated use of his medium, rather than the medium's use of him through imposition of inflexible standards. An understanding of basic elements was useful mainly for the purpose of the expression of meaning or original ideas, or to fulfill an aesthetic ideal.

Regarding the dance of the future, most of the students expressed positive feelings. All of them felt dance would continue to grow and change, though they differed in their opinions of the nature of the growth. Answers fell into two large groupings: those concerned with the role of dance in society as a whole; and those interested in the evolution of dance as a separate art form.

Among those concerned with the role of dance in the wider society, three themes stood out. The first theme was that dance will become more widespread, popular, and necessary to others in the future. Dance has become more popular in the last 10 years and will continue to become more popular. Its emphasis on space and movement will increase its popularity in this age now experimenting with three-dimensional art forms. On the other hand, as it becomes more popular, it may also become more commercial: "It will become more popular, commercialized . . . it will continue to grow until it reaches a peak." The second theme was that dance will become more accepted and understood by the general public. Dance will become more important in daily life: "It will reach a fuller, richer, development, become more universally accepted and appreciated." "It will continue to grow, to become important in our everyday life." Third, offshoots of dance, such as dance therapy, will become more important: "More people will become aware of dance through other fields opening to dance, dance therapy for the physically and mentally retarded, etc."

The second large group of answers had to do with the evolution of style within the field of dance itself. From these answers, two themes were apparent. The first stressed continuing invention and experimentation in dance, while the second emphasized the dangers of overabstraction in dance. The majority of the responses were concerned with further exploration in dance. These students felt that dance, like other art forms, would expand, grow, invent new styles, and become more experimental. Dance will follow its own evolution and find new techniques, just as jazz dancing evolved from ballet. Style will become freer and will follow the times, becoming more chaotic, less old-fashioned and romantic. New horizons will come into view; modern dance will become more and more important: "Dance will progress as all other forms, branching into new fields, new ideas." Some felt dance would consolidate its gains, combining emotion and inventive, abstract dance, and integrating different styles: "It will evolve more slowly and carefully with stabilizing forces, such as a universal dance notation to preserve tradition."

A few, however, were more pessimistic about the future of dance. These students saw a danger in some of the trends in dance toward overabstract, mechanical movement. Dance may lose its simplicity, warmth, and connection with human feeling: "It will become more and more technical with less and less emphasis on the emotions, as much as I hate to say it."

Most of the students, then, saw dance and their future in dance as expanding, becoming more popular and part of daily life, experimenting with movement and new forms, with an awareness of the dangers of technical, mechanical originality lacking in meaning. They did not see dance as static or routinized but rather as a growing, exciting art in whose growth they, presumably, would participate.

For the student dancers, then, the purpose of art in general and dance in particular was to provide forms for the expression of universal principles of life, oneself, spirituality, that would allow the artist to share his experience with others, enriching their lives as well as his own. Dance, like other arts, was for them a medium, a craft, requiring skill and application for its development and having a language and set of formal rules of its own. The elements of dance, however, were to be used to further goals of self-expression, communication, or aesthetic harmony. The creator of dance was basically he who used formal elements flexibly and originally to further his own ends.

VI. How Dancers Describe Themselves

A simple technique for obtaining self-descriptions was employed in conjunction with the questionnaire given to the dancers. A list of 300 adjectives referring to personal traits was filled out by each student (the Gough Adjective Check List, Gough, 1958), under instructions to check the adjectives that clearly applied to oneself. The results are shown in Table 17. (Fifteen dance students from Mills College were added to the female sample.)

Perhaps the best way to begin to describe the female dancers is to characterize them as women with a lot of "steam." Active, energetic, emotional, and excitable, they would tend to react strongly and deeply to their environment and to themselves. This energy has a certain driving quality to it; they describe themselves as determined, ambitious, and capable, and need to succeed in their chosen field. Their goals, however, are not the usual and cannot be pursued within the normal channels of endeavor. Individualistic, original, and independent, they tend to be headstrong and follow their own lead in developing themselves. Their development, however, is most likely construed by them in highly personal terms: There is a serious side to them—sincere, thoughtful, and reflective—and they have a thirst for experience that is perhaps related to a need for meaning in their existence. In pursuit of goals and self, they are adaptable, changeable, and adventurous; far-ranging in interests; and versatile in applying themselves. Individualism is tempered by an appreciation of the most basic social virtues: they describe themselves also as considerate, reasonable, civilized, responsible, and tolerant. Their femininity would be more of the generous, affectionate, understanding, and appreciative type, rather than the more conservative, submissive, deferring, and passive feminine nature. Their openness to themselves and their feelings, however, includes also an awareness of discord and anxiety. Nonetheless, they have considerable ability to use their dissatisfactions in creative ways, describing themselves as idealistic, imaginative, sensitive, and artistic.

The kinds of adjectives checked by the male dancer tell us more about the kind of person he is. From his self-description, he is much like his female counterpart, though more complicated, conflicted, and flamboyant.

He has the same steam and emotionality as she does, describing himself as active, energetic, excitable, enthusiastic, and emotional. His lability, however, has more of an impulsive, show-off, and sometimes hostile quality to it. He sees himself as mischievous, rebellious, zany, frank. He is flirtatious, pleasure seeking, and good looking, and may draw attention to himself through wit and humor. At the same time, however, he may also be outspoken, impatient, touchy, and fault finding. His excesses may stem more from difficulty in controlling the more hostile, moody, and defensive aspects of his personality, rather than from a need to compete and assert the self, as with the female. More restless and less confident than the woman, he nonetheless is equally ambitious. He can be capable, logical, and persistent in pursuing his goals; and like her, he is flexible, curious, adventurous, and versatile, seeking change and new experience. His emotionality appears socially as warmth, affection, joviality. He has a compassionate side, describing himself as forgiving, appreciative, and helpful. Despite his pique and moodiness, he sees himself as obliging, mannerly, and mild. Like the female, he accepts those basic values necessary for social life, including reliability, responsibility, tact, honesty, and tolerance. He is, however, painfully aware of conflict, doubts, and inferiorities. He describes himself as worrying, self-pitying, and self-punishing. His conflicts seem to appear not so much as timidity, as rather an alternation between temperamental outbursts, withdrawn moodiness, and enthusiastic giving.

CHAPTER NINE

Two Case Studies of Student Writers

A young man and a young woman who were students of creative writing took part in an "assessment" at the Institute of Personality Assessment and Research, University of California, Berkeley, some 10 years ago. They belong to a different generation of students than the ones we know now—less assertive of their individuality, less self-confident, less unconventional, less politically concerned. Were they also less creative, more inhibited by neurosis? Neither of them succeeded in being published after their student days, so their potential must be considered unrealized so far as professional success is concerned. But because they were studied in some depth by a method that combines measurement with interview, they may serve as examples of how the neurotic barriers to creative expression may be understood. The presentation of their cases is intended to serve also as an illustration of method and as an occasion for introducing the reader to more of the kinds of psychological techniques useful in research on the arts. Finally, there is a certain historical interest in seeing how the culture itself at a given moment in time may facilitate or inhibit creativity.

I. The Assessment Method

First, we present a few notes about assessment procedures not already described in preceding chapters.

A. USE OF ADJECTIVES, TRAIT RATINGS, Q SORTS

The Gough Adjective Checklist is employed in assessment as a way of obtaining a description of the person as seen by the assessment staff. Each staff member checks the list after the two or three days of acquaintance with the subject, and these descriptions are collated to yield an overall staff impression in adjectival terms. A similar procedure is followed in rating traits (Dominance, Flexibility, etc.). The Q sort consists of 100 phrases descriptive of possible personal functioning, and these are arranged in nine groups expressing degree of saliency of the characteristic in the person's behavior and way of being. These too are used by the staff to record individual impressions, and are then collated.

B. PROJECTIVE TECHNIQUES

The Rorschach Psychodiagnostic Test, Thematic Apperception Test, and Dramatic Productions Test are interpreted as reflecting a person's fantasy, preoccupations, needs, cognitive style, and so on.

1. The Rorschach Psychodiagnostic Test

This test was developed by a Swiss psychiatrist, Herman Rorschach. A description of its development may be found in Rorschach's monograph, *Psychodiagnostic: A Diagnostic Test based on Perception,* which is published in Berne, Switzerland, by the Huber Company, and is available in an English translation by P. Lemkan and B. Kronenburg.

The test consists of 10 inkblots, some in black and white and some containing color. These 10 blots were selected by Rorschach after extensive experimentation with many other blots. They are presented to the subject one at a time, and he is asked to describe all that he can see in each blot before going on to the next one.

An inkblot can be many things to many people, just as clouds can be, or shadowy objects in the night, or a drop of oil in a puddle of water. For that matter, a person can be many things to many people, and so can the world itself: a carnival, a grim struggle, a prison, a fascinating pageant, an interval. It is not the inkblot that the psychologist cares about, at least when he is being a psychologist, but rather the interpretation placed upon it by the subject. What the subject sees or imagines, and also what he does not see or imagine, is what concerns the psychologist.

Psychologists often speak of *norms* for tests, by which they mean statistical averages that are arrived at by gathering information in a systematic manner so that the responses of people in general will be accurately represented. In trying to understand an individual, it is helpful to know to what extent he differs from the norm. In interpreting the Rorschach, such norms are customarily employed, sometimes informally rather than formally. The interpreter also tries to understand the unique inner life and subjective experience of the person taking the test; he does so by paying close attention to the emotional tone of responses, to sequences that may reveal strong associational patterns or ways of dealing with troublesome thoughts, and finally to the meanings of symbols.

2. The Thematic Apperception Test (TAT)

In this test, the subject is presented with a picture calculated to evoke some sort of dramatic fantasy, and he is then asked to make up a story based on the picture. In the standard form of the test, 20 pictures are used, with some slight differences in the sets for men and for women. The second 10 are given to the subject on a later day than the first 10. One picture midway in the second set is not a picture at all, but simply a blank white card. The basic aim of the test is to stimulate the verbalization of complexes from the unconscious so that insight may be gained into determinants of behavior that the subject himself cannot report directly. At the same time, of course, one may observe the subject's skill in the use of words, his inventiveness, power of synthesis, and the like.

The pictures themselves were assembled from a variety of sources, ranging from story illustrations in popular magazines to noted works of art. From a very large initial collection, the authors of the test, Christina Morgan and Henry A. Murray, selected the final set of pictures to be used. Murray concurrently was evolving his intricate and ingenious scheme of personality needs (Murray, 1938), an attempt at a comprehensive theory of personality based on individual needs and the demands and stresses (or "presses") of internal and external environments. Valiant efforts to achieve a reliable system of scoring for these needs and presses from the Thematic Apperception Test stories have been made by Murray and his colleagues and students, but the scoring is so demanding in terms of skill, time, and dedication that norms are difficult to establish and to use. Nevertheless, the experienced TAT interpreter can readily discern the emergence of unusual themes, and from small signs he can often detect the presence of important conflicts revealed by the subject's stories. As with the Rorschach, the psychologist's sensitivity to emotional tone, associational patterns, indicators of repression, and symbolic meaning is most important in "getting the most out of" the TAT. The trouble with this, as with all interpretation of fantasy material, is that one may easily get more out of it than is in it. William James once called Freud's use of symbol interpretation "a very dangerous method," and reliance upon one's intuition of the meaning of symbols is even more chancy when personal associations to the symbols are not obtained.

3. The Dramatic Productions Test

In this test, a miniature stage is provided to the subject, together with hundreds of "props" and a wide choice of stage scenery. The test was first used by Erik Erikson in the pioneer assessment studies at the Harvard Psychological Clinic in the 1930's (Murray, 1938). The present version of it was constructed by Phyllis Diebenkorn, and the scenery was dashed off by her husband, Richard Diebenkorn. The props consisted of a wide variety of toys, human and animal figures, houses, bridges, trees, cars, planes, and so on. The instructions were simply to make up a play and to set the scene for it with the materials at hand.

C. QUESTIONNAIRES

Besides the MMPI, CPI, and SVIB, with which the reader is now familiar, the assessment included the Myers–Briggs Jungian Type Indicator and the Inventory of Fantasies.

The Myers-Briggs is based on Jungian theory and yields scores on Introversion-Extroversion, Thinking-Feeling, Sensing-Intuiting, and Perceiving-Judging, all of which are conceived as polar opposites rather than as independently varying dimensions.

The Inventory of Fantasies simply lists many possible fantasies and inquires into their frequency and intensity in the fantasy life of the respondent. It is not scored but is interpreted in terms of content.

D. TESTS OF INTELLIGENCE AND CREATIVE ABILITIES

Several tests of both convergent and divergent thinking abilities were employed in the assessment.

1. Convergent

The Concept Mastery Test, developed by Terman and his associates at Stanford to measure intelligence in adults in the high I.Q. ranges, is essentially a test of verbal comprehension and analogical reasoning. The Gottschaldt Figures Test calls for the ability to perceive a simple figure masked by or imbedded in a more complex one. It involves reasoning as well as perceptual discrimination. The Match Problems Test is based on the familiar puzzle in which one is required to make a new figure from a given number of matchsticks. Both Gottschaldt and Match Problems have been shown in a factor-analytic study to be measures of adaptive flexibility (Barron *et al.,* 1957). This was originally considered by Guilford to be a divergent thinking ability, but further analysis by Thorndike (1966) furnished a plausible basis for interpreting it as convergent.

2. Divergent

These tests present an open-ended problem for which there are many possible answers, no one of which is "the right answer." The Consequences Test, for example, invites the subject to consider an improbable state of affairs, or some remote contingency, and to imagine the consequences should the event occur. Unusual Uses presents the name of a common object and gives its most common use, then asks the respondent to suggest other uses. Plot Titles presents the synopsis of a short story and asks for suggested titles. The Barron Symbol Equivalents Test, as we have already seen, presents an image, such as "leaves being blown in the wind," and asks for equivalent or formally similar images (such as, "a civilian population fleeing chaotically before an invading army").

And so to the case of Edward, a man in his mid-twenties who aspires to write plays and is attempting to gain experience and knowledge by taking a university course in creative writing.

II. The Case of Edward

A. STAFF IMPRESSIONS

Edward arrived for assessment promptly (one or two minutes early). He was more formally dressed than most other subjects; he wore a suit and a regular dress shirt and necktie rather than a sports shirt (the more common attire of the male subjects). His manner was friendly and he smiled readily, but at the same time he appeared temperate, deliberate, and somewhat reserved.

Staff adjective descriptions of Edward at the end of the assessment stressed the following adjectives: cooperative (7 of 10 raters); conservative, deliberate, friendly, and moderate (6 out of 10); anxious, conscientious, considerate, obliging, tactful (5 out of 10); adaptable, alert, ambitious, confused, defensive, dependable, good-natured, industrious, inhibited, intelligent, mannerly, mild, painstaking, rational, self-controlled, serious, slow, thorough (4 out of 10).

The staff composite Q-sort description of Edward emphasized as *most characteristic* of him the following traits: calm, relaxed in manner; behaves in ethically consistent manner, is consistent with own personal standards; has high aspiration level for self; appears straightforward, candid, forthright in dealing with others; has social poise and presence, appears socially at ease. *Most uncharacteristic* of him were these qualities: rapid personal tempo; unpredictable and changeable in behavior and attitudes; rebellious and nonconforming; expresses hostile feelings directly; various needs tend toward relatively direct and uncontrolled expression, unable to delay gratification.

Staff rankings of these 10 subjects placed Edward at the extremes on the following variables: Masculinity (rank of 1); Rigidity (2); Dominance (9); Cognitive Flexibility (9); Impulsivity (9.5); Intellectual Competence (9.5); Social Acuity (10); Rejection of Sociocultural Conventions (10); Originality (10). There was an unusual degree of agreement that he was the least original subject, his average being 9.11, with half of the raters ranking him tenth.

B. PERSONALITY INVENTORIES

1. Minnesota Multiphasic Personality Inventory

L-50; *F*-48; *K*-55; *Hs*-48; *D*-47; *Hy*-58; *Pd*-55; *Mf*-73; *Pa*-52; *Pt*-47; *Sc*-40; *Ma*-52; *Es*-64.

Since scores on all of the clinical scales are within one standard deviation of the mean, the profile indicates freedom from serious psychological problems and a high degree of personal soundness and stability. Such an inference is supported by the score of 64 on *Es*; Edward appears from the MMPI to have a strong ego and relatively minor psychopathology. There is, however, a certain amount of overemphasis on repression as a characteristic mechanism for the handling of impulse; the highest score on the clinical scales is *Hy,* which, taken in conjunction with the very low *Sc* and the below-average *F* in a person of good intelligence and education, suggests an unwillingness to entertain fantasy or unusual perceptions and opinions.

The score of 73 on *Mf* deserves special consideration. In a man of broad interests and cultural sophistication some degree of elevation on *Mf* may be expected. However, a score of 73 is in the borderline region where some problems of sexual identity may be indicated.

2. California Psychological Inventory

D-66; Cs-64; Sy-42; Sp-53; Sa-55; Wb-54; Re-60; So-51; Sc-47; To-59; Gi-50; Cm-49; Ac-62; Ai-58; Ie-60; Py-58; Fx-59; Fe-60.

That Edward's highest score is on achievement via conformance sets him apart from most of the other subjects in this group of writers, who generally score much higher on Achievement via Independence than on Achievement via Conformance. However, his score on the former scale is well above average; since both scores are high, the combination appears favorable for achievement in a setting in which one may work within some organizational or institutional framework that rewards both conformance and independence.

Other CPI scores reflect a quite favorable pattern of adjustment and competence; elevations in the neighborhood of one standard deviation from the mean on such traits as Responsibility, Flexibility, Intellectual Efficiency, Tolerance, and Psychological-mindedness, and somewhat above-average scores on Dominance, Self-acceptance, Sense of Well-Being, Capacity for Status, and Socialization. This pattern does not indicate outstanding effectiveness, but does point to a moderate, firmly based competence and self-confidence.

The score of 60 on Femininity, taken in conjunction with the MMPI Mf score of 73, suggests a definite although not severe problem in the area of sexual identifications.

3. Strong Vocational Interest Blank

Scores in the A range, in order of decreasing magnitude: Musician, Minister, Physician, Social Science High School Teacher, Architect, Printer, Advertising man, Social Worker, YMCA Physical Director, Clinical Psychologist. Scores in the B+ range: Psychologist, Artist, Author-journalist, Psychiatrist, Vocational Counselor, YMCA Secretary. On the Masculinity–Femininity key, Edward earned a T score of 41 (nearly one sigma from the mean in the feminine direction), a result consistent with his scores on the MMPI and CPI.

A strong social-service drive seems indicated by the scores on Minister, Social Worker, Physician, Psychiatrist, Clinical Psychologist, Social Science Teacher, YMCA Physical Director, and Secretary. It would appear that one of Edward's manifest needs is to be nurturant. Accompanying that pattern of interests is another pattern related to creative or artistic expressions: Musician, Architect, Artist, Author-journalist, and Advertising man.

4. Myers–Briggs Jungian Type Indicator

E-I, 70; S-N, 86; T-F, 46; J-P, 60. Type: INtP (introverted thinking with extroverted intuition and preference of the perceptive to the judgmental function). This type of person is described in Jung's theory as follows: analytical and impersonal, interested primarily in underlying principles; outwardly quiet, reserved, detached, perhaps even aloof except with intimates; inwardly-absorbed in problems; likely to be persevering and to be independent of external circumstances; fond of organizing concepts and ideas.

C. Tests of Intelligence and Creative Abilities

Concept Mastery Test, 118; Gottschald Figures Test, 16; Plot Titles *A*, 5; Consequences *A,* 8; Unusual Uses, 23; Match Problems Test, 9; Barron Symbol Equivalents Test *A*, 19; Barron-Welsh Art Scale, 39.

These scores place Edward about two standard deviations above the general population mean in terms of verbal comprehension and adaptive flexibility. However, on almost all tests relevant to originality and fluency of ideas he is below average for this group (he ranks ninth on both Plot Titles and Consequences, for example). In the Unusual Uses test he gives extremely common responses for the most part, but occasionally he gives a very uncommon one, and it is worthy of remark that his uncommon responses involve hostile or destructive uses: a safety pin "to poison someone (child!) (mother)," for example, and a button "as a murder instrument." On both Plot Titles and Consequences he gives relatively few responses, all of them of low quality. In his preferences for figures on the Barron–Welsh Art Scale he scores just slightly below the mean of artists.

D. Projective Tests

1. Rorschach

M-3; FM-0; m-0 + 1; k-0; FK-0; F-12; Fc-3; c-2 + 1; C'-0 + 2; FC-0 + 1; CF-2; C/F-6; C-0. Total responses: 28; total time: 46 minutes; P-2 + 1; O-0; W-64%; D-32%; Dd-4%; S-0%.

The Rorschach report written by the Rorschach examiner is as follows.

The most outstanding feature of Edward's Rorschach performance is the evidence it provides about his way of experiencing affect. Particularly with respect to anger, and probably with most other emotions as well, his expression is shallow, superficial, and almost totally unrelated to his "real" emotion. The latter is felt, if at all, in a primitive and undifferentiated way. The result is that his public emotional responses seem to flow in a reasonably appropriate way, but provide no real gratification for him, and probably on close contact with another person would seem artificial. Since his emotional responses are not particularly related to his "real" affect, they are free to vary with the situation, and he need express only more socially acceptable and agreeable feelings. The result is behavior which is superficially always agreeable and friendly, and in which fear, anger, and other less acceptable emotions get expressed only indirectly.

The evidence for this is both in his test behavior and the test responses themselves. Almost every remark he made during the test was friendly, apologetic, or self-critical on the surface, and hostile and critical in implication. Possibly he was particularly threatened by the Rorschach: possibly he was angry about the assessment in general, but he seemed to be basically angry; and the angrier he got, the more friendly and self-critical became his remarks. With regard to content of his responses, there was special emphasis on bone structure, which in my experience is highly related to the denied and distorted expression of anger. With regard to determinants, the emphasis on C/F responses—color used in an arbitrary and artificial way—is thought to be related to superficiality and artificiality of emotional experience. His phrasing at times also suggests denial of strong emotion. Twice he referred to percepts which "*could* be used as fear images" and several times hastened to assure me that his percepts were "just decorative—just decorations."

2. Thematic Apperception Test

The subject's stories, in his own words, were as follows:

Picture No. 6.   A young veteran reveals to a mother the death of her son and his friend in battle. He wonders how to break the news, or to tell her that he was responsible for the death. He is capable of work about the farm and resolves in this instant to offer his services. There could be some pressure upon her from other sources which will further motivate him. She will forgive him.

Picture No. 12.   The young woman is a wealthy, accomplished wife of a politician, who measures himself against social standards. The hag is the old world prejudice against truth. She is the symbol of prejudice to which the wife returns eventually.

Picture No. 13.   This is the machine age—modern architecture, concrete and steel which dwarfs the nearly nonexistent woman. The odd angles, accent on architecture, suggest a setting for the Adding Machine or a situation in which a vibrant person turns away from life to become part of a mechanism. There is pathos of nonentity here, and she will be defeated by her environment.

Picture No. 19. A storm and wind situation in winter. A barren place somehow related to the north with rather incongruous fear symbols (too graphic). This is a child's vision of night (possibly Hallowe'en) with thrashing limbs, isolation, pitiless force of elements. The child is told a story of witches in a house across the valley and is sent at night to secure help from the inhabitant. The window eyes stare at her, etc. She discovers an old lady without fear characteristics.

Picture No. 20. The lonely life of a city dweller in the park at night. He is the situation that a youth must pass to cross Central Park at night. Again, the situation has terror only in reading into it. The boy faces the situation by walking squarely up to the apparition. The lights suggest the Christmas season, and the man could wish him well as he passes.

The figure could have appeared here many times as he watched from his window, accumulated these fear connotations, and the crisis came of his own volition to challenge it.

The examiner's report is as follows:

The fear and anger suggested by the Rorschach seem to find expression also in Edward's TAT performance. Affect is relatively isolated in the first story, although responsibility for his friend's death is imputed to the central male figure, who also has the task of breaking the news to the dead man's mother. The "death in battle" theme suggests the possibility that the fantasy is related to the death of his own father, an army officer, and to unconscious guilt as well as to fear of the mother's reaction. Fear, anger, and depression characterize the last three stories, and the word "fear" itself is used in a peculiar way: "fear symbols," "an old lady without fear characteristics," "accumulated these fear connotations."

3. Dramatic Productions

Edward made a scene for a play in approximately 10 minutes. He began by picking up some blocks and arranging them in the center of the table. He made a rock altar and a cavern, and placed a tree behind and somewhat to one side of the altar. He said there was an imagined background of foliage. The characters in the play were Seneca, Nero, a captain of a troop of soldiers (who proves to be an assassin), and many soldiers. The hero is Seneca, who is described by Edward as a Stoic playwright "who writes of war and its horrors but views death passively." Nero, "a strutting, vain figure," orders the death of Seneca. The captain must carry out the imperial orders of Nero, but he also identifies with Seneca and thus is in conflict about the necessity to kill Seneca.

Use of space appeared rather constricted, and the scene at first was made very symmetrical, but later was modified to asymmetry.

The theme is perhaps related to the fact that Edward's father was a captain in the army (a captain of troops). Seneca presumably would be Edward himself, who is much preoccupied with war and aggression in his fantasy. Nero and the captain may be different aspects of the father image; Nero is phallic exhibitionistic, sadistic, and irresponsible, while the captain is the unwilling agent who, in spite of hidden sympathy, must do his duty and dispatch the son in the interest of inevitable hostility. The production seems not to warrant any detailed interpretation, but points again to the subject's involvement with the Oedipal theme and its close connection with the expression of aggression and with writing.

E. Dreams, Fantasies, Suggestibility, Closeness to the Unconscious

1. Inventory of Fantasies

Frequent current fantasies, in the form of daydreams, include becoming a creative artist and thereby winning immortal fame; benefiting mankind by creating art forms; putting aside selfish ambitions in order to devote himself wholly to an elevated ideal or worthy cause; someday attaining a state in which one becomes aware of absolute truth, beauty, and goodness; possessing great knowledge, profound understanding, sagacity; being a wise guide, philosopher, and counselor of men and women. These daydreams fit well with the pattern of interests indicated by results on the Strong Vocational Interest Blank. Edward's strongest conscious fear is lacking, losing, or being deprived of money; two fears during early manhood were that he would show lack of courage, be humiliated and subjected to scorn and ridicule, and that he would be injured, crippled, or disfigured.

2. Fantasy Interview

The comments written by the interviewer are as follows:

Subject was relatively at ease and appeared eager to put himself across in a way that would sound interesting, even be arresting. Almost all of his impressive inner experiences are connected with war. In reference to extrasensory communication, for example, he reported that in a crisis in combat he frequently felt that he could detect the presence of an enemy who was completely unseen. He became quite excited as he talked about this. He believes in premonitions and preordinances, and describes himself as "superstitious to some extent" in believing in "preestablished patterns and interconnections." He considers himself to be an especially lucky person, and he counts on this luck in especially critical situations. He has had intense experiences of mystical communion with God (in church) and also overwhelming experiences of emptiness, desolation, and the like. He has found himself in "righteous rages" in which he is "capable of committing violence." He has fantasied committing murder and has had ideas of suicide. He has had especially vivid daydreams, but no hallucinations or visions. He has few night dreams; on the average, he dreams less than once a month. His dreams are in natural color, not vivid, and he says that no unusual or fantastic motifs appear. He pays little attention to his dreams.

As we went along, Edward realized that he has two levels of answers for most of the questions about the non-rational; one from a common-sense view, the other more permissive to the unexplainable. When he writes on religious or occult themes he identifies completely with this latter attitude for the moment.

He would make many of the questions difficult to ask by subtly belittling, by making them seem unclear, not well expressed, not to the point, etc. I sense in this man a great deal of difficulty with aggression and hostility, which comes out only indirectly and unintentionally.

I get the impression of a quite restricted fantasy, and a tendency to be rationalistic and philosophical. His tolerance for the nonrational comes as a surprise to him, and concerns mostly his ideas of preordinance. One feels the predominance of neurotic qualities in this man's presentation of himself.

3. Suggestibility

Edward proved resistant to suggestion, showing no effects when suggestions were given that he would be unable to unclasp his hands or open his eyes. He said of the Ouija board that he did not believe in it, but he agreed to try it. He gave up after 2 minutes. He had tried to remember the name of a woman who was a friend of his mother's. His muscles began to get tense on one side and the board seemed to move for a second, but he decided that it was just a chance tensing of muscles, so he gave up. Then he asked, "Do I have a resistance to this? I'm afraid I can't admit of these extrasensory perceptions."

He reported that someone had once tried to hypnotize him, but was not able to do so. He said that he would not have liked the experience, and that he really did not want to be hypnotized. He said, however, that he would be willing to be a subject if it would prove anything, but that he was convinced it would not. His strong resistance to being hypnotized was obvious, but he evidently did not want to be openly uncooperative. After much debate and conflict, he finally said he would rather not be a subject in the experiment.

Edward is a sound and regular sleeper, getting 9 hours sleep a night, which is about what he requires. He usually retires at 11 and arises about 7 or 8. In answer to the question, "How often do you wake up in the course of a night?" he replied, "I just about die. I seldom wake up." He never takes sleeping pills, and rarely naps during the day. He can usually fall asleep readily even if he has been writing just before going to bed, though it may take a little longer.

F. PROFESSIONAL IDENTITY AND GOALS

Edward cites the fact that his mother is a writer as being most important in determining his own aspirations to achieve success in that medium. Most of his training has been in visual arts, but he says that he had always done very well in English classes in school, and he turned to writing because he felt that, like his mother, he could win recognition and financial reward thereby. That writing is a better-paid artistic medium than painting was definitely an important motivation for him. He remarked that Faulkner feels that writing for profit is a sound motivation, and he was glad to hear of such a statement from a preeminent creative writer.

He has not as yet published any of his short stories, although he has submitted a number of them to magazines. He says he "almost" sold a story on the destruction of a church during the war. Most of his stories deal with warfare, and they are based on notes from his own experience. He has written some poetry, he said, "mostly to gain command of the language." He became interested in writing plays as a result of teaching dramatics in high school.

The poetic play, he feels, represents the last degree of excellence in writing. The model for his own work is the *Oresteia,* a trilogy that represents, as he says, the three states of Hellenistic philosophy. He remarks that he himself had conceived a similar drama, and then added with a laugh, "Not that I want to shoot my mother."

Edward's current plans are to get a master of arts degree in the dramatic arts department, and to teach in a local high school. He intends to write "on the side." Teaching is very important to him, he says, and he would wish to continue it even if he became very successful as a writer.

In response to the question, "To whom are you writing?" he answered, "My mother wrote a lot of adventure stories, and I would like to do that too. But I want to try for the works—if you measure yourself less than that you'll never be any good. You should aim for perfection; qualitatively you should seek to write 'up to' the tradition." In brief, he aspires to do more than his mother, while yet following part of her pattern. He spoke again of the importance of financial success to him, and in this connection referred to the possibility of "getting into television."

The play he is now working on is, he says "a dialectic—body, mind, and soul—in the individual and in civilization." It concerns the relation of "the well-ordered man" to society. He stressed the importance of social ideals. The play is a one-act play in verse, which has involved him in problems of meter and dissonance in speech. The play deals with his own youthful experiences in developing "an ideal philosophy" out of his "individual relationship to society." Concerning it, he said: "I have no interest in the heightening of the emotional response of the individual for its own sake. That's not my nature; my ideal is classical form and the balanced philosophy. Rationality, reality, and objectivity are the things I value. I don't like 'free expression' in the arts. I like structure to begin with—intense conflict in the individual is *not* what I like. I just don't like the existentialist approach. But don't get me wrong—I want to draw the violence in human nature—to demonstrate its contrast with the ideal—to show where the error lies."

G. Summary

1. Analysis

The main points that seem to emerge from these observations of Edward are the following.

1. He appears in ordinary social situations to be a cooperative, straightforward, and relaxed individual, but in close personal interactions a subtly negativistic and obstructionist tendency shows itself. When he is angry he becomes self-critical and appears friendly toward the person at whom he is angry, but the consequence of his actual behavior is to frustrate the other person and to criticize by implication. In brief, his anger gets expressed but he himself does not experience it as a feeling.

2. On the occasions when he is able to feel righteously indignant or when direct aggression is sanctioned by some social authority or by morality, he becomes freer in his fantasy. When he is angry but feels the anger blameworthy or dangerous (in the sense that it would bring retaliation), his fantasy is blocked.

3. He appears to have a problem in sexual identity that is probably related both to his problem with aggression and his capacity for creative work. On the surface he seems relatively masculine, and many of his traits are similar to those one might expect to find in a competent military officer; at the same time, there is evidence of identification with the mother and competition with her. From some source has come a great fear of death and a fear of the unconscious and the irrational. There is some suggestion in the projective test material that passivity is equated to death, and it will be recalled that he said that he "just about dies" when he goes to sleep, that is, when he loses conscious control and the unconscious is closer to being known to him. The most obvious inference from the Dramatic Productions Test would be that the unconscious impulse is to be "put to death" by the father (that is, be made a woman of by castration). However, it is noteworthy that when he "just about dies" upon going to sleep he thereby defends himself against awareness of his dreams. In brief, it appears that the passive impulse serves as a defense, and from the rest of the material one gets the impression that the more basic impulse is the aggressive one. However, his aggression cannot be expressed so long as it is "bad" aggression, that is, aggression that might indeed destroy the object, which in this case would mean to bring about the death of the father. Such speculation is probably idle in the absence of detailed information, but the material does point in that direction. The identification with the mother might then come about by way of denying the aggressive impulse toward the father and at the same time handling the fear that is experienced upon being left at the mercy of the mother when the father has actually died (killing by the son's magic, in terms of the unconscious).

2. Implications for Creativity

The most obvious indication from the interview material is that Edward's motivation to engage in creative work comes from his identification with his mother, and from his need to compete with her and surpass her as well as be like her. One might think that if the neurotic aspects of his relationship to her were to be cleared up, he would no longer need to define himself as someone to whom his own creativity is important. However, it is questionable whether he is really very creative when his work is determined by the identification with his mother. Actually, he appears more original and creative when his aggression, which is essentially masculine and directed against the father, can find free expression because morally sanctioned. One might expect in this case, therefore, that the neurosis operates directly against the individual's creativity, and that Edward would work at his creative best if he were to cease to cathect the Oedipus complex. He would then be able to experience anger directly without fear, his fantasy thus being freed for creative expression. At the same time, the motivation to engage in behavior that claims to be creative would lose its neurotic aspects, and if he continued to occupy himself with writing he would do so on a more genuine and integrated basis.

It should be noted that in this case neurosis seems specifically related to creativity. Edward appears to function effectively in the life situations he has found for himself, and he is undoubtedly a capable and socially responsible person. Such neurotic incapacity as he is burdened with seems to be linked precisely to that area of functioning that the neurosis itself impels him to remain involved with.

III. The Case of Janus

A. STAFF IMPRESSIONS

Janus throughout the assessment was dressed in a neat, conventional manner, and made an attempt to be friendly to those with whom she came in contact. She was quite concerned with the view of herself that was emerging to the staff, and at the conclusion of the period felt that she had not adequately represented herself. She became quite concerned over the fact that she had not been able to be hypnotized, and felt that this was another reflection of what she feared, namely, that she was not really a creative person and had been included in the group for comparison purposes. She believed that she had not measured up to the Institute's standards of a creative person.

Staff adjective descriptions of Janus characterized her as being highstrung (8 out of 9 raters); alert, imaginative, intelligent, and sincere (7 out of 9); anxious, awkward, complicated, confused, conscientious, emotional, idealistic, and sensitive (6 out of 9); affectionate, appreciative, nervous, quiet, sympathetic, and tense (5 out of 9); artistic, changeable, despondent, forgiving, honest, immature, impulsive, inhibited, kind, pleasant, shy, spunky, unaffected, unstable, worrying (4 out of 9).

The staff composite Q-sort description of Janus saw the following traits as being most characteristic: (1) concerned with own adequacy as a person, at either conscious or unconscious levels; (2) values own independence and autonomy; (3) is basically anxious; (4) thinks and associates to ideas in unusual ways, has unconventional thought processes; (5) engages in personal fantasy and daydreams, fictional speculations; (6) has a readiness to feel guilty; (7) genuinely values intellectual and cognitive matters; (8) has a high aspiration level for self; (9) has fluctuating moods. We may note that numbers 1, 2, 4, and 8 were rated as being most characteristic of the group as a whole, while numbers 3, 5, and 9 were rated as next most characteristic of the entire group. Thus in these seven traits Janus is similar to the group studied. However, in the case of number 6 (has a readiness to feel guilty) Janus differs a good deal from the group, as this trait was found third least characteristic of the composite group.

Those statements found most *uncharacteristic* of Janus were the following: (1) is subjectively unaware of self-concern, feels satisfied with self; (2) creates and exploits dependency in people; (3) is emotionally bland, has flattened affect; (4) is genuinely submissive, accepts domination comfortably; (5) shows condescending behavior in relation with others; (6) is calm, relaxed in manner; (7) emphasizes communication through action and nonverbal behavior. In relation to the group, numbers 2 and 4 were also least characteristic, while numbers 1 and 7 were next least characteristic.

Staff rankings of the 10 subjects placed Janus tenth on Sense of Destiny; on Dominance she was placed ninth; she was ranked as eighth on the following variables: Cognitive Flexibility, Breadth of Interests, Ego-strength, Rejection of Sociocultural Conventions, and Masculinity (of the five women subjects she was ranked third). On her high ratings, she was ranked second on Social Acuity, and third on Inquiringness, Aesthetic Sensitivity, Introspectiveness, and Warmth. On Originality she was ranked 4.5; on Predicted Achievement she was placed at 7.5. Relative to her own other traits, her originality was most conspicuous, even though unremarkable in the group as a whole.

B. PERSONALITY INVENTORIES

1. Minnesota Multiphasic Personality Inventory

L-46; F-55; K-59; Hs-46; D-59; Hy-54; Pd-60; Mf-34; Pa-59; Pt-66; Sc-63; Ma-58; Si-51.

This profile shows Janus to be relatively normal, but indicates the presence of a problem of self-alienation and anxiety. She feels herself to be "different;" she is vaguely apprehensive and on edge.

The Pd–Mf contrast hints at a "pulling for trouble" predilection—a kind of masochistic bent. She seeks (unconsciously) punishment and thus views herself as rather martyrlike and heroic. A behavioral manifestation of this tendency was found in her work for the play-writing class from which the group of assessees was chosen. The main project of the semester was to create and complete an original play. Having written a considerable amount of the drama, Janus became dissatisfied with it, and shortly before it was to be turned in to the instructor, she prevented her completion of the project by tearing up the manuscript.

2. California Psychological Inventory

Do-38; Cs-61; Sy-47; Sp-53; Sa-61; Wb-35; Re-31; So-27; Sc-42; To-50; Gi-40; Cm-28; Ac-34; Ai-68; Ie-54; Py-46; Fx-76; Fe-44.

The very low scores on Socialization and Communality (two standard deviations below the mean) and the high scores on Achievement via Independence and Flexibility (approximately two standard deviations above the mean) indicate that Janus not only has a feeling of *being* different but is, indeed, different. These scores indicate that she is original, complex, and clever, but that coupled with these characteristics favorable for a writer is another cluster of traits that might possibly hamper her effectiveness. The latter traits characterize her as impatient, rebellious, and headstrong. When we further consider that her lowest cluster of scores is in the socialization and cultural maturity realm, it seems that this lack of responsibility and of conscientiousness may be a real problem in Janus' creative development. As in the MMPI, these scores indicate self-defeating behavior and an under-use of talent.

As in the case of the MMPI, she tends toward masculine modes of behavior; but since she is rather low on the Dominance scale, this evidently does not appear in "strong-armed" behavior, but may be more characteristic of her general perception of the world.

3. Strong Vocation Interest Blank

Scores in the *A* range, in order of decreasing magnitude: Musician, Advertising Man, Author-Journalist, Architect, Artist, Clinical Psychologist, Psychologist, Physician.

Scores in the *B*+ range: Minister, Vocational Counselor, Psychiatrist, Social Science High School Teacher, Real Estate Salesman, Personnel Director, VA Clinical Psychologist.

Janus' score on the *M–F* scale is not consistent with those on similar scales in the MMPI and the CPI, where she scores in the masculine direction. On the Strong scale, she had a *T* score of 19, nearly three standard deviations from the mean in the feminine direction.

These scores generally indicate strong interest in the creative, artistic pursuits, with a slightly lesser interest in the area of human relations and social service.

4. Myers–Briggs Jungian Type Indicator

E-I 35; *S-N* 90; *T-F* 88, *J-P* 79. Type: EN*t*P. This type is described as being extroverted intuition with feeling introverted. Such a person, according to Jungian theory, is especially alert to possibilities and is likely to show initiative and originality. There is some tendency towards hasty judgment and impulsiveness, however, with difficulty in bringing to a satisfactory conclusion what has been initiated with enthusiasm. The allure of the possible outruns realization. Such a person is often versatile, clever, full of ideas, and is potentially very creative.

C. TESTS OF INTELLIGENCE AND CREATIVE ABILITIES

Concept Mastery Test 101; Gottschaldt Figures Test, 15; Plot Titles *A*, 26; Consequences, 33; Unusual Uses, 31; Match Problems, 10; Barron Symbol Equivalents Test, 25; Barron-Welsh Art Scale, 40.

Janus falls at the mean of undergraduate students for the Terman test. She scored well above the mean, however, in the Gottschaldt Figures; her score on this last test was earned by finding half (5) of the solutions in the first section and all 10 in the second, indicating that she may have been initially blocked, but once underway she could be quite flexible.

In the tests of originality, Janus ranked fourth in the number of Plot Titles produced, as she did in the Consequences and Barron Symbol Equivalents Tests. In Unusual Uses she ranked third, with her responses being of very high grade. Her lowest performance came in the Symbol Production Test, where she ranked tenth. Her score on the Barron–Welsh Art Scale is only one point below the mean of artists, and well above the general population mean.

D. PROJECTIVE TESTS

1. Rorschach

M-7; *FM*-2 + 3; *m*-0 + 1; *k*-0; *K*-0 + 1; *FK*-0; *F*-12 + 1; *Fc*-2 + 1; *c*-0 + 3; *C'*-0 + 1; *FC*-0; *Cf*-2 + 5; *C*-0. Total responses: 25; Total time: 55 minutes: *P*-4; *O*-3; *W*-28%; *D*-52%; *d*-4%; *S*-16%.

The interpretation of these scores by the Rorschach examiner follows.

The overall impression from Janus' Rorschach protocol is that of an adolescent struggling toward some kind of individual identity. She was clearly self-instructed to produce original responses. In her strain to do this, she sometimes overlooked the more obvious, popular response possibilities, though she saw enough of these to indicate that she could perceive in normal ways, if so set. She showed a strong tendency, in her attempts at uniqueness, to reverse figure and ground by seeing objects in the white spaces, and background in the blots. (Card V was the most extreme example of this; a white detail at the bottom was seen as a rocket, about to take off into the clouds represented by the black blot.) The usual Rorschach interpretation of this tendency—that it indicates negativism—is probably appropriate here; she almost certainly views her striving for individuation as a battle against adults who would suppress her if they could. Her response to Card II suggests a specific fantasy related to this struggle; the popular response to this card is two animals engaged in some action, usually identical. Her twist was to see two buffalo fighting; one, the old head of the herd, the other, a young contender. There is some suggestion in this that her striving for individuation is complicated by guilt, and a feeling that it is a direct attack on her parents.

2. Thematic Apperception Test

The subject's stories, in her own words, were as follows:

Picture No. 6.   Elise, the mother of the young man, had decided to tell him the story of what had happened to her husband. Elise is styled of another age, a more truly aristocratic one than the one to which Rance is accustomed, and she is deeply affected. She had informed Rance that his father had won his empire through extremely unscrupulous means, although he was much respected at his death. (The governor had spoken at his funeral.)

Rance, a young person of ideals, has taken this information deeply and is now about to depart, as shown by his hat. He is going to find out the truth, however unpleasant, and set it right.

Elise knows he shall not return, and she faces years of loneliness as a result.

Picture No. 12. Rhea is upset by her aloneness. The ugly bag is her future, and Rhea knows that she is also her past. Yet, paradoxically, the two often blend into an indivisible duality. What is to happen next, Rhea does not know.

To the bright, to the good, Rhea is a duality. To the cautious, the fearful, she is the hag. But to Rhea only is she herself. Knowing this, she continues to live in dread. Hag is unsure whether this usurpation can continue for the many years she desires.

Only when the hag is eyeless and Rhea is soulless will either die. Yet the hag sees well, and Rhea's soul is disgustingly healthy. Rhea contemplates more drastic measures. Am I the only one who perceives this?

Picture No. 13.   The unknown city had not been visited, nor devastated, for as long as the lifetime of an elm. Nobody knew even the existence of it.

Hattie was a simple tourist who decided to go her independent way and some erring instinct guided her to the gates of the city. Finding the place isolated, Hattie cautiously wended her way through the vacant streets to the most imposing structures she saw. She entered the formal garden in front and has now come to the geometrical stairs to one side.

She is expectant of the sight she will see from that perspective. When she reaches the top, an even higher plane than she expected, she absorbs the surroundings with awe. What will she tell the tour guide, let alone the world at home?

Picture No. 19.   "Something has gone wrong here." That was the first reaction we felt, but even that impression itself seemed wrong after retrospection.

This was a macrocosm of all aberrations, all mistakes, all nightmares. The childlike, fairytalelike quality is only a part of the madness gathered together. For it is Northern Lights, nightmares, and a stomach ache all seen at one glance.

Who can withstand this manifestation of destruction and desolation save creatures of the same ilk? That is true, all the creatures with any of the elements paid homage one at a time, after a pilgrimage crossing under the gashes of terror. Each tries to destroy the destruction, and each fails (sic) only in restoring it.

Picture No. 20.   All the Yard knew that Jenson was a good, steady worker. And Jenson knew it. As he stood under the glowing street lamp, he knew that his steadiness in work was about to come to an end. Not suddenly, of course, but through gradation in a continuum of regression. It would begin with a dropped wrench, and go from there to a mangled piece of work. This was his prospect.

The darkness in which he stood was his situation, and the lights through the trees were his past. But Jenson could not return to his past, only continue his decided path.

Jenson decided not to return to work, or to home, for his steadiness has worked into him until he could not possibly avoid going into a life of insanity.

The examiner's report is as follows:

The first picture (#6) clearly states what was suggested by the Rorschach—the struggles against the old and against the parental figure. This same theme appears in #13, where the girl decides to go her "independent way." The struggle between old and new, or past and future, also appears in #12. In general, there seems to be a problem of the necessity of a splitting of the past from the future.

The other main idea centers on the emptiness of life resulting from an absence of personal relations and the inability of communicating with others. Thus in #13 the girl visits an isolated, empty city. In #12 her heroine alone knows herself, and in #13 she worries how she will communicate her feelings to the tour guide and to the "world at home."

The stories themselves show Janus to be close to the most creative writer in the group assessed. During the TAT session she seemed to be having difficulty, being tense and perspiring and also withdrawn. The stories suggest depression, which seemed to gain in magnitude as the session progressed (especially #19).

3. Dramatic Productions

The setting of Janus' dramatic production scene is an isolated city, a sort of ghost town, strewn with newspapers. On the left is a pile of green shrubs, behind which are eight chairs. Placed on each of seven of the chairs is a "vessel." On one chair there is, beneath a piece of shrubbery, a mirror, a clock, the *Bible, Time Magazine,* a bouquet of flowers, and *It's Later Than You Think,* all of which represent "values." Hung on the set above the characters is a large piece of clay, with an anchor ground into it.

Three characters enter the scene: a man, a woman, and a nun. The man and woman represent mankind, only they have towel racks attached to their arms to show their individuality. There is no definite relationship between them; they are merely companions. The nun is not necessarily a religious symbol; rather, a symbol for "other." She is a sympathizer with the man and woman. When these two do not know what to do, she offers them advice, which they do not accept. The group travels through the city in the direction indicated by a pointer (dog) until they come to the shrubbery, which they admire. They are looking for something, which perhaps the nun could give them, but they do not accept it from her.

They continue their path past the chairs with the vessels, using both a magnifying glass and field glasses for their search. They look inside the "vessels" and then remove the shrubbery and look at themselves in the mirror. "They don't realize it is self-reversed. They, like everyone at the usual level of thinking, think it is a reflection of themselves and not just the opposite."

Then they discover all the values: time and eternity (represented by the clock); beauty (bouquet of flowers); religion and morality "and all that" (*Holy Bible*); and knowledge (*Time Magazine,* although something else would have been chosen, if available). When they come to *It's Later Than You Think,* Janus says "It's about time the man is doing what he wanted to do, and the woman, and the nun." In reply to the question of what it is they want to do, she states, "I haven't decided." But the characters, themselves, *do* know.

While the man and the woman examine the values, the weapon above (clay and anchor) drops on them, covering them and the values. "The clay is elemental: 'Dust thou art and to dust thou returnest.' "

At this point, a doctor and nurse enter the scene (although the town has until this time been entirely empty). The nurse has a chain attached to her arm; "This is her means of restoring to them what they had before or correcting it and doing whatever nursing she is going to do." The doctor and nurse go about trying to "fix" the people, but do not see the items of value. In the end, however, the people die.

Janus was the only one of the subjects to move her characters about during the discussion of the production. Her actions expressed feelings of aggression and hostility, as in the grinding of the sharp anchor into the clay, and the pleasure in dropping the clay on the characters. In addition, she completely destroyed the original finished production by knocking down, running over, and bumping into the various elaborate architectural and decorative props she had included in the scene. When she left, the stage was in shambles.

Evident in this production again are the feelings of emptiness and of lack of personal relatedness. Also, there is the symbol of the old people offering unwanted advice, and of the contemporary individuals searching for an unknown something. Another note enters here—that, having found certain values, the outcome will be destruction, in this case, death.

E. Dreams, Fantasies, Suggestibility, Closeness to the Unconscious

1. Inventory of Fantasies

Currently, Janus engages in the following daydreams: feeling inferiority, lack of courage, humiliation, scorn, ridicule, failure to achieve purpose; being disturbed by the possibility of one's own suicide; withdrawing to a shared or solitary dwelling and living like a hermit; voyaging by land, sea, or air to distant or unknown region, seeing or discovering new places, being a great traveler, adventurer, or explorer; marrying a rich man; becoming a creative artist, musician, writer, poet, and thereby winning immortal fame; being of the same nature as, or in accord with, or very similar to, or sympathetically imitating some object of nature. Fantasies that are both daydreamed about and consciously feared included being disturbed by the shortness of life's span, the inevitability of death; accepting death (or permanent departure) of father, of mother, of sibling; fantasies of current fears are losing one or both parents by separation, divorce, death; running away from home, escaping monotony, old humiliations, or conflicts; roving over the earth; living like a carefree hobo; going to sea; or migrating to another place.

2. Fantasy Interview

At the conclusion of the session, the interviewer made the following comments.

> Subject was somewhat ill at ease, tense; she gave the appearance of wondering what sort of view of herself was emerging with her answers and what implications they had. She became frankly anxious with the questions on occult phenomena, with sighing restlessly and looking at her watch; more anxious than hostile, I felt.
>
> She has suffered rejective experiences, and on questions about desolation, wanted to confide a good deal about her rejection problem. She was weeping for several minutes, but blaming herself and trying to minimize it. She gave a generally depressed appearance, in contrast to what seemed her more customary buoyancy as revealed momentarily in her teasing me about my 'dimples.' I felt she reacts to her feeling of outsideness by making herself concede and conform in order to gain acceptance once more; this becomes a recognized and anxious choice between the discomfort of outsideness if she remains different, and the loss of her creative inner wellsprings if she conforms.
>
> I have the impression of a girl who would like to go along with what her imagination tells her, as in ideas about the occult, and is surreptitiously fascinated, but who keeps a firm control over such thoughts by rationalistic explanations mostly in intellectual psychological terms. I wondered if the anxiety related to such a conflict. She has misgivings that rationalism may have injured her creativity.

After the staff conference, discussing the total results of Janus' performance on the various tests and procedures, the interviewer had further comments:

> She fears that her own rationalistic bias is a cramp on her nonrational concerns. ... She would like to have mystic experiences because imaginative people do. I think this may be not so much a contrast of herself with others as a statement of her own potential. . . . I felt the poem of the Tower of Babel [mentioned in the interview] conveys the meaning and the affect in this issue; the beautiful soaring spiritual aspirations of the fantasy are torn down and destroyed by the mundane world; she is furious and appalled.
>
> The formulation of this conflict that suggests itself to me is that the overbearing rationalistic demand comes from a masculine component (Jung's animus), which may most probably derive from the mother, a teacher; from this complex she gets feelings of inadequacy, especially in intellectual matters; her depressions most probably stem from this complex. Her concession to this mother-derived masculine component tends to weaken her otherwise feminine creativity. . . . From her appearance and manner one is led to feel that her womanly nature should predominate more than it does, and that the masculine bias is not appropriate to her. The self-derogatory and self-defeating tendencies seem to arise naturally from this conflict, and her rebelliousness is a much needed item.

Regarding the lack of personal relatedness of the characters in her dramatic production, the interviewer wrote:

> This suggests not only that her rationalistic bias has had the upper hand, but that correspondingly her awareness of eros concerns has remained to an equal degree undeveloped.
>
> Despite the paucity of dream imagery and of concern about her inner fantasy life, I feel that she might develop these once the rationalistic-conformist cramp were removed, which might be done by her outgrowing the mother dominance.

3. Suggestibility

Janus reported that she requires 9 hours of sleep to feel fresh the next day; she does not always get this much rest, however, but in those cases makes up for it by naps in the afternoon. She is a sound sleeper, but sometimes wakes an hour before her arising time, after which she falls back asleep. When falling asleep she is often worrying, thinking she should be doing something else, such as studying, or considering the writing she has been working on.

She finds late evening (9:30–11:30) her best working time. When writing, she is not able to work for a long stretch without interruption. She will, after a period of 15–45 minutes, get up to consult an encyclopedia, get a drink, and so on. The radio does not bother her when she works, but a conversation does. If she becomes blocked in her writing, she reports she turns to something else, "instead of resolving the situation."

In response to the suggestion she should press her hands together and would not be able to get them apart, she was quite tense and tried too hard to comply. The suggestion had no effect.

When it was suggested that her eyelids would close and she could not open them, she reported that they felt heavy and exerted pressure on her eyeballs. The suggestion here was only slightly effective.

Janus was unresponsive to the hypnotic part of the session. She was skeptical about its outcome from the start, not wanting to take the experimenter's time. However, she changed her mind and agreed to be a subject, but was not at all influenced.

Likewise, she had no success with the Ouija board.

F. PROFESSIONAL IDENTITY AND GOALS

Janus began writing at the age of 9, composing a number of jingles. Before this, her parents had read to her a good deal, and she in turn had read to her sister. She reports, "I was such a bookworm as a child." She continued writing, mainly essays, until she was 14, when she wrote a melodramatic short story.

She prefers writing stories; her interest in drama is in social relationships. (But note the absence of these in her dramatic production.) She imagines her audience as upper middle-class, as her characters and their motives come from that group. She feels a play should correspond or appeal to some element that is vital in the audience, as an emotional tone, an intellectual problem, or a universal theme or conflict.

As to her personal closeness or identification with her characters, Janus says she embodies herself in them. While she denies that they enter her dreams, she occasionally overhears a remark that could well have come from one of her characters. She reports that her drama does not usually express a problem that exists for her outside of writing; although, in the case of her play about traditional versus progressive witches, Janus states that she also has a "basic conflict between tradition and progress." The characters that have the most appeal for her as ones to develop are two girls, one attractive but naive and wide-eyed, the other unattractive but flippant and clever. She adds that "these are probably two aspects of my own personality."

In regard to the characters of the play she was writing, but gave up on, she reports that "I was tired of living with them—they wouldn't act for me and I began to hate them."

G. SUMMARY

1. Analysis

The main characteristics of Janus' personality appear to be the following.

1. She is currently engaged in a conflict involving tradition versus progress, old versus new, and rationality versus emotionality. She presently chooses the first of these alternatives in each pair because to do so gives her a feeling of security. At the same time she is worried by this choice, as she realizes it may be a block to creative endeavors.

2. There is some indication that part of this conflict includes a struggle against adults, most likely her parents.

3. Another problem she is currently facing is that of establishing herself in the network of social interaction. An absence of affiliation with other humans characterizes her projective creations. This emptiness is not, however, something she desires. Rather, it stems from an insecurity of her place in life and from feelings that she would not be able to communicate adequately with others.

4. Accompanying these difficulties is a masochistic bent that certainly curtails her productive creativity and may delay her solution of the foregoing problem.

2. Implications for Creativity

At present, Janus' creative ventures are entwined with her own personal problems. Even as the latter have remained unsolved, so her creative work is often left uncompleted. One might expect that if her own perplexities were cleared up, she would be able to surge ahead and create a *whole* work. However, there is some indication that her underlying self-depreciation might prevent this.

While she shows herself to be an intelligent, alert, and aesthetically perceptive person, her present rationalistic bias greatly limits her fantasy and dream life. During the assessment period, it seemed she was beginning to reevaluate her choice of rationality over emotionality. If she should decide to deemphasize the former, it is likely both her creative work and her social functioning would become richer.

PART THREE

A MISCELLANY

CHAPTER TEN

Nonrational Experience in Creative Writers

Reason seems often to be the enemy of poetic imagination. Some poets perhaps would say that reason is *always* the enemy of poetic imagination, and some rationalists might even cheerfully agree with them. Logic, abstractions, classifications, laws, prescribed sequences of thought—all these sometimes good things are exercised by most of us at the expense of whimsy, impulse, intense feelings, the vivid disconnected image or emotion, the sense of validity of the singular event or the eccentric person or passion. At the expense of part of ourselves—would that be too much to say?

Poets and other creators—let us say *the poet,* in a generic sense—the poet forever struggles to get free of the prison of rational thought and the requirements of logic. One can most easily imagine this to be a matter of purpose, as the foregoing sentence implies; but perhaps it is not purpose at all, but simply the nature of the poetic imagination that its images are at play under quite different rules, though in the same house of self. We are all of us both rational and nonrational, sometimes in order and sometimes in disorder, as indeed the world itself is. Let us think then of *principles* of mental functioning and their *relative strengths* in any given person, "the poet" being a pure case, perhaps largely himself imaginary.

In the course of trying to untangle himself from the mess that the concept of the unconscious got him into, whether he knew it or not, Freud at one point offered the distinction between primary process and secondary process in thinking. Primary process is characterized by the ready occurrence of displacement, condensation, substitution, and symbolization of instinctual drives or impulses, arising in part because of the urgency of the impulses and their demand for immediate gratification. Secondary process is characterized by the ability to delay gratification voluntarily and to make plans for obtaining satisfaction directly with the object of the drive in real life rather than permitting substitution, displacement, and fantasy to deflect the drive from its actual object. Or, the drive may be renounced in reality. Secondary process is thus marked by tolerance of frustration, flexibility in finding real alternatives, and logical programming of behavior sequences on the way to the goal.

This distinction seems to me to be quite useful in looking at the nature of creative activity, and it may be entertained without getting into the sort of boundary disputes and difficulties that the assumption of unconscious and preconscious processes entails. Primary process phenomena include the following kinds of cognitive activities that fall outside the realm of the rational: dreams, especially recurring dreams, prophetic dreams, and dreams of a preternatural vividness and intensity; precognitions, telepathy, clairvoyance; the occurrence of unusual coincidences; falling in love, mystical experience of oneness with the universe, or its negative side, total forlornness; and so on.

An open-ended questionnaire that was completed in writing by a group of 26 creative writers provided an opportunity to study the occurrence of these phenomena. The reports were obtained in the course of more comprehensive studies already reported elsewhere (Barron, 1969). Detailed protocols upon which certain conclusions were based have not previously been published, however. Nothing comprehensive in terms of report of protocols is here intended (the raw data run to some 2000 typewritten pages), but it seems worthwhile and useful to give some examples of reports that led to the conclusion that creative people have an unusual openness to nonrational experience.

These reports showed a significant numerically greater frequency of occurrence in creative persons of the primary process activities we have cited, and they will be discussed in terms of those categories, from dreams to transcendental experiences. At the outset, however, we must take note of an important finding in this research: that secondary process thinking need not be sacrificed to primary process, and that in the creative individual *both* modes are utilized freely and effectively.

I. The Research with Writers

Although eventually this research included many professional groups, such as architects, mathematicians, and scientists, it began with the study of creative writers. Writers were chosen for study for several reasons: (1) writing is one of the most widely used and understood forms of communication of creative interpretations of experience; (2) the social impact of writers in forming public taste, influencing opinion, and advancing culture is considerable; and (3) language itself is part of the bodying forth of culture, and by studying its use and its most creative practitioners one studies creative forces in the culture itself.

The participants in the study as a whole were 56 professional writers. All were engaged in creative writing, though they did differ widely among themselves in the extent to which artistic purpose and aesthetic quality were characteristic of their published work. The group of 26 writers whose responses are reported here were designated as representative creative writers and were not selected especially for their originality or fame, as some who were studied by the living-in assessment method had been. In brief, they are representative of the many thousands of individuals who are dedicated to creation through the use of language, regardless of their popular success. In this respect they are like most of the other groups who have contributed to this research: artists in the process of development.

By creative writing, then, we mean the composition of stories, essays, novels, poems or plays whose intent is to communicate the author's distinctive interpretation of experience. The definition assumes that individual differences will be found in style, intent, quality, and reception of the work, and one goal of the research was to study the correlates of such individual differences. In this presentation, however, we shall not be concerned with individual differences, but with characteristics of creative writers as a class; or rather, as representatives and agents of the creative spirit.

Most, though not all, of these writers were studied individually by means of intensive interviews about their lives and their work. The psychologists who got to know them personally were later asked to describe them individually through the Q-sort method. What this amounts to, as we have already seen, is that each observer or interviewer is given a deck of 100 3- by 5-inch filing cards on each of which is printed a phrase (item) that conceivably could be used to describe a person. He is then asked to arrange these in nine piles, which are assumed to represent a continuum of *saliency of the traits* in the personality of the individual being described. Item placements are then averaged for all observers to arrive at a composite description of each writer, and these in turn are averaged to arrive at a composite description of the group.

When this was done, the five items most characteristic of the group of creative writers seen in living-in assessments were these:

1. Appears to have a high degree of intellectual capacity.
2. Genuinely values intellectual and cognitive matters.
3. Values own independence and autonomy.
4. Is verbally fluent; can express ideas well.
5. Enjoys aesthetic impressions; is aesthetically reactive.

The next eight most characteristic were:

1. Is productive; get things done.
2. Is concerned with philosophical problems; for example, religion, values, the meaning of life, and so forth.
3. Has high aspiration level for self.
4. Has a wide range of interests.
5. Thinks and associates to ideas in unusual ways; has unconventional thought processes.
6. Is an interesting, arresting person.
7. Appears straightforward, forthright, candid in dealings with others.
8. Behaves in an ethically consistent manner; is consistent with own personal standards.

These descriptions found psychometric support in very high scores on tests of conceptual thinking, aesthetic judgment, originality, and personal effectiveness and flexibility.

In spite of this picture of effectiveness personally, intellectually, and socially, the writers earned rather high scores on a questionnaire designed to measure psychopathological tendencies, the Minnesota Multiphasic Personality Inventory (MMPI). Specifically, they were well above the general population average on measures of schizophrenic tendency (the Schizophrenia scale) and Depression, and moderately high also on Hysteria and Psychopathic Deviation. This finding is especially intriguing because at the same time (and on the same test) they scored well above average in Ego-strength, which in the general population is negatively related to the cited measures of psychopathology.

A special difficulty that arises from the application of psychopathological indices to groups of persons who are not clinically ill psychologically must be recognized. The logic of construction of MMPI scales is not such that one may expect with assurance that scores will be interpretable within the normal range. The items in the clinical scales are known to differentiate psychiatric patients of the named diagnostic class (depressives, hypochondriacs, hysterics, psychopaths, schizophrenics, and so on) from people in general, but whether the scales measure dispositions toward such psychopathology throughout the total range of variation is another question. Essentially the assumption underlying the current interpretive conventions is that the measured variables are linear dimensions, and that if the bivariate correlation surface representing the relationship between each scale and the dimension itself *in nature* could be plotted, that surface would prove to be homoscedastic and normal. Whether such an assumption is justified is certainly open to question; it is quite possible, for example, that such diseases as schizophrenia and paranoia are not extreme expressions of dispositions present continuously throughout the total range of variation of behavior, but are really different in kind from any normal manifestations, however analogous superficially. If such discontinuities do exist, scales constructed by comparing the responses of diseased persons with those of normals could not be valid measures within the normal range of the tendencies that they identify in the abnormal.

In an effort to explore this matter further, a student of mine (Fritz, 1969) located a group of young artists highly regarded for their creativity and succeeded in establishing a comparison group of hospitalized mental patients who had been diagnosed as schizophrenic. The groups were matched quite precisely in terms of age, sex, education, and scores on the Schizophrenia scale of the MMPI, so that they differed only in that one group was in a mental hospital and the other group in an art school. The Schizophrenia scale was now analyzed item by item to discover items answered very differently by the two groups. (It must be remembered that *all* items on the scale presumably distinguish "schizophrenics" from "normals.") The items located by this analysis are as follows.

A.   Characteristic of hospital patients but not of artists:

1.   Most of the time I feel blue.
2.   I don't seem to care what happens to me.
3.   Most of the time I wish I were dead.
4.   I cannot understand what I read as well as I used to.
5.   There is something wrong with my mind.
6.   I am afraid of losing my mind.
7.   I am worried about sex matters.
8.   At one or more times in my life I have felt that someone was making me do things by hypnotizing me.

9. I have strange and peculiar thoughts.
10. Almost every day something happens to frighten me.
11. I have more trouble concentrating than others seem to have.
12. I find it hard to keep my mind on a task or job.
13. Once a week or oftener I become very excited.

B. Responses more characteristic of artists than of hospital patients:

1. My daily life is full of things that keep me interested.
2. I enjoy children.
3. I worry over money and business.
4. I get all the sympathy I should.
5. My hands have not become clumsy or awkward.

These factors seem to be involved:

1. Clinical schizophrenia is marked by apathy, despair, dread, and a sort of spiritual death.
2. In schizophrenia there is confusion, bizarre ideation, delusions of control by others, and a loss of stable self-regulation of mood.
3. The artist, by contrast, finds joy in life, is not self-pitying, is reasonably worried about practical matters, and functions well physically.

It must, of course, be noted that an art school is enough different, as an institution, from a mental hospital to produce through sheer environmental effects a different sort of mood in the inmates. Who would not be more cheerful in an art school than in the locked ward of a psychiatric hospital? What could be more supportive of the bizarre in oneself than a community of artists? Conversely, what worse social judgment can be passed upon one than to be locked up and labeled insane?

Although the observed differences may in part be a function of environmental influences, they also would themselves be . sufficient to produce the contrasting environmental and institutional destinations of the two groups, given something else in common. And they do have something else in common, of course, since 60 of the 78 items of the Schizophrenia scale revealed no differences between the patients and the artists.

We are left, then, with psychometric indication of an unusual state of affairs psychically in creative artists, characterized by the incorporation of psychotic-like experiences and dispositional tendencies in a matrix of rationality, very high conceptual intelligence, honesty, and personal effectiveness.

Let us turn now to the reports, in their own words, of the kinds of experiences that lead us to rate creative writers high in primary process thinking, even while they are notably efficient in secondary process as well.

II. Manifestations of Primary Process

We shall begin with the most commonplace manifestation of primary process, the dream. What is a dream? Put simply, dreaming is thinking under the condition of sleep.

When the person sleeps, a sort of "censor" (though not the Freudian fellow, in this case) sleeps too. The revelry of the images in our dream life may go on because this censor has been caught napping and the stability and regularity that everyday logic and common sense enforce upon our thought patterns are temporarily undone. In dreams we may be irrational at no cost to our survival.

In the life of the creative individual, this safe irrationality of dreaming becomes the unsafe mode of thought that permits wild hunches, censorable images, unprintable words, "unthinkable" ideas, to merge with the thinking of the day. "Dreaming awake" may be an apt description of the creative reverie and of the usual mental life of the creative person.

Dreaming is almost a prototype of primary process thinking. Irrational (or, as I prefer to say, nonrational) thought processes are not necessarily unconscious, in the Freudian sense of the term. Dreams themselves are not unconscious. When Freud pointed to dreams as evidence for the existence of the unconscious, he was referring to an inferred latent structure of the dream, not the experienced manifest content. This distinction is sometimes not understood. Dreams are the royal road to the unconscious only because the life of impulse is less well disguised in our dreams. Nothing can so deceive as logic. It is when the rule of logic and common sense is temporarily abrogated that disguises fail and naked impulse is revealed. The conscious dream-life is simply a more easily penetrated disguise.

There is more to dream-thinking than that, of course (and more to logic as well). Freud's exclusive preoccupation with drive and defense and the underlying assumption of homeostasis led him to present a picture of thinking and "the ego" that emphasized control of impulse in the service at once of individual satisfaction and social organization. *His* "censor" therefore stands guard at the gates of the unconscious and there exercises its repressive function. The dream itself, however, may be doing other things than serving the Freudian censor by disguising unconscious mental contents. The dream may be a song, a painting, a solution to a problem, a drama, an expression of love. The dream process is nonrational in the sense of not obeying the rules of waking logic, but it is not unconscious and need not stand for something unconscious. It may in fact be an expression of the self at a very high level of integration and wholeness. Indeed, there are some who believe that in dreams we may reach out with a higher self to experience that which is itself beyond the limits of our ordinary world.

A. RECURRING DREAMS

Recurring dreams had been experienced by 70% of the sample. Here are examples of the dreams from the interview records:

One writer had dreamt at least once a week for the past 15 years that he was swallowing something indigestible, "usually watch gears or glass." The dreams are so vivid and realistic that often "I wake up my wife and urge her to get help." Built into the dream is a rather complex mechanism: "this has always been just a dream before, but this time it has really happened."

Another writer has a dream that has recurred for 30 years:

> Since the time my eldest son started to walk, I have dreamed that he was walking around the cornice of a high building; the wind is blowing a gale; he is balancing himself unsteadily. I try to speak quietly but I can make no sound. I am so frightened that I want to rush and grab him, but caution myself to move slowly. Then, as I am creeping carefully toward him the dream fades. He has never fallen and I have never rescued him.

In almost all cases, the dreams described have an intensely unpleasant, nightmarish quality and often terrify the dreamer. Often, the physical safety of the dreamer is threatened in the dream; this is an especially common characteristic of dreams that recur from childhood on.

One woman described two dreams of this nature. The first dream she experienced "in little girlhood" (often between the ages of three and six). "Huge apes grabbed me out of bed, hung me over a loop swing suspended from the enormous beams in an old Mexican house, and swatted my rear end with a big stick each time I swung back and forth." The second dream she experienced repeatedly during adolescence (between the ages of eleven and fifteen). "Slow thumping footsteps on [the] porch came upstairs. [A] creature like [a] giant amoeba stood beside my bed waiting to engulf me. I am unable to move or scream—finally [I] waken in [a] cold sweat."

In several of the dreams, the dreamer is assailed psychologically rather than physically.

One woman has two recurring dreams of this nature: "I wandered around from floor to floor of a large hotel, wearing a shabby bathrobe, unable to remember the number of my room." In the second dream, "I find myself in a college class without pen, pencil, notebook, or textbooks. These are agonizing dreams."

Two of the writers have had dreams that ceased to recur after they dreamed a resolution to the problem presented in the recurring dream.

One of these cases is a fairly simple and lucid example of a resolution of this kind.

I often dreamed of being stranded in the middle of a collapsing bridge, the Golden Gate Bridge, to be exact. The flooring of the bridge would be torn away. Finally one night I dreamed that I personally built myself a path of planks over the remaining framework of the bridge, and got across. The dream never recurred after that!

The second case of this type is more lengthy and complex, but highly interesting. I cite here the entire response of this woman.

My father died four months before my birth and my mother, my older sister, and I went to live with my maternal grandparents. My grandparents were very good to me and I had a reasonably happy childhood except that I longed, desperately, for a life "just like the other kids" . . . a home with a father in it, a mother who didn't work (this was before the day of "working mothers"), and perhaps some younger brothers and sisters. Many times, when I questioned my mother or my grandparents as to why something in my life was not like other children's, I would be told it was because my father was dead.

At a very early age—about five or six, I think—I began dreaming that my father was not dead. There was always some reasonable explanation for his absence—he had been exploring some foreign country, had been lost in a forest someplace . . . there were many varied "reasons" in these dreams but it was always something that seemed very logical. At any rate, he was now near me and this knowledge made me excited and happy because now everything was going to be all right and I would have a life more "normal" than I had had in the past. In my dream I would walk into a room hunting for my father, and I would see a chair rocking or a door closing and I would know he had just left the room. I would run to catch him but just as I reached the other room he would, again, be closing *that* door. I would go from room to room, never quite able to catch up with him. Sometimes he would be on a train, bus, or streetcar and I would run trying to catch it but it always was just a little beyond me.

These dreams left me feeling sick, depressed and shaken all the following day and as weary as if I had actually run all night. I think I dreamed this—or a variation of it—about once a month all through my childhood. As I reached high school age I found life increasingly interesting and rewarding and the dream began to occur less frequently. About this time I would awaken shortly after the dream started and would realize that I was having the old nightmare but could never awaken to the point that I could prevent it. I remember thinking, with a sense of hopelessness, "Oh, tonight I'm going to have to run!"

After I was married I almost never had the dream. I was happy in my home life, I was doing the work I wanted to do, and although we lost several premature babies we still hoped to raise a family. Only when I was ill did I have an occasional "running dream" in which I searched for my father and the next day I felt tired and a little depressed but not to the extent that I had felt tired and depressed when I had the nightmare during my childhood and adolescence.

In April, 1945, I received word that my father's sister was going to Iowa to see my paternal grandmother as she had been in poor health the past few months. This did not affect me greatly as I scarcely knew this grandmother and had not seen her for 15 years. On April 12, my birthday, I was entertaining friends in my home and was cutting my birthday cake when word came of President Roosevelt's death. Some of my guests began to cry and my "party" disintegrated at once. I felt caught up in the emotional upheaval that gripped the nation that day and felt a rather childish resentment that it had happened on my birthday ... an attitude that horrified me even as I experienced it.

That night, for the first time in several years, I dreamed that my father was alive. I thought I received a letter from my mother telling me he had been ill in a tuberculosis sanitorium all these years but that he was now well, and was coming to visit me. At this point, as usual, I half-wakened and thought, "Oh, I am so tired, I've had a hard day and I do wish I didn't have to run tonight!" I managed, this time, to wake up enough to go out to the kitchen and get a drink of water, then I went back to bed and the dream continued. Only *this* time it was different—for the first time I saw a train coming *in*. Even in my dream I could not understand why it was not the same as I had dreamed before. I stood on the station platform and watched the passengers disembark. Finally I saw a man get off and knew he was my father, although he looked much older than the pictures I had seen of him. (He died at the age of 30 and the man getting off the train looked to be about 60, the age my father would have been at the time.) He came over to me and I put my hands on either side of his face and looked at him for a long time. I thought I asked him a great many questions and he answered them—in my dream we discussed books, my writing, philosophy, religion. In a sense, I seemed to be "soaking up" his presence. I pleaded with him to stay but he told me he could not and I did not question it or ask him again to stay. He smiled at me and then I woke up abruptly feeling as happy as if I had really conversed with him. I had a great sense of peace and happiness . . . I received a telegram from my aunt stating that my grandmother (my father's mother) had died during the night. The news did not surprise me nor did it affect my feeling of unusual happiness. For weeks afterwards I had a feeling of great contentment and release from some unnamed pressure.

I never dreamed of my father again. Even after 15 years the dream is so vivid that I can recall our "conversation" almost word for word. Several times when I have been speaking with someone about one of the topics my father and I discussed in my dream I have caught myself on the point of saying, "My father told me . . ." and wanting to quote something he said in the dream. Each time this happens I am startled by it and am not pleased that I should come so close to quoting a dream as if it were reality. If it occurred very often I think I would seek psychiatric advice but it only happens once every two or three years or so and I have always been able to "catch myself" before I actually quote my father to someone else.

One of the writers who usually has difficulty recalling his dreams and does not remember having had dreams that have recurred, described one recent dream that he feels

. . . stayed in my conscious mind because of an unusual line: I had killed someone and a man, presumably a friend, took me to an outlaw's lair, remote, hidden even from the air. I was warned not to come out for any reason. I was anxious about the food supply and said "But we'll starve!" The outlaw spoke up, solemnly, as if making a profound observation, like a philosopher-economist: "Starving is a waste of hunger." The remark was enough to wake me.

B. PROPHETIC DREAMS

Just under 20% of the writers reported that they had had dreams that proved prophetic. Some of these might be considered as instances of precognition, while others were more readily susceptible of interpretation as natural occurrences based on intuitive grasp of future possibilities.

One writer, after being offered a contract by a movie director, was waiting to receive the contract by mail. He had a dream in which "the director rode into a small mountain town in an open car and as he bowed to the villagers he tore up a document (the contract?) and threw the pieces on the ground at his feet." This writer never got the contract and wonders whether the dream was actually prophetic or a review of his own fears. A second writer recounted a dream he had had during the war: "In the Argonne in World War I, I saw a bridge over a stream and a large boulder behind which were two German machine gun nests." By moving downstream and edging up through the shallows, he was able to take the prisoners without firing a shot. "I've often wondered whether providence forewarned me to save *me* or the Germans."

A third writer recounts a dream that "seems to be" prophetic.

> A few months ago I dreamed that our only child, a married daughter, had died. I wakened, so terribly depressed and grief-stricken that I got up and went to the bathroom and noted the time as about four in the morning. The next day our daughter called and told of wakening in the night before, strangling and unable to breathe. She lost her voice for a few hours. Though the doctor found no real explanation [for this]. This happened at about four in the morning, the same time I awakened from my dream.

One woman writer has had prophetic dreams "not often, but occasionally. They are not usually personal," she says, "but concern places." For instance:

> About a year ago I had a vivid dream about an earthquake. I "saw" it happening high in the mountains where there were big trees. The trees twisted and fell and a lake was created. About a month later there was an earthquake in Yellowstone National Park, and a lake was formed. No one I knew had any connection with the disaster.

The same respondent recounted a second dream:

> When we sold our home in San Francisco three years ago and were looking for a house on the peninsula, I had a dream that we had found a place on Massachusetts Avenue. I didn't know such a street existed. We were all ready to buy a totally different place when the agent said a new listing had come in. On Massachusetts Avenue. Everything about it was right for us and we bought it.

A second woman dreamed of driving through an English street. She could not think of any reason the next morning why she would have dreamed of England. Shortly before noon that day she received a letter from her literary agent in London telling her of a sale he had made. She had not thought of him or heard from him for several months.

None of the other female respondents have had prophetic dreams, although one woman recounts that she dreamed three or four lines of one of her best poems. This dream had a "pompous, prophetic tone," she claims. Another woman responded that although she has not had a prophetic dream, she "like most people, frequently experiences things in real life that [she] seems to have dreamed before."

From the responses, it seems that prophetic dreams are quite rare and perhaps occur to some people more often than to others. It is noteworthy that the three men who claim to pay close attention to their dreams answered affirmatively to this question. The two women who have had prophetic dreams also attend closely to their dreams.

C. Extrasensory Communication

This question was put to the writers: Have you ever had an experience which made you think that extrasensory communication is possible?

There is a wide variance in the nature, intensity, and frequency of the experiences recounted in reply. The experiences range from relatively common interpersonal exchanges to much more unusual psychic occurrences.

Several of the experiences recounted were of a unique and striking nature, and seem to be inexplicable on a naturalistic basis. One writer gave the following account:

> Once when in the Navy I was to be sent for several months to the South Pacific and the Orient. My mother had fallen in love with a man who disappeared the day before I left. I was deeply disturbed, leaving my mother in a desperate broken-hearted condition. About two months later, I was tending a midnight search light watch on the aft search light. A beautiful full moon had turned the placid waters of the Pacific to a golden color. Suddenly almost as if I heard someone plainly speaking, I was informed of this man's whereabouts, and before retiring, I wrote my mother, telling her she could meet him at the Navy gate in Brooklyn, giving the exact hour and day she would meet him. My mother immediately boarded a train from San Francisco for Brooklyn, met her fiance exactly as I had described and they were married.

Two of the women described unusual experiences of extrasensory perception, two of which are particularly striking. One woman was reading *Crime and Punishment* on an auto trip. She reported the following:

> We parked and locked the car. Just previous to this, I thought, "If we stop in this town and leave the car, it will be broken into, and my new coat will be stolen." When we returned, this had happened. . . .

The second woman recounts an incident that occurred to her when she was about 19 years old and her younger sister was ill with pneumonia and was not expected to survive.

> At the time, my father was out on the Navajo Indian reservation and could not be located. He did not know Barbara was ill. I set about trying to get in touch with Dad, telephoning traders, etc., but none of them knew where he was. Twenty-four hours later, he came home. No one had told him that my sister was near death. He thought that *I* was ill. He said that in the remote desert house where he had spent the night, I had appeared to him in a sort of vision and begged him to come home. He was not asleep at the time. He got up and started driving at once, expecting to find *me* ill. Actually, I had been the one who was trying to contact him, and apparently I did, mentally.

D. PECULIAR COINCIDENCES

To elicit the accounts that follow, the question was put: Can you recall any especially peculiar coincidence which has occurred in your life? If so, how do you explain it? Nearly two-thirds of the writers reported unusual coincidences, but nine-tenths of these were imputed simply to chance. There were some striking exceptions, however.

One writer had made an agreement with his best friend, immediately prior to the friend's embarkation on a naval ship, to meet in a certain spot at a certain date and hour five years hence, "no matter how hard it would be to do so." The appointed date and location was written on the two halves of a card.

Sometime after this agreement was made, the respondent received word from his friend that he was sailing for home on the *Cyclops*; "the *Cyclops* has never been heard from since. . . . [It] is believed she carried nitrates and blew up. . . ." Nevertheless, the respondent kept his word, "arrived at the agreed location and waited a full hour, fully aware I would not see him." He did find, however, in the "accumulation of papers, dust and rubbish" a "stained square of business card paper that had once been white." It was the other half of his friend's card!

The respondent speculates upon the explanation of this incident:

> Is there a logical explanation to this? Had W. dropped his half (I thought I had seen him place it in his wallet) and had the wind blown it into a crevice to rest there five years to the day we were to meet and match the torn edges of the two halves. Or—is there some other explanation, wherein we can say he *was* there in some form—spiritual or otherwise?

Another writer, who had never been in Texas until he was sent there to join a regiment at Fort Sam Houston, found himself "as familiar with the old town of San Antonio as with the little town where I was born." He learned many years later that his father had been born in Texas.

Almost all the respondents who had had such peculiar experiences dismissed them as "merely coincidences," however, or had no lucid explanations for them.

E. HALLUCINATIONS

The following question was asked: Have you ever had a vivid sensory experience of something that was not really there? What were the circumstances?

More than half of the male writers have had vivid sensory experiences of something that was not really there. Most of these experiences are of a visual nature. One respondent was recently sitting by a radio that was not turned on; around the switch and speaker he seemed to see a blue flickering light. At times, this same respondent has seen a disappearing figure with the feeling that this figure was not unfriendly. Another respondent recounts an experience that occurred one moonlit night while he was sitting on a rock on Glacier Point above Yosemite Valley.

> Several ghostlike figures floated past, white, one to three feet tall, vague of outline. . . . I was with another man who saw these figures as vividly as I did! The night was cloudless and [there was] no apparent mist. Reason

tells me there's a logical explanation for this, but I've never been able to pin it down.

A third respondent, under a dose of iodine given to him by his doctor, saw a woman enter his room. The hallucination was so vivid that he spoke to her and heard her answer him.

Two of the respondents have experienced olfactory sensations of something that was not really there. One smelled lilacs or hyacinths "quite clearly." Another respondent thought he witnessed a visitation, but discovered it was not a valid visitation. "Since I had every subjective feeling that I would have had if the visitation had been genuine," he wonders, "just what was the criterion for . . . psychic experience?"

One of the respondents who has not had a sensory hallucination has had various sensory experiences (olfactory, visual, audible) that were validated in reality. For example, he detected the odor of deer, and later found their nesting place; he had heard the cry of a mountain lion at dusk, and later seen the lion. He admitted to the common visual illusory experience, however, of fallaciously identifying an object; he had mistaken a tree stump for a bear, two trees rubbing against each other for a mountain lion.

The women respondents seem to be more susceptible to illusory sensory experiences; two-thirds of them have had such experiences. Unlike those of men, the most common hallucination is of an olfactory nature; four of the women have had olfactory hallucinations. One woman often smells heliotrope fragrance when no heliotrope "is anywhere near." "It was my mother's favorite flower," she recounts, "and grew below my bedroom window when I was a child." It has been since the death of her mother that the respondent has experienced the illusion. She can not explain it and does not try to. Another respondent smelled paint and wet wool, neither of which was actually present, while she was in the acute stage of the mumps. A third woman only remembers one illusory experience: "I repeatedly thought that I could hear crackling and could smell burning wood and I thought the house was afire, but this was during a pregnancy and we were living in a rural community with only one fire department, so I worried about it."

Only one of the respondents recounted a visual hallucinatory experience: "I have seen many mirages in the desert with such realistic trees and water that I knew they couldn't possibly be mirages. But they were, and they eventually disappeared."

Three reported sensations of something that was not really there; that is, they experienced the vivid feeling of a presence. One of the respondents "awoke suddenly one night, feeling certain that there was someone in the room." She turned on the light expecting to see someone and even looked under the bed and into the closet, but found no one in the room. A second woman reports that as a young widow of 24, she strongly felt the presence of her husband on several occasions immediately following his death. The same feeling occurred after the death of her mother, but only once. "I did not 'see' anything; but it was as though each had come through the door, crossed the room, and stood beside me for awhile, a reassuring presence. I felt certain they—or the essence of them—was there."

The third woman felt the presence of her deceased mother-in-law, to whom she had been very devoted. She describes the incident as follows.

> She was a tiny little woman with small gentle hands. Often, when we were sitting side by side on a sofa she would reach over and hold my hand.... Five or six years after her death I nearly died during childbirth. The baby did not live and it appeared likely that I would not survive. During this time it seemed to me that I could feel the hands of my mother-in-law on my forehead and I recall feeling that if I opened my eyes I would see her standing by my bed, but could not quite summon the effort to open my eyes.

F. MYSTICAL EXPERIENCE

Half of the male writers reported that they have had intense experiences of mystical communion. The conditions for such an experience, and the explanations proffered by the respondents, are markedly varied. One of the writers remarked tersely that he experiences a mystical communion whenever he paints. A second respondent had several experiences "consisting primarily of a consciousness of 'belonging'" while he was studying hatha-yoga. "I have achieved an emotionless objectivity regarding acts of the world," he states. "In their way, these experiences of objectivity contain the same mystical feeling."

Three of the respondents do not explain the conditions under which they have had mystical experiences; one of the three, however, explains at length why such experiences occur. He feels that "frequently such experiences are premeditated or self-inflicted." Under the proper conditions, placing one's self in a self-hypnotic state will place one in a position to solve properly any problem confronting him. "This follows the natural law that all things are a oneness with all things in the universe and that all things that affect our destiny are those things that we gather to ourselves from the storehouses of infinite supply."

Another respondent stated that "when surrounded by nature and not distracted by people" he often has the feeling "of God's full attention." He even hears a voice within his head saying "Be still and know that I am God."

Half of the women writers profess to have had mystical experiences. Their accounts are also quite varied as to the nature of the experiences and the conditions under which the experiences occurred.

One woman reported that when she was with her husband on their first pack trip into the High Sierras, "We were so breathless with awe and the vision of beauty before us that we almost ceased to exist." She has had other such experiences in the mountains since then, but never one of quite such intensity.

A second woman, while listening to a recording of Richard Strauss's "Death and Transfiguration," "seemed to become a part of the music itself" and felt that she understood "completely the mystical truths the composer experienced."

A third respondent recounted a childhood experience of a mystical nature. One night when her mother was extremely ill and near death, the respondent sat by her bedroom window "knowing" that if she "could keep the sound of her breathing until the sun came up" her mother would be all right. When the sun rose, she went peacefully to bed feeling confident that her mother would live, for so the sun had "told" her.

A fourth woman recounts that she has had moments of intellectual clarity, mind expansion, and expansion of the physical world, when "paradoxically ... [she] seemed to have stopped thinking completely" and was simply "being." The experience was accompanied by a sense of brilliance and light.

Two of the respondents feel that mystical communion is a continual experience. One feels "as if God were constantly beside me." The other, that "communion with the universe or whatever is continuous but is intensified when you concentrate on it—never accidentally or at random."

G. THE SENSE OF DESOLATION

The following question was asked of our subjects: Have you ever experienced a tremendous, quite overwhelming sense of emptiness, desolation, aloneness, forsakenness?

Over half of the male writers responded in the affirmative to this question. Again, the nature of the experiences that aroused feelings of emptiness, desolation, aloneness, and/or forsakenness are quite varied. Two of the men have somewhat similar conditions for such feelings: One senses a feeling of emptiness and desolation "often, when the day ends, when the sun sets, when evening comes on." Another feels aloneness and "awe in the night alone watching the stars." A third writer professes to experience such desolation and forsakenness very frequently. "Most stories I write," he says, "use characters who become aware of their utter 'aloneness,' their inability to communicate or to share themselves. I think of the skin as a cage from which we can escape only by death."

Two of the men recounted specific incidents in their lives that precipitated an overwhelming sense of emptiness, aloneness, forsakenness, desolation. One of the men had such an experience when he was 17 and left home. "Los Angeles was a lonely place for a boy fresh off the farm." The second, when he faced death in the crash of a military plane he was flying in World War I, experienced an intense feeling as described in the question.

As was the case with the men writers, over half of the women writers said they had experienced a tremendous sense of emptiness, desolation, aloneness, forsakenness. Two of the women feel that their emotional state is very closely linked with their work. "I seem to have no identity except through achievement," one woman reports, "so that at times of failure, I have experienced an annihilation, which must be assimilated so that I can go on." The second respondent recounts a similar experience:

> After a period of repeated failures at work, the feeling of failure was so pervasive, I thought I had failed in every area of my life. [I] took a beach cottage for a month by myself. [The] first few days were a sheer hell involving all the above elements, but for no reason I can ascribe it to, my whole approach to life suddenly seemed overwhelmingly egotistical and downright ludicrous and I snapped out of it. I went back to work on a long piece of writing I had laid aside.

A third respondent experienced the emotions specified when her husband left to report "back to camp." "I knew we had said our last goodbye and he was on his way overseas. At about 5 A.M. a long loud train whistle, which could have been his train taking him to war and out of my life forever, swamped me in desolation."

III. Discussion

As the terminology implies, primary process thinking was held by Freud to occur earlier developmentally than secondary process and to predominate in infancy and earlier childhood, yielding gradually to domination by secondary process. The distinction is analogous to that proposed by Jean Piaget between animistic and scientific modes of thought, the animistic being characteristic of young children and gradually being supplanted, beginning around age five or six, by the scientific mode. This transition had of course not gone unnoticed through the centuries, and an analogy in the moral sphere is provided by the old doctrine of the Catholic Church that sin (and repentance, conveniently) becomes possible when one reaches "the age of reason," generally fixed at age six.

This temporal sequence allows introduction of the concept of regression, and the psychoanalytic theorist Ernst Kris introduced the memorable phrase "regression in the service of the ego" to describe the production of the sort of phenomena we have here presented as manifestations of primary process. This is of a piece with the common observation that artistic perception is childlike and that genius is "to madness near allied."

Such usage is lazy, and the application of the concept of regression seems to me to be misleading. Primary process thinking is a *capability* that *may* be weakened in some individuals as they grow from childhood to adulthood. I emphasize *may* because I think we do not know that this is so. Its expression *may* also simply become muted, or be altogether behaviorally silent, while the capability remains. This is an empirical question, and one that badly needs basic research efforts on the part of psychologists.

As for the childlike quality of creative perception, we need to remember that creative power—the force of that which is created—increases with age in about the same way that general intelligence does. Qualities of freshness and spontaneity that seem more common in children before they realize that they are fated are retained by creative individuals, who remain, as it were, "innocent in the face of Fate." But this is not regression, it is courageous progression. In the creative act we witness neither dissociation nor mere bisociation, but integration and synthesis. The whole self creates.

CHAPTER ELEVEN

King Lear and His Fool: A Study of the Conception and Enactment of Dramatic Role in Relation to Self-Conception

This chapter describes an approach to the study of role interpretation and enactment in drama through the use of the technique of personality assessment, including psychological tests and interviews. To illustrate the approach and the methodological problems it generates, we have chosen to treat in detail the study of two characters whose relationship to one another in the Shakespearean drama *King Lear* presents a perennially fascinating problem for actors. The solution, in terms of the actual performance, was in this instance considered by audience, critics, and director an unusually creative one.

A Shakespearean role offers a challenge to an actor that is of special interest to students of creative imagination: it demands exercise of the actor's talents as a performer and it taxes the resources of his personality in a way that few assumed roles do. In *King Lear,* particularly in the roles of Lear and the Fool, the actor's capacity to conceptualize, experience, and project a complex ambiguous character is tested to the limit.

The casting, rehearsal, and production of *King Lear* at the University of California in Berkeley offered us, through the cooperation of the director, Professor Robert Goldsby, and his actors, an opportunity to investigate a behavior dynamic that had long interested us (Rosenberg, 1961; Barron, 1969): the development and potentialities of a highly complex identity. The problem is related to the process of self-realization in a creative person, as well as to the conceptualization and enactment of a dramatic role in the theater.

All of the major roles in *Lear* were examined in our study, but we have chosen to concentrate on Lear and the Fool. These are the most complex of the play's characters, and they embody an opposition and reciprocation symptomatic of the tragedy's dialectic form. Lear, the great king and father, is at the other extreme from the poor tolerated Fool. King and Fool exchange bickering and hurt, but they are closest to each other in sympathy, and their identities begin to merge.

I. Methodology and Design of the Research

The personality assessment method, combining a standardized battery of personality tests with depth interviews, was used in the study, with certain important modifications. The actors who had been chosen to play ten major parts in *King Lear* were first asked, immediately after casting, to participate in an assessment as themselves. Then they were asked to take the same tests as the character they were to play. Four months later, shortly after the final performance of the play, which had 12 public performances, they were asked once again to go through the assessment procedures as the character. Following this, they were given individual interviews, two to three hours in length, on the process of character creation as they had experienced it in their part in *King Lear*.

The emphasis was thus upon their changing conception of the character as it might relate to their own personalities. In retrospect, it seemed apparent that there were, at least in some cases, changes in the personalities of the actors themselves, although no direct information from test scores was available.

The testing procedures that are considered in this report are the Gough Adjective Check List (a list of 300 common personality traits) and the California Psychological Inventory.

II. Test Results

Some insight into the process of art and the artist may be discerned in the parallelisms and differences that seem to emerge from a comparison of the tests of Lear and the Fool, the role conceptualizations, and the performances.

A. KING LEAR

1. The Actor Himself

The role of King Lear was played by a married graduate student in dramatic art. In the psychological testing session he appeared reserved, thoughtful, temperate, of serious if not grave demeanor. This impression was heightened by somewhat melancholy eyes deep set in a bony face. His frame was somewhat spare but muscular, and he was well above average in height. He used relatively few adjectives to describe himself on the Gough Adjective Check List; the most outstanding characteristics he listed, in terms of their singularity for graduate students, were awkward, clever, courageous, dreamy, fussy, gloomy, individualistic, irritable, original, painstaking, sensitive, shy, steady, temperamental, thoughtful, and touchy. On the California Psychological Inventory, he made indicative low scores on scales for Self-acceptance and Social Presence, and he scored quite low also on scales designed to measure Self-control, Tolerance, Responsibility, and Ability to make a Good Impression. He was also rather low on Flexibility, and high on Femininity.

2. Actor's Conceptualization of the Role

On the Gough Adjective Check List, at time of casting (*t*-1), the actor described Lear by three clearly different sets of adjectives that together suggested the complexity and ambiguity of the character. He saw Lear as (1) possessed of considerable energy and aggressiveness (active, argumentative, arrogant, assertive, blustery, conceited, confident, courageous, forceful, hard-headed, headstrong, individualistic, intolerant, loud, opinionated, self-centered, show-off, sophisticated, stubborn, and tough); (2) somewhat confused, anxious, troubled (absent-minded, aloof, anxious, confused, dependent, distractible, distrustful, dreamy, fearful, foolish, fussy, high-strung, preoccupied, suggestible, and touchy); (3) a good person withal (frank, honest, idealistic, insightful, outspoken, serious, warm, and wise). When the actor was asked to submit three adjectives of his own choosing not represented on the check list, he offered suffering, guilt-ridden, willful.

On the California Psychological Inventory, the actor at time of casting, taking the test as though he were Lear, earned a profile of scores of which the following were high or low enough to be considered indicative: High—Self-acceptance, Dominance, Social Presence, Sociability; low—Sense of Well-Being, Self-control, Tolerance, Intellectual Efficiency, and Socialization.

It is apparent that the actor's conception of himself and of Lear revealed some similarity: he, like Lear, was low on Self-control and Tolerance; and among the few adjectives he chose to describe himself, he found almost a third also in the Lear character: courageous, dreamy, fussy, individualistic, touchy. The suggestion is that while the actor had, like all his fellow players, to summon to a stage characterization qualities he did not find in himself, he also shared some identity with the character he conceptualized.

He played the role more as man than monarch: he was more Lear than King Lear. In the history of the theater, many well-known actors, from Garrick on, have similarly emphasized Lear's simpler humanity. This conception shortens the great descent from kingship to fool, and more quickly shapes the King-Fool roles toward two-of-a-kind, as happened in this production. Significantly, in the final interview with the Lear actor, after the completion of his quite successful performance, he said that he had not wanted the Lear role and had not intended to try out for it—he had wanted to be the Fool. The director's intuition had found in this actor special qualities that made him so effective a Lear.

So far as statistical results are concerned (i.e., in peformance on these standardized tests), the actor played Lear much as he had conceived him originally, and his role conception did get across clearly to the audience. This is shown by test results following the final performance, and by the results of the tests when taken by a skilled clinical psychologist on the basis of the final performance of the play itself.

On the California Psychological Inventory, the actor after the final performance earned a pattern of scores as King Lear almost identical with the pattern four months earlier. Of the four indicative high points at t-1, three remained as highest scores at t-2: Dominance, Self-acceptance, and Sociability. And of the low scores, five remained lowest at t-2 and in almost the same order: Sense of Well-Being lowest, followed by Intellectual Efficiency, Self-control, Tolerance, and Socialization.

As suggested by his extensive listing of adjectives on the checklist, the actor had sensed at the beginning the extreme complexity of the character's dimensions, and the rehearsals were a process of exploring their limits. Critics, or other actors, might well have argued that Lear could be perceived (as this actor perceived him) as high in Self-acceptance only at the very beginning of the play; from the midpoint to the end Lear can hardly bear the self that he comes to confront. (This reflects a problem with the test itself: it may only be reliable at given points in a play, since the Shakespearean character is a dynamic and reflects a series of radically different self-images as it experiences tragedy.) Certainly the Lear of this production, in the last three acts, had—except in his madness—very little self-regard.

The clinician in the audience, taking the test for Lear as projected in the performance, earned indicative high scores on Dominance, Self-acceptance, Social Presence, Sociability, and Psychological-mindedness (a newcomer), while the indicative low scores were on Socialization, Self-control, Sense of Well-Being, and Achievement via Conformance (also new). The degree of agreement is quite impressive, and indicates a consistency of role interpretation and acting by the actor. (It also shows astuteness of observation on the part of the clinician, of course.)

B. THE FOOL

1. The Actor Himself

The young man who played the Fool seemed somewhat inclined to play the fool in real life. Short and sturdy, generous in gesture, he was sometimes whimsical and elliptical, as well as as voluble, in his thought and speech. In the Gough test he chose on the one hand many adjectives for himself that were the same as those he later picked for the Fool: most significantly foolish, but also bitter, charming, cynical, daring, dreamy, egotistical, fickle, hasty, humorous, immature, peculiar, polished, rude, sarcastic, sensitive, sharp-witted, soft-hearted, superstitious, temperamental, unconventional, witty, zany. On the other hand, he reserved for himself alone boastful, cowardly, demanding, flirtatious, quarrelsome, self-pitying, unstable, and weak. Two of his adjectives for the Fool matched the other actor's choice of descriptives for Lear: foolish and dreamy.

On the CPI, the actor's responses (he wrote on the test, "Only a fool would answer these questions") earned extremely high scores on Flexibility, Femininity, and Self-acceptance. These jibe quite well with his manner and attitude in the assessment. He not only manifested a skipping wit but had a tendency to vanish from testing sessions and to be elusive in interview through quick changes of subject and esoteric allusions. He earned quite high scores also on Social Presence and on Psychological-mindedness on the CPI, and these traits, too, were certainly in evidence.

The actor's very low scores were on Self-control and Good Impression. Also low enough to be considered indicative were his scores on Responsibility, Socialization, and Achievement via Conformance.

All in all, the actor was, as we have suggested, already familiar with the role of fool, understanding "fool" in this instance to refer to a deliberate posture not unlike the classical conception of the King's jester.

2. Actor's Conceptualization of the Role

On the adjective check list, as observed above, the actor at t-1 described the Fool by many of the adjectives he had used to describe himself. He sees the Fool as like himself in his role as a jester, but stronger underneath, more of a self-determined person.

In taking the CPI as if he were the Fool, the actor earned these indicative high scores: Social Presence, Flexibility, Psychological-mindedness, and Good Impression. The first three are traits that he represents as his own, while the fourth is one that he possesses to a notably low degree. Missing from the high scores in this role conception compared with actual self is Femininity. He sees the Fool as relatively masculine (more so than about 80% of men).

The most indicative low scores were on Responsibility, sense of Communality with others, Sense of Well-Being, Intellectual Efficiency, and Socialization. Three of these (Re, Wb, and So) are traits in which the actor himself is also lacking, according to the test. The two exceptions are Communality and Intellectual Efficiency.

In summary, there is to begin with a certain fit between the actor's real-life representation of self and his conception of the Fool. There are some important differences, however, and these, as we shall see, entered in a significant fashion into the creative process during the period of rehearsals and in the course of the performances. The differences are that the actor himself scores quite high on Femininity but thinks of the Fool as rather masculine, and he represents himself both as more intellectually efficient and more like other people than he represents the Fool.

The Fool's second CPI, at the end of the run, showed significant change. In the first test, the character emerged as rather masculine: in the second, it was being experienced as noticeably feminine (a rise of 20 standard score points, or 2 standard deviations, on the Femininity scale). Communality had now risen from 22 to 55, a move through 3 standard deviations, and Responsibility had risen some 30 points. These changes accorded with the actor's style and development in the role. In the early rehearsals, as he felt his way, he played mainly—and masculinely—for the Fool's bite, emphasizing the hardness of the clever verbal assaults. But as the relationship with Lear ripened, tones of plaintiveness and compassion, of a tenderness almost in spite of itself, softened the Fool, made him, in a subtle and moving characterization, poignantly sensitive to Lear's suffering and able to offer an affection that was as close as Lear could then come to the filial love the daughters would not give him.

What remains to be noted here, so far as the CPI evidence is concerned, is that the skilled clinical observer, on the basis of the final performance of the play and taking the CPI now for the Fool as projected, earned highest scores on Flexibility and Femininity but rather low scores on Communality and Responsibility. While the actor felt that he was portraying a more responsible Fool, and certainly in human terms of sympathy for a fellow being *in extremis* he was so, the observer, attempting to empathize with the performance, saw the Fool as being out of touch with ordinary human attitudes and irresponsible socially.

While we must guard against overinterpretation in this instance, since either the actor or the observer in the audience may simply have erred in translating his conception into test responses, the discrepancy is suggestive of an interesting possibility. In terms of the play, the actor was right in *feeling himself* to be more responsible as he remained loyal to the man who needed him so desperately, whereas to a dispassionate observer the Fool's characteristic appearance of taunting might be taken as a rejection of his social responsibilities, a fact rather than a mask.

Interestingly enough, with the exception of femininity, the picture of the Fool that the actor did convey to the observer was quite consistent with his initial conception of the role, the similarity extending even to the three other most indicative variables, Socialization, Sense of Well-Being, and Intellectual Efficiency. What had changed in the interim were the actor's feelings about a character who would behave as the Fool did in relation to Lear. This is an important point and reflects the philosophy of the director of this production. Professor Goldsby's rehearsal process is akin to the creative process itself. Actors and director together explore the implications of the character as they go along; there is no dictation, no rigid preconception; all share responsibility for the final artwork. Here, the director's intuition in making this actor his Fool was confirmed by the evident sympathy that emerged between actor and role, not as the actor originally conceived it, but as he came to know it by living with it.

Most significantly, in terms of the relationship of the two roles, the CPI's taken by the actors as characters suggested latent resemblances that did not show up in the adjective check lists. Both King and Fool tested low on Sense of Well-Being, Intellectual Efficiency, and Socialization. (Lear was also low on Self-control and Tolerance, the Fool on Responsibility and sense of

Communality.) Here the tests seem to confirm the implications of Shakespeare's poetic dialectic: the figure at the top of the royal chain of being shares the alienation and insecurity of the marginal Fool at the other extreme, and can understandably exchange roles with him.

As the rehearsa! went on, the relationship between King and Fool became steadily more reciprocal, interdependent; the two often huddled together against the hostility of men and weather, until the troubled Lear began to take on some of the riddling, erratic (and erotic) imagery of the Fool; whereupon the Fool gave way and was seen no more. He "went to bed at noon": and Lear, in his madness, played the Fool.

III. Discussion

A. METHODOLOGY

The novel features of this study as a method of research in theater arts are the following.

1. Standardized psychological tests are used to elicit an actor's conception of a role he has undertaken to play.

2. The relationship between the actor's conception of the role and his conception of himself can now be expressed in quantitative terms (test profile similarity, e.g.) as well as by way of clinical or depth psychology formulation.

3. The success of the performance is studied by comparing the actor's conception of the role with a clinician's projection of it by way of the same standardized test. Discrepancies may now be given special attention for their meaning in terms of the creative process in development of the role.

Certain difficulties should be noted:

(a) Coefficients of similarity between test profiles have little meaning in themselves; they must be referred to a distribution of such coefficients for people in general (the person in relation to himself on different occasions, and persons in relation to one another, e.g.). The establishment of such empirical sampling distribution for the tests under study would have made these data more meaningful statistically, but it was beyond the scope of this research to develop such distributions for this specific purpose, and they are not otherwise available.

(b) This study assumes high validity in the test instruments. If the test were not valid, the suggested criterion of success of performance (i.e., correlation of observer's conception of the role with actor's conception of it) would be without merit. That there was very high agreement between observer and actor in this study argues for the validity of the test as well as the merit of this criterion of success. We must note as well, however, that the validity of the observer is assumed, too; if the observer fails to grasp what is in fact being projected in the actor's performance, the lack of correlation would be his failure to comprehend rather than the actor's failure to enact.

B. IMPLICATIONS

We are not suggesting here a method for use by a director in casting or directing a play, even though a director with proper training in psychological testing might indeed be able to use the tests for those purposes. Rather, we are suggesting a research method for the study of the process of role conceptualization and development and for the study of certain specific problems. Questions that might be studied by this method include:

1. Is there a point at which degree of dissimilarity between actor and character counterindicates success in performance?
2. Is ability as an actor related to the "distance" he can bridge between himself and the role?
3. Can operational meaning be given to the concept of "scope as an actor" by studying the number of highly dissimilar roles an actor can play?
4. Are there specific variables that are particular stumbling blocks for particular actors (Masculinity-femininity, e.g., or Dominance, or Flexibility)?

One of us (Barron) has put this general method to use in another way in teaching a course in the psychology of literature. The students were asked to read 10 novels or dramatic poems depicting American life from the 1600's to the present (from Benet's *Western Star* to Capote's *In Cold Blood* and Mailer's *Why Are We in Vietnam*). Then they were asked to take the psychological tests, first as self and then as protagonist in the work of fiction. Pairs of students, one male and one female, then reported their individual results to the class, after themselves studying their own differences in projecting the character through the tests. As pedagogy the method was unquestionably successful, for the students learned about the tests, themselves, American character, and perhaps even the process of character creation in fiction.

CHAPTER TWELVE

Twin Resemblances in Creative Thinking and Aesthetic Judgment

The material for education is always a person, the student. The process of education takes the student as given, and does the best it can to develop innate potentialities. Thus in a certain practical sense the question of talent is irrelevant to the general task education sets for itself, though obviously not to individual differences in the quality of the product.

From this point of view, the question of whether talent is inherited rarely need arise. It is more out of scientific curiosity than for any practical pedagogic reasons, therefore, that we put the questions to which this chapter addresses itself: Is aesthetic judgment inherited? Is the ability to think creatively inherited? The present study claims nothing conclusive in response, for reasons that we shall shortly try to make evident; yet at any rate we do here make a beginning on a problem that does need scientific study.

Although the heritability of general intelligence as measured by the conventional IQ test has already been the subject of much study and can be considered to be well established (though precise quantitative statement is not warranted), the heritability of specific factors in intellectual functioning has not yet been the object of such intense scientific inquiry.

The recent work of Robert C. Nichols (see Vandenberg, 1965), utilizing a large sample of twins from the National Merit Scholarship testing program and employing a battery of tests measuring achievement in five different academic areas, is an excellent pioneering study. Nichols used a composite score derived from the five subtests, presuming this score to be a measure of general ability, and he found that identical twins were much more alike than fraternal twins with respect to the composite score; about 70% of the variance in the composite could be attributed to heredity. [This estimate is based on the ratio h^2 proposed by Holzinger (1929), where $h^2 = r_{mz} - r_{dz}$ divided by $1 - r_{dz}$. Both Holzinger's ratio and Nichols' ratio HR, where $HR = 2(r_{mz} - r_{dz})$ divided by r_{mz}, were calculated for our own data in this study. However, as Lerner (1969) has pointed out, these ratios rest on assumptions that are rarely known to be met, simply because of interaction effects between genetic and environmental influences. We refer in the title, therefore, to *twin resemblances* rather than *heritability*; the latter term is used in this chapter to refer to the ratios employed and is subject to the strictures noted.] The novel result of Nichols' investigation is his discovery that the specific subject areas also have significant heritability components in the sense of the term denoted by the applied ratios. When the influence of the composite general ability upon subtests was removed statistically, the residual subtest scores also showed considerable heritability.

A limitation of the Nichols findings is that the subtests do not offer any potential theoretical link to basic factors in mental functioning. Such measures may be provided by the fundamental factor-analytic explorations of J. P. Guilford and his associates during the past 20 years, however. Since our own interest has been in the area of creative thinking and aesthetic judgment, we have restricted ourselves in the present investigation to the use of tests in those areas whose factorial classification has been studied previously.

I. Method and Subjects

Tests for the following factors were employed: (1) Adaptive Flexibility; (2) Expressional Fluency; (3) Ideational Fluency; (4) Originality; (5) Aesthetic Judgment for Visual Displays.

A word about this last factor test is in order. The factor was identified in a study done jointly by the present author and the Guilford group (see Barron *et al.*, 1957). However, the authors were of two minds about its interpretation. The highest loading of the factor was on the Barron–Welsh Art Scale, the set of geometrical figures and drawings already described, whose preference rank for professional artists had been established independently and whose scoring expresses the degree of agreement of the respondent with professional artistic judgment. The standardization would thus justify the factor name given above. A complication stems from the fact that virtually all the figures ranked high by artists are of greater complexity than those they rank low, and it is possible to interpret the measure as basically a preference for complexity, as the present author has done (Barron, 1953a). The factor might therefore be understood simply as "preference for complex visual displays." As we shall see, this may be an important point for the interpretation of the findings to be reported.

Our measure for the Adaptive Flexibility factor is the Crutchfield revision of the Gottschaldt Figures Test, in which the task is to discover in a complex figure a simpler embedded one. This, too, was taken as the test of choice because of its high loading on Adaptive Flexibility in the earlier factor analysis (Barron *et al.*, 1957).

The present investigation employed, in addition to the Barron-Welsh Art Scale and the Gottschaldt Figures Test, the following tests from the Guilford battery: Expressional Fluency, Unusual Uses, Consequences, and Barron Symbol Equivalents Test. The last three tests are scored for Ideational Fluency (low quality score, or a simple count of the number of acceptable but not highly original or clever responses) and for Originality (number of responses scored 4 or 5 on a 5-point scale of Originality).

Two samples of adolescent twins were employed: one group of Italian twins whose cooperation was secured through the good offices of the Mendel Institute in Rome and the Institute for Medical Genetics in Florence, and a second group of American twins studied at the Institute of Personality Assessment and Research, University of California, Berkeley. In the Italian sample, diagnoses were arrived at from medical data, including blood tests, and it is safe to assume they are highly accurate. The American sample was classified as to zygosity on the basis of their responses to the questionnaire developed by Nichols in the research cited previously. While the method can be expected to result in some misclassification, Nichols reported 93% accuracy against the blood grouping criterion. Error in diagnosis should lead to a higher intraclass correlation for dizygotic (DZ) twins and a lower intraclass correlation for monozygotic (MZ) twins for inherited traits, so that heritability will be underestimated rather than overestimated on the average when errors of classification do occur.

The Italian sample consisted of 59 pairs of like-sexed twins: 30 MZ pairs,

15 male and 15 female; and 29 DZ pairs, 14 male and 15 female. One female DZ pair had to be eliminated later because of incomplete test results. The average age of the sample was 17.04; all subjects were secondary school students or graduates. The American sample consisted of 57 pairs of like-sexed twins: 29 MZ pairs, 14 male and 15 female; and 28 DZ pairs, 13 male and 15 female. The average age of the sample was 17.42, and all were either recent high school graduates or seniors.

II. Results

Results are reported first for the Italian sample and then for the American, as this was the actual order of work and a preliminary partial report on the Italian sample has already been made (Barron, 1969). A statistical summary of results for both samples is given in Table 20.

A. ADAPTIVE FLEXIBILITY

As we have indicated, the form of the Gottschaldt Figures Test employed as a measure of this factor is the Crutchfield revision (MacKinnon *et al.,* 1958). The test is well adapted for group administration and is closely timed. The task is to discover in a complex figure a specific simpler figure embedded in it. Fifteen problems are presented.

Scores in the Italian sample ranged from 0 to 15, with a mean of 7.16. The intraclass correlation for the MZ group was .86; for the DZ group, .35. Both correlations are significantly different from zero, and they are significantly different from one another as well (t of 4.79, p less than .01). The Holzinger heritability coefficient h^2 was .79 (correlations not corrected for attenuation).

In the American sample, the mean score was 7.81, not significantly different from the Italian mean. The MZ intraclass correlation was .49; DZ, .13; giving h^2 of .41. The two correlations are significantly different from one another, as in the Italian sample, and the indications are for a significant degree of heritability in the intellectual function measured by this test.

B. EXPRESSIONAL FLUENCY

This is a test from the Guilford battery in which the subject is given the initial letters of four words in sequence and asked to complete the words in such a manner as to form a sentence. His score is the number of complete sentences he can form in a given time.

In the Italian sample, the MZ correlation was .92, the DZ correlation .70, yielding a Holzinger coefficient of .75. In the American sample, however, the finding did not hold. The MZ correlation was −.28, the DZ .76, yielding a value of −4.33 for h^2.

C. IDEATIONAL FLUENCY

Here again the findings were inconsistent and heritability was not indicated. Low quality scores for Consequences, Symbol Equivalence, and Unusual Uses for the two samples showed the results given in Table 18.

D. ORIGINALITY

The results for the "high quality" scoring of these tests were as shown in Table 19. It should be noted that these tests of expressive verbal behavior independent of verbal comprehension and reasoning are not scored objectively, as the other tests in the battery are, but rather by subjective ratings. Their reliabilities are correspondingly lower, revealing interrater agreement in the range from .40 to .70. Inconsistencies in the findings may thus be in part a function of scoring error.

E. AESTHETIC JUDGMENT OF VISUAL DISPLAYS

In the Italian sample, the MZ intraclass correlation was .58; the DZ, .07. The MZ correlation is significantly different from zero, but the DZ is not. They are significantly different from one another (t of 3.05, p less than .01), and a high heritability component is indicated by the h^2 value of .55.

This finding was strongly confirmed in the American sample. The MZ intraclass correlation was .66, the DZ, −.02, a highly signficant difference. The corresponding h^2 value is .67.

III. Discussion

Leaving aside for the moment the hypothesized factorial structure for which some of these tests are presumably measures, the most obvious feature of the results is that the tests calling for expressive verbal behavior show, for the most part, substantial similarity of all twin pairs, MZ and DZ alike. The tests calling for visual discrimination of complex forms, as well as reasoning and judgment in the visual sphere, reveal significant differences between MZ and DZ twins, however, with the correlations being much higher in the MZ samples.

Since expressive verbal behavior is much more likely to be influenced both by imitation and propinquity than are purely visual discrimination and reasoning, which are largely silent and unobserved because of their infrequent practical consequences and a lack of social need for their expression, it does make sense that simply being part of the environment called twinship would produce high correlations in the first set of behaviors, while the second would be unaffected by the social environment. Thus, the findings create a strong argument for the existence of a significant hereditary component in visual judgment. The possible significance of this for aesthetics needs clarification, however, since the Gottschaldt Figures Test, on the face of it, calls for discrimination and reasoning but not aesthetic judgment, whereas the Barron–Welsh Art Scale, although known to be relevant to aesthetic judgment and creativity, has not been studied from the point of view of the respondent's *capacity* to discriminate form and to reason about patterns, but only from the point of view of the correlates of his *preferences*. The question arises, can one exhibit good taste in preferences without having the capacity to discriminate and reason about the stimulus material in which the problem of choice is presented? Could these considerations play a part in the analysis of creative mathematical reasoning, which traditionally has employed aesthetic criteria in judging of the fitness of a solution, or the degree of promise of steps toward a solution? Certainly further study of these effects and their implications is needed, both in new studies with the twin method and with expanded test measures in the figural sphere, as well as with individuals of noteworthy ability in the arts and in mathematics.

IV. The Design of Future Twin Studies

The living-in assessment method offers some intriguing possibilities for new wrinkles in the design of twin studies. The unique feature of the method is that several individuals, generally from 5 to 15, are collected in a group for two or three days and studied with respect to their social behavior and the kinds of personal relationships they establish with other group members and with the assessment staff. Imagine 10 twin A's in one assessment center and their counterparts in a group of 10 in another assessment center (imagine twin assessors, too, if you like). A sample of 100 pairs of like-sexed twins of the same age, half of them male and half of them female, studied by such a method would make possible all sorts of experiments and observations never yet attempted in research with twins. The application of sociometric procedures, for example, could shed light on the genetic bases for likability and for the determinants of preferences in persons. Mood variables could be rated, as well as measured by tests, and of course all sorts of expressive behaviors could be rated and thrown into the hopper, including dancing, singing, motility of behavior in charades, reaction to alcohol (given the usual predinner cocktails), reaction to marijuana under proper experimental conditions and with careful safeguards, or what have you. The study of similarity of sleep and dreaming patterns, as well as content of dreams, would be made especially convenient, and the study of telepathic communication in dreams, using variations of the Krippner (1969) methods, would at least be feasible. Members of twin pairs could also be asked to describe one another, and even to take some tests as if they were the other, or at least as they might think their twin would take the tests. The study of aesthetic values, choices, and expressive behavior in such an experimental situation could be greatly enriched. Cinematic documentation of selected parts of the proceedings could provide a data pool for later studies, using different observers. That 7% of dizygotic twins who mistakenly think they are monozygotic might also be included in the sample, providing a control for "set to be similar to one's twin."

Both the twin method and the living-in assessment method would become much more powerful if thus conjoined. The validity of assessment ratings would be opened to a new kind of scrutiny, and the study of the distorting effect of transference and countertransference could become much more telling.

Acknowledgments

We are especially indebted to Drs. Luigi Gedda and Paolo Parisi, of the staff of the Mendel Institute in Rome, and Dr. H. B. Young, of the Harvard Florence Project for the material used in this chapter. Other members of the Mendel Institute staff, including especially Dr. Lucio Braconi, also contributed time and effort to the research in a spirit of generosity that we found most memorable. The work in Florence also owes much to Dr. A. Noferi, who interviewed the subjects and administered the tests. The Institute for Medical Genetics in Florence and the Institute for Applied Psychology there also contributed their facilities and technical help.

The research in Berkeley was accomplished with the valuable help of Drs. Arnold Mordkoff and Ann-Marie Allerand Bloch, the interviewing and test-scoring assistance of

Barbara Bell, Lorraine Granit, Jerrell Kraus, and Isabel Conti, and the statistical advice and labors of Dr. Wallace Hall and Susan Hopkin.

The research was initiated with the financial help and support of the Richardson Foundation, and parts of it were made possible by a grant from the United States Office of Education for basic research in aesthetics. The latter aspect of the work is continuing with valuable support from the Arts and Humanities Division of that agency.

CHAPTER THIRTEEN

A College for Aesthetic Education

The educational experiment based on the "cluster college" concept at the University of California, Santa Cruz, provided an opportunity to develop a new kind of college, one devoted specifically to aesthetic education. Colleges on that campus are built in clusters of four, each with a distinctive theme that unifies faculty and student interests and provides a common core for the college curriculum. The first three colleges were devoted, respectively, to the humanities, the social sciences, and the natural sciences. The fourth focused on problems of poverty at home and underdevelopment abroad. The fifth college, as described in the 1969–1970 catalog, "addresses the arts, the fine arts and the popular arts in the 20th century, with special attention to creativity and to the identification of talent."

A brand new faculty and administration set to work in high spirits in the fall of 1969 to create this new thing. Nine months later a squalling infant was indeed on hand. Clearly there was no single pair of parents, but *in loco parentis* there were some 30 faculty Fellows who had accepted responsibility—existentially, indeed, *were responsible*—for bringing baby up. It may prove instructive to others to review here some of the lessons learned from conception to parturition, and to seek to anticipate on the basis of this first experience some of the problems still ahead, for this college and for others like it.

I. The Cluster College

It might be added that, whatever the problems, the opportunity to develop a college devoted specifically to aesthetic education can hardly exist without the support of a campus-wide structure that includes colleges with other aims as well as the traditional disciplines that look beyond both college and campus. The rarity of the opportunity is attested by recent research reported in the April, 1970, issue of the *Journal of Aesthetic Education*. Allen Shields writes there that

> Research in the literature has failed to disclose a four-year program in aesthetic studies in any university or college in the United States at the present time. . . . There is some kind of basic vacuum among the arts in the training of young college people that must be filled [p. 134].

Shields goes on to say that a basic objective of this sort of new curriculum should be to introduce changes in general education, first at the college level and then, through the training of teachers by the college, at all levels of education. The goal, in brief, is to bring an aesthetic perspective to the entire school system, with emphasis not simply on training in the arts but infusion of the educational process with *the spirit of art.*

What he was picturing, and what our new college for aesthetic studies at Santa Cruz may yet help to make a reality, is a new force in education, basically different from such traditional art colleges as the San Francisco Art Institute or the Rhode Island School of Design or the Boston Conservatory of Music, or for that matter any of the usual art departments within a college or university. This new force aims at changing the fabric of education, from the nursery school through to college itself. As such, it may very well need a new kind of student as well as a new curriculum and a faculty with a new perspective on general education. Later in this chapter we shall see what research can tell us about the kind of student this new college is in fact attracting. The crucial issue of the effect of the curriculum on the students is also under study, and if all goes as planned we should soon have some evidence to report.

II. The Core Course

Each college at Santa Cruz organizes, for freshmen at least, a two- or three-quarter course that introduces students to the intellectual activity relevant to the college theme. It does this by way of a "core course," usually taught by several faculty members; theoretically, all could contribute to this.

In a college for aesthetic education, the core course properly combines studio work with theory. In this particular college, the studio work includes sculpture, painting, graphics, musical composition, poetry, dance, photography, mixed media, and jazz. The studios are called "workshops," and a pre-enrollment poll of entering freshmen showed that photography, drama, dance, film, and creative writing are popular preferences, whereas drawing, painting, sculpture, and musical composition and performance rank low.

Do these preferences mean something about the distribution of talents in the student body? Perhaps so, for those arts in which talent is a prerequisite if one is not to fall visibly on one's face are not much opted for. This in turn reflects the method of selection of students for the college. All students who meet the campus-wide requirements are given the opportunity to indicate a college preference. If the college can admit all students who rank it first in preference, it does so. If its expected enrollment will not be filled by taking all who wish to enter, it takes others, who then become students of the college willy-nilly.

In the case of this college of aesthetic education, only one third of its first-year enrollment chose it; the others were assigned to it. But, this was apparently due in large part to the fact that the news had not gotten around that a college with a major in aesthetic studies was on the way. In the second year, more than half of the students were enrolled in the college by choice, and in the third year (as of this writing), it appears that the number will rise to 80 or 90 percent.

Midway in the second year of the college's life we were able to test 49 students, 23 male and 26 female, who were at the college by choice. They were recruited for testing through announcement of the testing program in lower division studio courses and in a psychology course; all were volunteers, and except for a sprinkling of upper division transfer students, they were freshmen or sophomores. Although the test battery was somewhat more limited than that used with San Francisco Art Institute students, tests on which we have especially relied in other research were included, making possible a comparison of students in the College for Aesthetic Studies and the San Francisco Art Institute. The numerical results are given in detail in Tables 21, 22, and 23 of the Appendix.

III. Student Characteristics as Shown by Test Results

A. THE STRONG VOCATIONAL INTEREST BLANK

For six scales of the Vocational Interest Blank, the *average* score of these students is in the A range. These A scores are, in descending order of magnitude, Musician, Physician, Artist, Author, Architect, and Psychologist. The scale for Advertising Man just barely misses being included in the A range, and is followed in rank in this sample by that of Lawyer. These eight scales are precisely the same as the top eight for the San Francisco Art Institute sample, though with Physician and Psychologist ranking a bit higher. At the other end of the scale, we find very low scores for Purchasing Agent, Army Officer, Office Worker, Accountant, Carpenter, Industrial Arts Teacher, Veterinarian, Banker, Credit Manager, Policeman, and Mortician, all in the C range. Again, there is an almost complete correspondence between Art Institute students and the College of Aesthetic Studies students, this time in shunned vocations.

B. THE CALIFORNIA PSYCHOLOGICAL INVENTORY

In personality, too, the College of Aesthetic Studies students are very similar to students at the San Francisco Art Institute. Flexibility and motivation to achieve by independent means rather than by conformance are the outstanding traits in both groups. They are alike too in being relatively high on Self-acceptance but relatively low on Sense of Well-being. The latter scale seems to reflect a sense of contentment with things as they are; low scores indicate discontent with external arrangements rather than with oneself, and so can very well go along with high scores on Self-acceptance. Both groups also are consistently low on scales measuring sense of social responsibility, self-control, socialization, and effort to make a good impression. As we have suggested earlier, such scale scores, and indeed the very names of the scales, must be interpreted with an eye to the social context, and this kind of profile has consistently turned up in our earlier research as associated with creativity. One does not expect the Left Bank to be the same as the Right Bank, and the traits possessed by these students, on the average, are socially appropriate to their self-chosen context. As one of the professors in the aesthetic studies college put it upon seeing these test results, "I'm not surprised". The most interesting thing about these results is that there is so little difference in vocational interests and in social attitudes and personality between art students and students who are pursuing general educational objectives but with an emphasis on the arts.

C. Tests of Aesthetic Judgment and Preferences

(Barron-Welsh Art Scale, Gottschaldt Figures, Hall Mosaic Judgment Test and Child Aesthetic Judgment Test.)

Once again, the two groups are very similar and are very much like artists, creative writers, and architects and very different from the usual college or high school sample.

Art Institute students score 34.4 on the Barron-Welsh Art Scale, on the average; College of Aesthetic Studies students score 33.46, and the difference is not statistically significant. The reader is again referred to Table 5 in the Appendix for comparative statistics for other groups for this scale.

On the Child Aesthetic Judgment Test too there is not a significant difference between San Francisco Art Institute students and College of Aesthetic Studies students (57.4 vs. 56.5). The same finding of no significant differences between the two groups obtains for all the variables of the Hall Mosaic Judgment Test. On the Gottschaldt Figures, however, the latter group is slightly but significantly superior (14.26 vs. 11.2), with standard deviations of 4.99 and 5.05 respectively.

IV. Lectures and Seminars

Three main sources of lectures and seminars broadly relevant to aesthetic education are provided the student:

1. a special open lecture series allied to the core course, given by Fellows of the college, focusing on "The Work of Art," "The Historical Context of Art," "Art and the Future," and similar topics of a theoretical, speculative, or scholarly nature;

2. college offerings by Fellows, usually seminars for upper-division students rather than freshmen, often based on aesthetic avocational interests of college faculty members whose primary disciplines were not in the arts (a psychologist teaching a course on the American character as revealed in historical fiction, e.g., or a geologist on the aesthetics of natural forms);

3. campus-wide offerings relevant to aesthetics in boards of studies such as literature, the language arts, philosophy, psychology, history, sociology, theater arts (including dance and film); for example, Creative Writing, Literary Interpretation, Modern Drama, *The Divine Comedy,* The French Novel, Twentieth-Century German Drama, *The Iliad,* Modern American Writing, Philosophy in Literature, Aesthetics, Psychology of Creativity, Art History, Sociology of Art, The Ancient City, Studies in Acting, Dance,

History and Aesthetics of Cinema, Anthropological Basis of Dance, Drawing, Painting, Sculpture, Art in the Twentieth Century, Byzantine Art and Aesthetics.

Certainly there was no dearth of regular course offerings and lectures that could readily be made to constitute a college major in aesthetic education. One lack proved to be in the field of education itself! However, this was due largely to the fact that no board of studies in education yet existed on the campus, and only a scattering of courses offered by a transitional committee on education was available. This situation was remedied in the second year and a college major was developed by the faculty and approved by all the necessary campus agencies. A statement of the requirements for the major was prepared by the present author and Pavel Machotka, another psychologist in the College, for faculty approval, and upon recommendation by the Provost, James B. Hall, it was subsequently adopted. It reads as follows:

College Major in Aesthetic Studies

The College major in Aesthetic Studies is intended to provide a unique focus for the studies of our College's students whose primary interest is in the arts. It is specifically intended for students who (a) wish to devote concentrated study to certain fields of aesthetics such as art history, sociology of art, or aesthetic theory and psychology; or (b) who wish to devote themselves to the practice of arts not represented by full Boards of Study and degree programs, or who need greater flexibility in combining the practice of several related arts.

Requirements

Four distinct "paths" exist within the major in Aesthetic Studies: a Studio-Performance path, an Aesthetic Theory and Psychology path, a History of Art path, and an Art and Society path. A student must complete *six* upper-division courses within *one* of the paths and one course each in the other three paths (a total of nine courses).

In addition to these requirements, each student must (a) take a Sophomore Studio (one quarter); (b) complete an individual Senior Project relevant to his path of specialization, which must be deemed sufficiently competent by a jury of two Fellows. A student taking the Studio-Performance path will exhibit his work or give a public performance; a student in one of the other paths will write a major essay or research paper. Independent study (one quarter) is the appropriate vehicle only for the Senior Project.

If the student chooses the Studio-Performance path, at least three of his six required courses must be in one of the arts, but his other courses may range more widely.

A total of 56 upper-division courses will be offered by the college faculty in the four paths. In addition, some 40 other relevant courses are offered by various boards and can be elected by students to fulfill the requirements for the major in Aesthetic Studies.

V. Some Possible Improvements

That the experiment in developing a college for aesthetic education is viable has been made clear. Even with the division of faculty time between College and Board, there are ample personnel to man a college major that includes studio work in drawing and painting, sculpture, movie making and photography, classical musical composition and performance, dance, jazz composition and performance, creative writing in poetry, the short story, and the novel, the psychology, sociology, and philosophy of art, and art history.

Nevertheless, there are some ways in which the situation could be improved:

1. Provision should be made in the college budget for full-time nontenured positions that could be used to attract distinguished visiting artists and scholars for short periods of time (from one quarter to a year). The existence of three or four such budgeted positions would greatly increase the flexibility of the program and make it more attractive because of the excitement of having a changing slate of lively visitors.

2. Psychological testing should be used for recruitment of students. At a minimum, the Strong Vocational Interest Blank should be administered on a campus-wide basis, and scores on it should lead to recommendations for the assignment of students to given colleges in those cases where assignment is necessary. Some of the performance tests discussed in this book might be used if talent also can be taken into account in the selection decision.

3. Continuing research should be conducted into the changes brought about by the educational experience, as well as the question of the identification of talent. Learning situations that stimulate creativity should be sought. The process of evaluation by teachers, students, and administrators should be built into the whole educational program. Again, provision of budget support for research and evaluation is essential. A full-time research psychologist whose job is to carry on a continuous program of research, which might involve interviewing, counseling, and troubleshooting in general, could be a great asset to the college. (He could also help provide research training for the students.)

4. Genuine curriculum innovation should be effected. The aesthetic vision of life contains within it certain prescriptive elements for education, and one should expect that these would animate all curricula. Basic to this is the expressive rather than repressive regulatory mode in the classroom; this in turn has many implications for physical structures, time schedules, spacing and facing of students and teachers, and the like. But content, too, should be affected. Sensorial variegation in the learning environment should be sought, and the full use of the senses encouraged. Could one not learn better use of the faculties of hearing, seeing, smelling, tasting, touching? Could one not learn to dream more often and more richly, and in more sensory modes? Why should we not teach methods for inducing creative reverie, for meditation, for learning to break set, to reverse figure and ground, to make the familiar strange and the strange familiar? Strategies for enhancing ideational fluency and originality are being developed in nonacademic settings; why can they not be incorporated into special curricula in the college? The genuine breadth of "aesthetic education" would be realized if the implications of creativity for the very process of learning were embodied in educational techniques.

5. Career opportunities in the school system and the community for the college graduate with an AB in aesthetic education should be actively stimulated. The problem of career choice is obviously related to the real possibilities in the world at large for the artist and the aesthetic educator to make a living. The school systems usually have no place for the specialist in aesthetic education or in art. There is no demand as yet for what the college is on the verge of being able to supply. Perhaps it is paying the penalty for being ahead of its time. Although it is fashionable to decry the apparent increase of art in popularity in the United States as reflecting nothing but American materialism, the fact is that there has been a general and quite noticeable increase in popular taste, and in appreciation for the aesthetic qualities of the environment, over the past two decades. This is shown in the flood of superb reproductions of paintings, drawings, etchings, primitive and classical sculpture and jewelry, and so on, as well as in the attention to good design in manufactured products, homes and office buildings, transit systems, packaging, clothing, and all the other appurtenances of "the good life," material though it be.

The college devoted solely to aesthetic education may be a bit premature, but surely not much so. The time is coming when aesthetic education must reach down to the elementary and preschool levels, through special training programs for teachers, and reach out from the schools as we know them now to a broader community school in which education will employ all its means to honor the artistic impulse in people in all walks of life.

Appendix

Tables

TABLE 1

California Psychological Inventory Scale Statistics, Students of Art

Scale		Mean	S.D.
Do (Dominance)	Total sample	24.16	5.91
	Males	24.09	5.90
	Females	24.27	5.91
Cs (Capacity for Status)	Total sample	18.27	3.79
	Males	17.91	3.88
	Females	18.88	3.56
Sy (Sociability)	Total sample	20.49	5.10
	Males	20.77	5.26
	Females	20.00	4.76

TABLE 1 (*continued*)

Scale		Mean	S.D.
Sp (Social Presence)	Total sample	36.51	6.59
	Males	36.04	6.16
	Females	37.31	7.18
Sa (Self-Acceptance)	Total sample	21.54	3.68
	Males	21.45	3.76
	Females	21.69	3.53
Wb (Sense of Well-Being)	Total sample	30.67	6.13
	Males	30.09	6.48
	Females	31.65	5.35
Re (Responsibility)	Total sample	21.83	4.23
	Males	21.34	4.03
	Females	22.65	4.41
So (Socialization)	Total sample	30.24	5.09
	Males	29.77	4.80
	Females	31.04	5.45
Sc (Self-Control)	Total sample	21.49	6.69
	Males	20.97	6.85
	Females	22.34	6.32
To (Tolerance)	Total sample	17.93	5.22
	Males	16.98	5.32
	Females	19.54	4.63
Gi (Good Impression)	Total sample	12.84	4.91
	Males	13.30	4.97
	Females	12.08	4.71
Cm (Communality)	Total sample	23.00	3.03
	Males	22.56	3.42
	Females	23.73	2.03
Ac (Achievement via Conformance)	Total sample	20.86	3.86
	Males	20.43	3.83
	Females	21.58	3.79
Ai (Achievement via Independence)	Total sample	20.04	3.91
	Males	19.77	4.01
	Females	20.50	3.69

TABLE 1 (continued)

Scale		Mean	S.D.
Ie (Intellectual Efficiency)	Total sample	35.51	5.65
	Males	34.89	5.13
	Females	36.58	6.30
Py (Psychological-Mindedness)	Total sample	11.01	2.54
	Males	10.98	2.48
	Females	11.08	2.64
Fx (Flexibility)	Total sample	13.74	4.36
	Males	13.34	4.46
	Females	14.42	4.10
Fe (Femininity)	Total sample	(deleted)	
	Males	18.31	4.25
	Females	23.96	2.88

Note: Only two significant sex differences are found in this table: Females score higher on Tolerance (t of 2.01, $p < .05$) and on Femininity (t of 4.87, $p < .01$).

TABLE 2

Minnesota Multiphasic Personality Inventory Scales: Student Artists

	Males ($N = 88$)			Females ($N = 65$)		
	Raw scores		T Score	Raw scores		T score
Scale	X	S.D.	T	X	S.D.	T
L (Lie)	3.31	2.04	48	3.34	1.79	48
F (Validity)	7.09	4.26	60	7.31	5.63	61
K (Positive self-presentation)	13.86	4.29	52	12.98	3.72	51
Hs (Hypochondriasis) (+.5K)	12.90	3.65	53	13.62	4.58	51
D (Depression)	18.44	4.76	54	19.39	5.78	49
Hy (Hysteria)	21.59	4.60	59	22.80	5.21	56
Pd (Psychopathic deviation) (+.4K)	22.82	4.51	59	21.94	4.57	56
Mf (Masculinity-femininity)	28.30	6.02	65	38.03	4.25	47
Pa (Paranoia)	10.58	3.19	57	10.36	3.44	57
Pt (Psychasthenia) (+1K)	28.25	5.62	60	28.92	5.58	55
Sc (Schizophrenia) (+1K)	29.75	6.74	64	29.50	7.24	60
Ma (Hypomania) (+.2K)	22.53	3.91	51	22.58	4.83	54
Es (Ego-strength)	48.57	5.94	60	45.94	6.36	57

TABLE 3

Strong Vocational Interest Blank (Men's Form) Scores: Entering Studio Students, San Francisco Art Institute, 1968[a]

Occupation or scale		Mean	S.D.
Group I			
Artist	Total sample	54.9	8.61
	Males	53.6	8.89
	Females	57.0	7.71
Psychologist	Total sample	41.5	8.40
	Males	41.6	8.06
	Females	41.3	8.88
Architect	Total sample	49.0	7.28
	Males	48.6	7.60
	Females	49.5	6.72
Physician	Total sample	44.8	9.81
	Males	44.7	10.16
	Females	44.9	9.26
Psychiatrist	Total sample	39.9	8.99
	Males	40.2	9.38
	Females	39.3	8.34
Osteopath	Total sample	34.8	9.40
	Males	34.7	9.70
	Females	35.1	8.93
Dentist	Total sample	36.5	7.30
	Males	36.7	7.09
	Females	36.3	7.61
Veterinarian	Total sample	16.8	9.13
	Males	16.3	9.35
	Females	17.7	8.73
Group II			
Mathematician	Total sample	32.6	7.33
	Males	33.0	7.56
	Females	32.2	6.95
Physicist	Total sample	29.2	8.04
	Males	30.0	8.63
	Females	28.0	6.88

***TABLE* 3** (*continued*)

Occupation or scale		Mean	S.D.
Group II (*cont.*)			
Chemist	Total sample	33.1	8.18
	Males	34.2	8.36
	Females	31.4	7.60
Engineer	Total sample	26.5	7.23
	Males	27.7	7.95
	Females	24.7	5.46
Group III			
Production Manager	Total sample	18.3	6.99
	Males	19.3	7.45
	Females	16.8	5.89
Group IV			
Farmer	Total sample	31.0	7.72
	Males	30.9	8.28
	Females	31.1	6.79
Carpenter	Total sample	19.7	9.79
	Males	20.7	10.06
	Females	18.1	9.13
Forest Service Man	Total sample	15.2	10.64
	Males	15.7	11.64
	Females	14.6	8.84
Aviator	Total sample	25.3	8.74
	Males	26.2	9.71
	Females	23.8	6.74
Printer	Total sample	34.8	8.27
	Males	35.2	8.72
	Females	34.2	7.47
Mathematics Science Teacher	Total sample	22.9	9.79
	Males	24.4	10.56
	Females	20.7	7.98
Industrial Arts Teacher	Total sample	11.2	11.12
	Males	13.1	11.76
	Females	8.3	9.36

TABLE 3 (continued)

Occupation or scale		Mean	S.D.
Group IV (*cont.*)			
Vocational Agriculture Teacher	Total sample	14.5	10.34
	Males	15.1	11.18
	Females	13.5	8.62
Policeman	Total sample	15.7	7.36
	Males	16.1	7.44
	Females	15.0	7.18
Army Officer	Total sample	6.8	10.79
	Males	8.4	11.40
	Females	4.3	9.26
Group V			
YMCA Physical Director	Total sample	18.6	8.88
	Males	19.2	10.09
	Females	17.8	6.55
Public Administrator	Total sample	28.5	8.08
	Males	28.6	8.83
	Females	28.3	6.77
Vocational Counselor	Total sample	26.9	8.66
	Males	27.4	9.88
	Females	26.1	6.28
Physical Therapist	Total sample	26.3	10.87
	Males	27.3	11.89
	Females	24.8	8.89
Social Worker	Total sample	32.4	9.05
	Males	32.3	10.12
	Females	32.4	7.10
Social Science Teacher	Total sample	24.3	9.06
	Males	24.6	10.13
	Females	23.7	7.09
Business Education Teacher	Total sample	17.6	10.11
	Males	18.6	11.04
	Females	16.1	8.28

TABLE 3 (continued)

Occupation or scale		Mean	S.D.
Group V (*cont.*)			
School Superintendent	Total sample	19.9	9.00
	Males	20.4	9.83
	Females	19.1	7.49
Minister	Total sample	29.2	9.32
	Males	29.1	10.61
	Females	29.3	6.87
Group VI			
Musician	Total sample	55.7	7.64
	Males	55.1	8.22
	Females	56.7	6.52
Music Teacher	Total sample	37.1	9.20
	Males	37.1	10.38
	Females	37.0	7.04
Group VII			
CPA Owner	Total sample	26.4	7.26
	Males	26.7	7.36
	Females	26.1	7.10
Group VIII			
Senior CPA	Total sample	17.3	9.43
	Males	18.4	10.09
	Females	15.7	8.05
Accountant	Total sample	8.2	8.53
	Males	9.1	9.12
	Females	6.7	7.31
Office Worker	Total sample	14.3	8.14
	Males	15.1	8.40
	Females	13.0	7.55
Credit Manager	Total sample	14.8	9.39
	Males	15.8	10.31
	Females	13.4	7.57

TABLE 3 (continued)

Occupation or scale		Mean	S.D.
Group VIII (*cont.*)			
Purchasing Agent	Total sample	10.3	8.45
	Males	11.5	8.48
	Females	8.5	8.08
Banker	Total sample	16.1	6.23
	Males	16.2	5.88
	Females	16.1	6.72
Pharmacist	Total sample	26.6	6.64
	Males	27.2	6.52
	Females	25.7	7.72
Mortician	Total sample	21.0	7.09
	Males	20.9	6.70
	Females	21.0	7.64
Group IX			
Sales Manager	Total sample	22.6	6.80
	Males	22.9	7.47
	Females	22.1	5.59
Real Estate Salesman	Total sample	37.1	6.26
	Males	36.4	6.84
	Females	38.2	5.05
Life Insurance Salesman	Total sample	29.3	6.66
	Males	29.0	6.95
	Females	29.8	6.15
Group X			
Advertising man	Total sample	47.8	7.16
	Males	46.8	7.65
	Females	49.3	6.01
Lawyer	Total sample	40.5	6.95
	Males	39.5	6.98
	Females	42.0	6.64
Author-journalist	Total sample	51.5	7.85
	Males	50.4	8.25
	Females	53.2	6.85

TABLE 3 (*continued*)

Occupation or scale		Mean	S.D.
Group XI			
President, manufacturing concern	Total sample	34.0	7.32
	Males	33.9	8.11
	Females	34.1	5.90
Group I	Total sample	58.8	6.33
	Males	58.2	6.43
	Females	59.6	6.07
Group II	Total sample	34.4	7.01
	Males	35.4	7.43
	Females	32.9	6.01
Group V	Total sample	35.5	7.26
	Males	35.9	8.33
	Females	34.9	5.18
Group VIII	Total sample	10.7	8.46
	Males	11.6	8.34
	Females	9.4	8.47
Group IX	Total sample	34.1	6.01
	Males	33.7	6.48
	Females	34.8	5.13
Specialization Level	Total sample	44.0	7.84
	Males	43.06	7.71
	Females	44.06	8.00
Interest Maturity	Total sample	44.9	6.43
	Males	45.0	7.14
	Females	44.8	5.17
Occupational Level	Total sample	57.2	7.06
	Males	57.5	5.90
	Females	56.8	8.51
Masculinity-femininity	Males	30.0	7.56
(Masculinity scored high)	Females	23.8	6.87

[a] N = 91 total sample; 55 males; 36 females.

TABLE 4

Comparison of Art Students with Other Groups on Artistic
Values (Preferences for Complexity) Scale

Occupation or scale	N	Mean	S.D.
Group			
Art Students			
Total sample	76	32.0	4.60
Males	46	31.8	4.74
Females	30	32.3	4.37
Military officers	343	17.4	4.30
Female college students			
"Unselected"	113	23.9	2.77
"Creative"	22	27.1	4.78
Writers			
Representative	29	23.9	4.00
"Creative"	26	31.3	4.35

TABLE 5

Mean Scores on the Barron-Welsh Art Scale for the Samples Indicated

Sample	N	Mean	S.D.
Artists			
Standardization group[a]	80	40.3	12.9
First cross-validation group[a]	30	39.1	13.8
Architects I ("creative" architects)	40	37.1	9.8
Student artists: San Francisco Art Institute	103	34.4	10.30
Team member of first American expedition to			
attempt Mount Everest	15	31.5	12.1
Research scientist I ("creative" scientists)	15	30.7	6.3
Architects II (control sample for Architects I)	43	29.5	10.1
Women mathematicians I ("creative")	16	28.1	12.5
Women mathematicians II ("representative")	28	26.9	15.4
Men mathematicians I ("creative")	26	26.9	12.7
Architects III ("representative" American			
architects)	41	26.1	12.1
Research scientists II ("less creative")	15	22.1	14.1
Men mathematicians II ("less creative")	21	19.4	10.1
Scientists III ("least creative")	15	19.2	8.7
Unselected adult males	343	13.9	11.2

[a] After the initial standardization, three items were found to be nondiscriminating on further item analysis and therefore were dropped from the scale, bringing it to its present 62-item form. Therefore, the corrected means are slightly lower than those given here for the first two groups of artists.

TABLE 6

Significant Correlates of the Perceptual Acuity Test

Variable	r	N	Significance level
Gottschaldt Figures Test	.29	83	.01
Mosaic judgment: Originality	.30	83	.01
CPI			
Self-acceptance	.26	70	.05
Socialization	.27	70	.05
Symbol equivalents			
Fluency	.27	83	.05
Originality	.22	83	.05

TABLE 7

Significant Correlates of the Barron M-Threshold Inkblot Form Test Scales of Part II

Variable	r	N	Significance level
1. Total M responses			
Adjective self-description: Total score,			
Artist scale	.392	85	.01
Self-rating			
There is something in my work which			
escapes explanation.	.245	85	.05
I like my own work.	−.235	85	.05
Mosaic judgment: Good use of color	.265	85	.05
SVIB			
Psychiatrist	.233	85	.05
Vocational Counselor	.245	85	.05
Social Worker	.300	85	.01
Social Science Teacher	.223	85	.05
Minister	.237	85	.05
Musician	.335	85	.01
Music Teacher	.265	85	.05
President, manufacturing concern	−.217	85	.05
Inkblot form test			
Part I, Threshold score	−.280	85	.01
Part I, Volume	.430	85	.01
Part II, Originality, non-M responses	−.410	85	.01
Part II, Originality, M responses	.480	85	.01

TABLE 7 (*continued*)

Variable	r	N	Significance level
Symbol equivalents test			
Part I, Total number unusual responses	.243	85	.05
Part I, Total weighted score	.231	85	.05
Inventory of Personal Philosophy: *CO*			
(Complexity of Outlook)	.434	76	.01
IPAR *CS* (Preference for Complexity)	.435	76	.01
IPAR *Ind* (Independence)	.296	76	.01
CPI *Ai* (Achievement via Independence)	.239	70	.05
Fx (Flexibility)	.430	70	.01
2. Originality, *M* responses			
Self-rating			
There is something in my work which			
escapes explanation.	.288	85	.01
Perceptual Acuity Test			
Illusion items, number correct	−.261	83	.05
Nonillusion items, number correct	.219	83	.05
SVIB			
Architect	.212	85	.05
Group I	.224	85	.05
Specialization level	−.226	85	.05
Consequences			
Part I, total number unusual responses	.213	85	.05
Inkblot form test			
Part II, Total *M* responses	.480	85	.01
CPI *Ac* (Achievement via Conformance)	−.305	70	.01
Mosaic judgment: Originality	.300	85	.01
SVIB			
Architect	.227	85	.05
Dentist	.244	85	.05
Mathematician	.285	85	.01
Physicist	.240	85	.05
Engineer	.262	85	.05
Group I	.243	85	.05
Group II	.231	85	.05
Inkblot form test			
Part I, Volume	−.224	85	.05
Part II, Total *M* responses	−.410	85	.01
Symbol equivalents			
Part I, Total weighted score	−.228	85	.05

TABLE 8

Significant Correlates of the Hall Mosaic Judgment Test

Variable	r	N	Significance level
1. Overall Artistic Merit			
Mosaic judgment			
Good Use of Form	−.292	86	.01
Total score on 50 pairs	.441	86	.01
SVIB			
Architect	−.210	86	.05
Vocational Counselor	.227	86	.05
Social Science Teacher	.290	86	.01
Business Education Teacher	.244	86	.05
School Superintendent	.369	86	.01
Music Teacher	.240	86	.05
Real Estate Salesman	−.298	86	.01
Group V	.233	86	.05
Franck Drawing Completion Test			
Expansion-contraction	.226	86	.05
First-Semester Grades			
Drawing	.328	66	.01
2. Good Use of Color			
Adjective self-description			
Total score, Artist scale	.271	86	.05
Self-rating			
I prefer working on my own rather than in class.	.333	86	.01
I am influenced by the work of other students.	−.219	86	.05
Mosaic judgment			
Total score on 50 pairs	.376	86	.01
SVIB			
Physician	.214	86	.05
Physicist	.299	86	.01
Purchasing Agent	−.239	86	.05
Group I	.248	86	.05
Group VIII	−.223	86	.05
Inkblot form test: Part II, Total M responses	.265	85	.05
Franck Drawing Completion			
Originality	.259	86	.05
Complexity-simplicity	.301	86	.01
Expansion-contraction	.281	86	.01
Inventory of Personal Philosophy: *CO* (Complexity of Outlook)	.321	76	.01

TABLE 8 (*continued*)

Variable	r	N	Significance level
2. Good Use of Color (*cont.*)			
IPAR *CS* (Preference for Complexity)	.347	76	.01
IPAR *Ind* (Independence)	.308	76	.01
CPI *Fx* (Flexibility)	.321	70	.01
3. Good Use of Form			
Adjective self-description: Total score	−.268	86	.05
Mosaic judgment: Overall artistic merit			
(10 pairs)	−.282	86	.01
CPI *Cm* (Communality)	.323	70	.01
First-semester grades: Drawing	−.289	66	.05
4. Originality			
Child Aesthetic Preference Test: Total score	.440	86	.01
Mosaic judgment			
Warmth and Vitality	.278	86	.01
Total score on 50 pairs	.524	86	.01
Perceptual Acuity Test			
Illusion items, number correct	.268	83	.05
Nonillusion items, number correct	.254	83	.05
Total weighted score	.297	83	.01
SVIB			
Osteopath	−.241	86	.05
Veterinarian	−.268	86	.05
Mathematician	.277	86	.01
Aviator	−.247	86	.05
Inkblot form test			
Part I, Volume	−.325	86	.01
Part II, Originality, non-*M* responses	.300	85	.01
CPI *Sp* (Social Presence)	−.252	70	.05
5. Warmth and Vitality			
Self-rating			
I like my own work.	−.213	86	.05
When compared to the work of other students at my level, my work is unusually creative.	−.232	86	.05
I can bring my emotional life into visual imagery.	−.219	86	.05
Barron–Welsh Art Scale: Total score	.285	86	.01
Gottschaldt Figures Test: Total score	−.377	86	.01
Mosaic judgment			
Originality (10 pairs)	.278	86	.01
Total score on 50 pairs	.465	86	.01

TABLE 8 (*continued*)

Variable	r	N	Significance level
5. Warmth and Vitality (*cont.*)			
SVIB			
Psychologist	−.257	86	.05
Architect	−.228	86	.05
Physician	−.213	86	.05
Physicist	−.270	86	.05
Chemist	−.321	86	.01
Engineer	−.312	86	.01
Forest Service Man	−.269	86	.05
Banker	.342	86	.01
Group II	−.356	86	.01
Franck Drawing Completion			
Originality	−.298	86	.01
Complexity-simplicity	−.302	86	.01
Expansion-contraction	−.271	86	.05
CPI			
Sy (Sociability)	−.308	70	.01
Sp (Social Presence)	−.278	70	.05
Ie (Intellectual Efficiency)	−.318	70	.01
Py (Psychological-mindedness)	−.299	70	.05
6. Total Score			
Self-rating: I prefer working on my own rather than in class.	.255	86	.05
Child Aesthetic Preference Test: Total score on 100 items (pairs)	.409	86	.01
Mosaic judgment			
Overall artistic merit (10 pairs)	.441	86	.01
Good Use of Color (10 pairs)	.376	86	.01
Originality (10 pairs)	.524	86	.01
Warmth and Vitality	.465	86	.01
SVIB			
Veterinarian	−.237	86	.05
Mathematician	.265	86	.05
Farmer	−.237	86	.05
Forest Service Man	−.344	86	.01
Aviator	−.322	86	.01
Inventory of Personal Philosophy: *CO* (Complexity of Outlook)	.278	76	.05
IPAR *CS* (Preference for Complexity)	.277	76	.05
CPI			
Fx (Flexibility)	.324	70	.01
Fe (Femininity)	.374	70	.01

TABLE 9

Intercorrelations of Rating Scales Based on Mean Ratings of Seven Judges

	Expr.	Geom.	Repr.	Blth.	Conf. dyn.	Chrom. dyn.
Geom.	−.43					
Repr.	−.62	−.44				
Blth.	.02	.11	−.12			
Conf. dyn.	.35	−.19	−.17	.06		
Chrom. dyn	−.07	.19	−.11	.38	.35	
Diff.	.43	.37	−.74	.26	.40	.18

TABLE 10

Significant (0.05 level) Correlates of the Representational Component in Painting

Name of variable	Product-moment correlation
Abstract expressive component	−.80
Configurational dynamism	−.53
Diffusion	−.63
Hall Mosaic Judgment Test	
Overall merit	−.54
Warmth and vitality	−.56
Total score	−.80
M-threshold inkblots: Originality	−.47
SVIB: Verbal originality	.58
CPI	
Capacity for Status	.62
Intellectual Efficiency	.51
School grades: Painting	.52
Portfolio, year-end	
Faculty rating	.57
IPAR staff rating	.62

TABLE 11

Significant (0.05 level) Correlates of the Abstract Expressive Component in Painting

Name of variable	Product-moment correlation
Representational component	−.80
Configurational dynamism	.66
Diffusion	.57
Blitheness	−.53
Barron–Welsh Art Scale	.55
Gottschaldt Figures Test	−.47
Hall Mosaic Judgment Test	
Total score	.50
SVIB	
Psychologist	−.52
Psychiatrist	−.53
Banker	.51
Franck Drawing Completion Test	
Originality	−.46
Barron Symbol Equivalence Test	
Unusualness	−.51
Total score	−.54
School grades: Drawing	.53
Portfolio, year-end: Faculty ratings	−.49
CPI	
Communality	.64
Socialization	.56

TABLE 12

*Significant (0.05 level) Correlates of the Geometrical
Component in Painting*

Name of variable	Product-moment correlation
Child Aesthetic Preference Test	.50
Hall Mosaic Judgment Test	
Total score	.51
Originality	.60
Portfolio	
At admission	.76
Year-end: IPAR staff ratings	.55
School grades	
Drawing	−.52
English composition	−.57
Self-rating	
I do my best work outside of class.	.54
There is something special about my work.	.54
CPI	
Communality	−.62
Good impression	.53
SVIB	
Production Manager	−.55
Sales Manager	−.55
Consequences: Ideational fluency	−.57

TABLE 13

Significant (0.05 level) Correlates of Chromatic Dynamism in Painting

Name of variable	Product-moment correlation
Self-rating	
I work spontaneously.	.70
I bring emotional life to my painting.	.49
Perceptual Acuity Test	
Illusions items correct	−.70
Total score	−.66
SVIB	
Mathematician	−.65
Chemist	−.69
Mortician	.71
Real Estate Salesman	.59
Hall Mosaic Judgment Test	
Good Use of Color	.49
Good Use of Form	−.52
Independence of Judgment	.58
CPI: Good Impression	.62
Consequences: Originality	−.57
Franck Drawing Completion Test	
Originality	−.47
Asymmetry	−.51

TABLE 14

Significant (0.05 level) Correlates of Configurational Dynamism in Painting

Name of variable	Product-moment correlation
Abstract expressive component	.67
Barron–Welsh Art Scale	.56
SVIB	
Psychologist	−.62
Psychiatrist	−.69
Public Administrator	−.54
School Superintendent	−.78
Minister	−.63
Music Teacher	−.61
Specialization Level	−.70
Verbal Originality	−.59
Barron Symbol Equivalents Test	
Fluency	−.52

TABLE 15

Significant (0.05 level) Correlates of Diffusion in Painting

Name of variable	Product-moment correlation
Representational component	−.63
Abstract expressive component	.57
Hall Mosaic Judgment Test	
Total score	.63
Franck Drawing Completion Test	
Expansiveness	.58
School grades: Sculpture	.94
Grade-point average	.54
Independence of Judgment	−.53

TABLE 16A

Commitment [a]

Category	Yes		Not yet		No		
	F	M	F	M	F	M	*N*
1. Do you consider yourself a dancer?							
Training, experience, standards met	12	2	7	1	–	–	22
Love of dance, motivation to							
succeed	11	3	–	–	1	–	15
Special talent	2	–	–	–	–	–	2
	25	5	7	1	1	–	39
2. Do you intend to continue dancing? As a professional?							
Professionally, as performer	19	6			–	–	25
Professionally, as teacher	2	–			–	–	2
Nonprofessionally	4	–			–	–	4
Not at all	–	–			1	–	1
	25	6			1	–	32

[a] The column headings F and M stand for female and male, respectively.

TABLE 16B

Education[a]

Category	F	M	*N*
1. Are there any aspects of dance you dislike?			
Rigidity, superficiality:			
Lack of expressiveness, technique without content	9	–	9
Set views on style, seeking to impose one's own			
style on others	3	–	3
Aspects of the dance world	5	–	5
Demands of training: fatigue	4	–	4
No complaints	6	5	11
	27	5	32
2. List the attributes of a good teacher.			
Knowledge, background			
Knowledge of technique, forms, experience,			
training	16	5	21
Broad background in fine arts	2	1	3
Knowledge of, sense for, music and rhythm	4	–	4
Knowledge of body, anatomy, movement	9	–	9
Knowledge of dance world	1	3	4
Attitude of teacher to profession			
Enthusiasm, love of profession	12	2	14
Attitude of learner	5	1	6
Energy, vitality	6	1	7
Attitude of teacher to pupil			
Understanding of, insight into people; interest			
in students	8	5	13
Observant, able to pick out individuality	3	–	3
Impartial, objective	2	–	2
Teaching manner			
Discipline: firm, strict, perfectionist	7	–	7
Patient, tactful	11	1	12
Persistent, foresightful, reliable, prompt, orderly	7	1	8
Ability to think and communicate clearly,			
precisely	9	1	10
Creative, imaginative	7	–	7
	109	21	130

TABLE 16B (continued)

Category	F	M	*N*
3. What are the attributes of a good class?			
Stimulating			
Inspiring, challenging; new learning	17	2	19
Sense of accomplishment; closer to perfection, new skills	4	3	7
Variety of techniques, interesting	5	–	5
Effects on body: build better body, warm-up, loosen body	13	1	14
Coherent, well-organized class	7	–	7
Creative, create new expressions	3	–	3
	49	6	55
4. What is a good dance student?			
Work and practice			
Hard working, practices regularly, persistent, disciplined	17	3	20
Perfection seeking, drive	5	–	5
Works in class, gets most out of class	4	1	5
Personal traits			
Receptive, attentive	6	–	6
Cooperative, open-minded, wants to learn	4	–	4
Patient with faults	7	1	8
Love of dance, devotion	4	–	4
Innate attributes			
Physical ability	5	–	5
Talent, feeling for line, dynamics	5	–	5
Creative nature, dance with feeling	3	–	3
	60	5	65
5. Do you feel you are a good student?			
Yes	11	2	13
Seek improvement	8	2	10
No	2	–	2
No answer	4	1	5
	25	5	30

[a] The column headings F and M stand for female and male, respectively.

Dance, Emotion, Motivation[a]

Category	F	M	*N*
2. Do you enjoy dancing more when you are in certain moods?			
Affected by mood			
When happy, excited, exuberant, inspired	9	1	10
Either happy, sad, or angry; any intense mood	5	1	6
Particularly when sad	3	–	3
Only when not depressed, only when feeling energetic	6	–	6
Not affected by mood			
Always enjoy dancing	1	3	4
Intellectual interests	2	1	3
	26	6	32
3. Does being tired affect your dancing?			
Affected by fatigue			
Lethargic, slow, muscles less responsive, loss of control	13	1	14
Loss of strength, endurance; possibility of injury	5	4	9
Loss of concentration	5	2	7
Frustration, loss of creativity	4	–	4
No; snaps out of it, becomes less tired	5	1	6
Not affected by fatigue	1	–	1
	33	8	41
4. Does being tense affect your dancing?			
Affected by tension			
Lack of fluidity, flow; sense of constraint	14	3	17
Loss of control; use of excess strength, energy	3	2	5
Inability to concentrate	4	1	5
Positive: vitalized dance, or dissipates through dance	4	–	4
No effect	4	–	4
	29	6	35
5. Does dancing affect your moods, tensions, fatigues?			
Dancing affects mood			
Dancing relieves moods, fatigues, tensions, makes one feel better	16	5	21
Evaluation of class performance and achievement leads to elation or depression	13	–	13
Dance leads to physical fatigue	3	–	3
No effect	1	1	2
	33	6	39

[a] The column headings F and M stand for female and male, respectively.

TABLE 16D

Dance and Personality[a]

Response	F	M	*N*
1. Do you consider yourself creative?			
Yes	14	4	18
Sometimes	6	–	6
No	5	1	6
	25	5	30

	Yes		Sometimes		No		
	F	M	F	M	F	M	*N*
2. Why or why not?							
Results, accomplishment, choreography, past achievement	7	2	3	–	1	–	13
Feelings, need to express self	4	1	1	–	–	–	6
Personal traits							
Receptive to the new; original, imaginative	5	1	2	–	1	1	10
Daring, sensitive; creative nature	3	–	1	–	1	–	5
Not creative, due to lack of training	3	–	–	–	–	–	3
	22	4	7	–	3	1	37

	F	M	*N*
3. Do you talk with your hands?			
Yes	18	4	22
Sometimes	3	1	4
No	4	1	5

	Yes		Sometimes		
	F	M	F	M	*N*
4. If so, when?					
Always (no elaboration)	3	3	–	–	6
For description	6	–	2	1	9
When excited	9	1	1	–	11
No, never noticed	4	1	–	–	5
	22	5	3	1	31

Response	F	M	N
5. Do you consider yourself normal?			
Yes	14	3	17
Somewhat	5	–	5
No	2	3	5
Rejects question	5	–	5
	26	6	32

	Yes		Somewhat		No		
	F	M	F	M	F	M	N
6. Why or why not?							
Emotional balance; or, more emotional than others	4	1	3	–	1	–	9
Ability to adjust, be with others, play social role	5	–	–	–	–	–	5
Meaning; living up to potential	2	–	–	–	–	–	2
Different because are artists	–	–	4	–	–	2	6
What is "normal"?	7	–	–	–	–	–	7
Pathology	–	–	–	–	–	1	1
	18	1	7	–	1	3	30

	F	M	N
7. What do you think of male dancers?[b]			
Role in profession			
Necessary to the art	5	1	6
As having a masculine role in dance	6	–	6
Same as other dancers; they are all individuals	5	3	8
Like/dislike: they are "good" people	5	2	7
As masculine or feminine	5	–	5
Do not know	2	–	2
	28	6	34
8. Why are there not more men dancers?[c]			
Social prejudice	24	5	29
Social isolation	2	–	2
Sex-linked traits	3	–	3
Do not know	–	1	1
	29	6	35

[a] The column headings F and M stand for female and male, respectively.

[b] Students responding to question 7 numbered 24 females and 6 males.

[c] Students responding to question 8 numbered 25 females and 6 males.

TABLE 16E

Dance as Art[a]

Response	F	M	N
1. Why is there art?			
Expression of self, life, emotion, spirit; need to create	16	4	20
To emphasize beauty; aesthetic purposes	6	1	7
Communication; to entertain	9	2	11
To reveal truth, give awareness	3	1	4
	34	8	42
2. Is dance an art as music, painting, and poetry are arts?			
Yes	26	6	32
No	–	–	–
	26	6	32
3. Why or why not?[b]			
Similarities between dance and other arts			
Expressiveness	19	5	24
As creative form of communication	5	–	5
Shares common elements with other forms	3	–	3
Has same reason for existing; has survived centuries	2	1	3
Differences between dancing and other arts			
Purely formal	7	–	7
Is living art	2	1	3
	38	7	45
4a. Are there any elements you think all dances should have?			
Yes	22	4	26
No	3	2	5
	25	6	31
4b. What are they?			
Should be expressive, have meaning	10	–	10
Use of all elements integral to medium	6	4	10
Creative, variety, personal touch	5	–	5
Unity, beauty	3	–	3
Should be left free	3	2	5
	27	6	33

TABLE 16E *(continued)*

Response	F	M	N
5. What do you think will happen to dance as an art in the future?			
Role of art in life			
Popularity will increase, become widespread	5	2	7
Be more accepted and understood, part of life	4	–	4
Use of new offshoots, dance therapy	2	–	2
Evolution of style			
Experiment, invent new styles, grow	13	3	16
Dangers of abstraction, too mechnical movement	4	2	6
	28	7	35

[a] The column headings F and M stand for female and male, respectively.

[b] Responses to this question were made by 26 female and 6 male students.

TABLE 17

Student Self-Descriptions

Females (N = 41)		Males (N = 6)	
Checked by	Adjective	Checked by	Adjective
100%	(None)	100%	Affectionate, anxious, determined, good-looking, intelligent, interests wide, mischievous
87.8%	Honest, active		
85.4%	Idealistic, imaginative, sincere	80%	Active, appreciative, artistic, clear-thinking, considerate, cooperative, curious, easy-going, emotional, energetic, enthusiastic, excitable, flirtatious, frank, friendly, gentle, good-natured, helpful, imaginative, informal, kind, logical, loyal, mannerly, mild, natural, peaceable, persistent, pleasant, pleasure-seeking, restless, self-punishing, sensitive, sentimental, sociable, talkative, thoughtful, understanding, versatile, witty
82.9%	Considerate, dependable, interests wide, sensitive		
80.5%	Appreciative, cooperative		
78%	Adaptable, curious, determined, understanding		
75.6%	Emotional, forgiving, healthy		
73.2%	Artistic, conscientious, energetic, individualistic, intelligent, reasonable, reliable, serious, thoughtful		

TABLE 17 (continued)

Females (N = 41)		Males (N = 6)	
Checked by	Adjective	Checked by	Adjective
70.7%	Civilized, generous, gentle, responsible	60%	Adventurous, ambitious, attractive, calm, capable, changeable, cheerful, civilized, defensive, dependable, dreamy, fault-finding, forgiving, formal, generous, healthy, honest, idealistic, impatient, impulsive, jolly, moody, obliging, patient, persevering, poised, warm, progressive, reasonable, rebellious, relaxed, reliable, responsible, sarcastic, self-pitying, serious, sincere, soft-hearted, spendthrift, spunky, sympathetic, tactful, tolerant, touchy, unaffected, worrying, zany
68.3%	Adventurous, affectionate, attractive, changeable, excitable, feminine, friendly, kind, loyal		
65.9%	Alert, ambitious, capable, cautious, cheerful, natural, original, sympathetic, warm		
63.4%	Good-natured, independent, reflective, sentimental, tolerant		
61%	Anxious, humorous, optimistic, versatile		

TABLE 18

	Italian sample			American sample		
	MZ	DZ	h^2	MZ	DZ	h^2
Consequences	.38	.71	−1.14	.45	.10	.39
Symbol equivalents	.42	.73	−1.17	.29	.36	−.11
Unusual uses	.72	.59	.31	.42	.45	−.06

TABLE 19

	Italian sample			American sample		
	MZ	DZ	h^2	MZ	DZ	h^2
Consequences	.72	.75	−.13	.42	.49	−.14
Symbol equivalents	.15	.58	−1.04	.22	.35	−.20
Unusual uses	.59	.47	.23	.38	.18	.24

TABLE 20

Comparison of Monozygotic with Dizygotic Twins on Measures of Aesthetic Judgment and Creativity

	Italian sample						American sample					
	MZ_r	DZ_r	MZ_{r_2}	DZ_{r_2}	h^2	HR	MZ_r	DZ_r	MZ_{r_2}	DZ_{r_2}	h^2	HR
Gottschaldt Figures												
Test	.86	.35	.74	.12	.78	1.186	.49	.13	.24	.02	.41	1.469
Expressional Fluency	.92	.70	.85	.49	.75	.485	.28	.76	.08	.58	−4.33	7.429
Consequences												
Fluency score	.38	.71	.15	.51	−1.14	−1.708	.45	.10	.20	.01	.39	1.556
Originality score	.72	.75	.52	.57	−.13	−.086	.42	.49	.18	.24	−.14	−.333
Symbol equivalents												
Fluency	.42	.73	.17	.53	−1.17	−1.506	.29	.36	.08	.13	−.11	−.483
Originality	.15	.58	.02	.34	−1.04	−5.634	.22	.35	.05	.12	−.20	−1.182
Unusual Uses												
Fluency	.72	.59	.52	.35	.31	.348	.42	.45	.18	.20	−.06	−.143
Originality	.59	.47	.35	.22	.23	.411	.38	.18	.14	.03	.24	1.053
Barron–Welsh Art												
Scale	.58	.07	.34	.01	.55	1.750	.66	−.02	.44	.00	.67	2.061

TABLE 21

Strong Vocational Interest Blank Results, Students at College for Aesthetic Studies, University of California, Santa Cruz (N = 49)

Scale	Mean	S.D.
Artist	51.35	8.67
Psychologist	46.69	8.15
Architect	47.02	8.60
Physician	51.49	10.00
Psychiatrist	46.16	8.26
Osteopath	40.31	10.01
Dentist	37.43	8.69
Veterinarian	20.76	9.23
Mathematician	34.84	8.92
Physicist	32.47	11.05
Chemist	39.04	10.52
Engineer	28.55	9.82
Production Manager	18.73	6.33
Farmer	33.82	7.14
Carpenter	19.59	9.44
Forest Service Man	21.51	7.24
Aviator	28.18	7.90
Printer	36.92	8.22
Mathematic Science Teacher	31.02	8.38
Industrial Arts Teacher	15.12	10.86
Vocational Agriculture Teacher	20.47	8.38
Policeman	18.59	5.95
Army Officer	13.35	10.45
Y.M.C.A. Physical Director	25.27	9.74
Personnel Manager	22.10	9.61
Public Administrator	34.47	8.18
Vocational Counselor	32.20	8.77
Physical Therapist	34.35	9.30
Social Worker	37.73	10.04
Social Science Teacher	28.49	9.85
Business Education Teacher	22.59	9.39
School Superintendent	24.49	8.82
Minister	34.53	10.86
Musician	56.57	8.81
Music Teacher	40.12	10.39
C.P.A. Owner	26.90	7.24
Senior C.P.A.	23.04	7.56
Accountant	10.78	7.38
Office Worker	16.27	7.18

TABLE 21 (*Continued*)

Scale	Mean	S.D.
Credit Manager	19.61	9.14
Purchasing Agent	7.63	5.40
Banker	16.12	6.00
Pharmacist	27.18	6.65
Mortician	18.76	8.01
Sales Manager	19.80	6.45
Real Estate Salesman	32.71	6.38
Life Insurance Salesman	26.43	8.57
Advertising Man	43.59	6.20
Lawyer	38.96	6.78
Author-Journalist	48.10	6.41
President Manufacturing Concern	29.76	7.04
Group I	58.47	6.94
Group II	38.29	9.84
Group V	40.12	8.77
Group VIII	11.53	7.20
Group IX	30.88	6.87
Specialization Level	47.20	6.88
Interest Maturity	48.16	5.64
Occupational Level	57.06	4.53
Masculinity-Femininity	28.53	8.71

TABLE 22

California Psychological Inventory Results, Students at College for Aesthetic Studies, University of California, Santa Cruz (N = 49)

Scale	Males		Females	
	Mean	S.D.	Mean	S.D.
Do (Dominance)	25.15	6.23	26.81	6.05
Cs (Capacity for Status)	20.67	3.80	21.19	3.21
Sy (Sociability)	22.96	5.27	22.81	4.49
Sp (Social Presence)	39.78	5.10	36.35	5.39
Sa (Self-Acceptance)	22.78	3.82	22.00	3.23
Wb (Sense of Well-Being)	33.89	4.24	31.31	7.12
Re (Responsibility)	24.89	4.96	27.19	3.66
So (Socialization)	32.59	4.75	34.96	6.27
Sc (Self-Control)	23.70	6.15	24.81	7.21
To (Tolerance)	21.82	4.22	22.39	4.46
Gi (Good Impression)	14.85	4.99	14.81	4.94
Cm (Communality)	23.78	1.99	23.00	3.44
Ac (Achievement via Conformance)	23.85	5.30	23.77	3.85
Ai (Achievement via Independence)	23.11	4.30	21.81	5.21
Ie (Intellectual Efficiency)	39.22	5.83	39.35	4.78
Py (Psychological-Mindedness)	12.11	2.52	12.54	2.93
Fx (Flexibility)	16.16	3.69	15.77	3.65
Fe (Femininity)	18.56	3.97	23.89	3.33

TABLE 23

Perceptual Test Results, Students at College for Aesthetic Studies, University of California, Santa Cruz (N = 49)

Test	Mean	S.D.
Child Aesthetic Judgment Test	56.59	5.78
Gottschaldt Figures	14.27	4.99
Barron-Welsh Art Scale	33.10	8.97

Variables from San Francisco Art Institute Testing

Adjective Self-Description
    1. Total score, Similarity to Artists

Artists Self-Rating (on 10-point scale)
    2. I completely lose myself while working, forgetting all other personal matters.
    3. I prefer working on my own rather than in class.
    4. I have definite feelings about most art works which I see.
    5. I work spontaneously, rather than deliberately.
    6. My work is unique.
    7. I value a good instructor's opinion of my work more highly than my own.
    8. I do better work in class than out of class.
    9. There is something in my work which escapes explanation.
    10. I like my own work.
    11. I am influenced by the work of other students.
    12. When compared to the work of other students at my level, my work is unusually creative.
    13. I can bring my emotional life into visual imagery.

Art Scale
    14. Barron–Welsh Art Scale, total score
    15. Welsh Revised Art Scale

Child Aesthetic Preference Test
    16. Total score (100 items)

Gottschaldt Figures Test
    17. Total score
    18. Ratio, part 1/total

Hall Mosaic Judgment Test
    19. Overall Artistic Merit
    20. Good Use of Color
    21. Good Use of Form
    22. Originality
    23. Warmth and Vitality
    24. Total score, 19–23.

Perceptual Acuity Test (Gough–McGurk Illusions)
   25. Nonillusion items, number correct
   26. Illusion items, number correct
   27. Total weighted score

Strong Vocational Interest Blank (SVIB)
   28. Artist
   29. Psychologist
   30. Architect
   31. Physician
   32. Psychiatrist
   33. Osteopath
   34. Dentist
   35. Veterinarian
   36. Mathematician
   37. Physicist
   38. Chemist
   39. Engineer
   40. Production Manager
   41. Farmer
   42. Carpenter
   43. Forest Service Man
   44. Aviator
   45. Printer
   46. Mathematics Science Teacher
   47. Industrial Arts Teacher
   48. Vocational Agriculture Teacher
   49. Policeman
   50. Army Officer
   51. YMCA Physical Director
   52. Personnel Manager
   53. Public Administrator
   54. Vocational Counselor
   55. Physical Therapist
   56. Social Worker
   57. Social Science Teacher
   58. Business Education Teacher
   59. School Superintendent
   60. Minister
   61. Musician
   62. Music Teacher
   63. CPA Owner
   64. Senior CPA
   65. Accountant
   66. Office Worker
   67. Credit Manager
   68. Purchasing Agent
   69. Banker
   70. Pharmacist
   71. Mortician
   72. Sales Manager
   73. Real Estate Salesman
   74. Life Insurance Salesman
   75. Advertising Man
   76. Lawyer
   77. Author-Journalist
   78. President, manufacturing concern
   79. Group I
   80. Group II
   81. Group V
   82. Group VIII
   83. Group IX
   84. Specialization level
   85. Interest maturity
   86. Occupational level
   87. Masculinity-femininity

Stick Figures Test (Hardyck)
   88. Total score

Consequences Test (Guilford)
89. Part I, total number of average responses
90. Part I, total number of unusual responses
91. Part I, total number of acceptable responses (sum of 89 and 90)
92. Part I, total weighted score
93. Part II, total score

Barron M-Threshold Inkblot Form Test
94. Part I, threshold score
95. Part I, volume
96. Part II, total, *M* responses
97. Part II, Originality, non-*M* responses
98. Part II, Originality, *M* responses

Franck Drawing Completion Test
99. Originality
101. Symmetry-asymmetry
103. Femininity
100. Complexity-simplicity
102. Expansion-contraction

Barron Symbol Equivalents Test
104. Part I, total number of average responses
105. Part I, total number of unusual responses
106. Part I, total number of acceptable responses (sum of 104 and 105)
107. Part I, total weighted score
108. Part II, total score

Inventory of Personal Philosophy (IPP)
109. *CO* (Complexity of Outlook)

Special IPAR Scales (see also 140 and 141)
110. *CS* (Preference for Complexity)
111. *Ind* (Independence)
112. SVIB Originality scale (Barron–Wolfe)

California Psychological Inventory (CPI)
113. *Do* (Dominance)
115. *Sy* (Sociability)
117. *Sa* (Self-Acceptance)
114. *Cs* (Capacity for Status)
116. *Sp* (Social Presence)
118. *Wb* (Sense of Well-Being)

119. *Re* (Responsibility)
120. *So* (Socialization)
121. *Sc* (Self-Control)
122. *To* (Tolerance)
123. *Gi* (Good Impression)
124. *Cm* (Communality)
125. *Ac* (Achievement via Conformance)
126. *Ai* (Achievement via Independence)
127. *Ie* (Intellectual Efficiency)
128. *Py* (Psychological-Mindedness)
129. *Fx* (Flexibility)
130. *Fe* (Femininity)

Portfolio Ratings at Time of Admission
131. San Francisco Art Institute, average faculty rating
132. IPAR average rating

First-Semester Grades
133. Grade point average
134. Drawing
135. Painting
136. Modern art history
137. English composition
138. Sculpture
139. Photography

Special IPAR Scales
140. *O-T* (Originality determinants: total, 0-1 through 0-5 scales)
141. *O-B* (Barron originality)

Means and Standard Deviations, San Francisco Art Institute Freshmen. October 1968 Testing

	Variable No.	N	Mean	S.D.	Variable No.	N	Mean	S.D.
Total	1	101	23.9	5.18	8	101	4.24	1.72
Males		62	23.3	5.37		62	4.18	1.77
Females		39	24.6	4.74		39	4.33	1.64
Total	2	102	7.00	2.08	9	100	5.80	2.62
Males		63	6.98	2.16		63	5.95	2.86
Females		39	7.02	1.93		37	5.57	2.14
Total	3	102	6.83	2.31	10	102	6.95	2.11
Males		63	6.94	2.34		63	7.27	1.99
Females		39	6.67	2.26		39	6.44	2.19
Total	4	101	7.75	2.10	11	101	4.42	2.14
Males		63	7.83	2.23		62	4.27	2.29
Females		38	7.63	1.86		39	4.64	1.85
Total	5	102	6.25	2.30	12	100	5.95	2.17
Males		63	5.87	2.43		61	6.34	2.18
Females		39	6.85	1.94		39	5.33	2.00
Total	6	101	6.44	2.16	13	99	6.64	2.44
Males		63	6.33	2.20		63	6.71	2.59
Females		38	6.61	2.10		36	6.50	2.14
Total	7	102	5.91	2.68	14	103	34.4	10.30
Males		63	5.89	2.67		64	33.0	11.03
Females		39	5.95	2.69		39	36.7	8.47
Total	15	103	34.6	10.43	27	83	18.2	5.34
Males		64	33.5	11.11		49	18.2	5.81
Females		39	36.3	8.91		34	18.2	4.57
Total	16	101	57.4	14.65	88	92	17.9	4.64
Males		62	55.3	15.62		55	18.2	4.47
Females		39	60.7	12.23		37	17.5	4.85
Total	17	99	11.2	5.05	89	86	46.0	16.44
Males		61	11.1	5.12		54	46.2	17.73
Females		38	11.3	4.94		32	45.8	13.99
Total	18	99	43.4	15.50	90	86	5.60	5.09
Males		61	41.8	15.14		54	5.44	4.92
Females		38	46.0	15.72		32	5.88	5.35
Total	19	86	4.79	1.61	91	86	51.7	18.49
Males		54	4.70	1.56		54	51.7	19.44
Females		32	4.93	1.69		32	51.6	16.76

Means and Standard Deviations (continued)

	Variable No.	N	Mean	S.D.	Variable No.	N	Mean	S.D.
Total	20	86	5.15	1.79	92	86	120.	46.80
Males		54	5.17	1.66		54	120.	47.10
Females		32	5.12	1.98		32	121.6	46.26
Total	21	86	5.57	1.47	93	83	37.4	9.81
Males		54	5.56	1.60		53	37.5	9.71
Females		32	5.59	1.25		30	37.2	9.97
Total	22	86	4.22	1.41	94	103	7.92	5.35
Males		54	4.22	1.19		64	8.73	5.81
Females		32	4.22	1.19		39	6.59	4.17
Total	23	86	4.09	1.70	95	103	7.72	3.62
Males		54	3.80	1.59		64	6.78	3.22
Females		32	4.59	1.75		39	9.26	3.73
Total	24	86	23.8	3.22	96	85	14.1	3.42
Males		54	23.4	3.15		54	13.3	3.35
Females		32	24.5	3.23		31	15.5	3.07
Total	25	83	1.83	1.12	97	84	1.46	1.06
Males		49	1.94	1.17		54	1.52	1.00
Females		34	1.68	1.02		31	1.35	1.15
Total	26	83	9.88	2.95	98	85	2.71	1.56
Males		49	9.86	3.16		54	2.50	1.62
Females		34	9.91	2.61		31	3.06	1.37
Total	99	86	8.41	6.56	112	91	23.4	4.13
Males		54	8.63	6.75		55	23.3	4.26
Females		32	8.03	6.21		36	23.5	3.92
Total	100	86	9.29	6.95	131	54	197.	44.76
Males		54	10.2	7.32		32	199.	43.71
Females		32	7.81	5.99		22	193.	46.02
Total	101	86	12.5	6.82	132	50	185.	55.71
Males		54	13.1	6.88		32	185.	58.89
Females		32	11.7	6.61		18	185.	49.54
Total	102	86	18.0	10.06	133	89	291.	76.10
Males		54	18.4	10.16		57	288.	83.36
Females		32	17.2	9.84		32	298.	60.47
Total	103	Mf			134	66	31.9	8.94
Males		Not				40	31.0	9.61
Females		Scored				26	33.2	7.61

Means and Standard Deviations (continued)

	Variable No.	N	Mean	S.D.	Variable No.	N	Mean	S.D.
Total	104	100	39.0	13.58	135	69	31.9	8.94
Males		61	39.5	12.86		46	31.8	9.69
Females		39	38.2	14.61		23	32.1	7.20
Total	105	100	5.79	4.22	136	53	17.0	12.47
Males		61	5.89	4.06		37	15.4	11.34
Females		39	5.64	4.45		16	20.8	14.04
Total	106	100	44.8	14.53	137	60	28.8	9.54
Males		61	45.4	13.58		36	25.9	10.60
Females		39	43.8	15.85		24	33.2	5.26
Total	107	100	102.	34.61	138	31	27.0	12.17
Males		61	103.	31.92		22	31.2	5.37
Females		39	100.	38.38		9	16.7	17.00
Total	108	92	20.5	4.40	139	24	35.9	4.70
Males		55	20.7	4.71		20	35.9	4.76
Females		37	20.3	3.87		4	35.8	4.38
Total	109	76	21.7	3.51	140	70	36.4	5.85
Males		46	21.5	3.54		44	36.3	5.94
Females		30	22.0	3.44		26	36.6	5.67
Total	110	76	32.0	4.60	141	70	27.4	5.33
Males		46	31.8	4.74		44	27.5	5.40
Females		30	32.3	4.37		26	27.3	5.21
Total	111	76	16.0	2.89				
Males		46	15.8	3.07				
Females		30	16.4	2.53				

References

Alsculer, R. H., & Hattwick, L. B. W. *Painting and personality.* 2nd ed., abridged. Chicago: University of Chicago Press, 1969.

Asch, S. E. *Social psychology.* New York: Prentice-Hall, 1952.

Barron, F. Personality style and perceptual choice. *Journal of Personality,* 1952, **20,** 385–401.

Barron, F. Complexity-simplicity as a personality dimension. *Journal of Abnormal & Social Psychology,* 1953, **48,** 163–172. (a)

Barron, F. Some personality correlates of independence of judgment. *Journal of Personality,* 1953, **21,** 287–297. (b)

Barron, F. Threshold for the production of human movement in inkblots. *Journal of Consulting Psychology,* 1955, **19,** 33–38.

Barron, F. *Creativity and psychological health.* Princeton, New Jersey: Van Nostrand-Reinhold, 1963. X, p. 292.

Barron, F. The generation gap. In *Creativity and personal freedom.* Princeton, New Jersey: Van Nostrand-Reinhold, 1968. Pp. 273–282.

Barron, F. *Creative person and creative process.* New York: Holt, 1969.

Barron, F., & Welsh, G. S. Artistic perception as a possible factor in personality style: Its measurement by a figure preference test. *Journal of Psychology,* 1952, **33,** 199–203.

Barron, F., Guilford, J. P., Christensen, P. R., Berger, R. M., & Kettner, N. W. Interrelations of various measures of creative traits. Technical Memorandum AF 18 (600)-8. Berkeley, California: Institute of Personality Assessment and Research, 1957.

Burt, C. The factorial analysis of emotional traits, Parts I and II. *Character and Personality,* 1939, 239-254, 275-299.

Burt, C. The general aesthetic factor. *British Journal of Psychology, Statistical Section,* 1960, III, 90-92.

Cardinet, J. Préférences esthétiques et personnalité. *Année Psychologique,* 1958, **58,** 45-69.

Child, I. L. Personal preferences as an expression of aesthetic sensitivity. *Journal of Personality,* 1962, **30,** 496-512.

Child, I. L. Observations on the meaning of some measures of aesthetic sensitivity. *Journal of Psychology,* 1964, **57,** 49-64.

Child, I. L. Aesthetics. In G. Lindzey and E. Aronson (Eds.), *The handbook of social psychology* (2nd ed.). Reading, Massachusetts: Addison-Wesley, 1969.

Eysenck, H. J. The general factor in aesthetic judgments. *British Journal of Psychology,* 1940, **31,** 94-102.

Eysenck, H. J. A critical and experimental study of colour preferences. *American Journal of Psychology,* 1941, **54,** 385-394.   (a)

Eysenck, H. J. The empirical determination of an aesthetic formula. *Psychology Review,* 1941, **48,** 83-92.   (b)

Eysenck, H. J. The experimental study of the "good Gestalt"–a new approach. *Psychology Review,* 1942, **48,** 344-364.

Fritz, S. H. The *Sc* scale: an analysis of the MMPI items answered in the scored direction by a group of creative individuals and a sample of psychiatric patients. Unpublished M.A. thesis, San Francisco State College, 1969.

Gordon, D. A. The artistic excellence of oil paintings as judged by experts and laymen. *Journal of Educational Research,* 1955, **48,** 579-588.

Gordon, D. A. Individual differences in the evaluation of art and the nature of art standards. *Journal of Educational Research,* 1956, **50,** 17-30.

Gordon, K. A study of aesthetic judgments. *Journal of Experimental Psychology,* 1923, **6,** 6-43.

Gottschaldt, K. On the influence of experience on the perception of figures, 2. *Psychologische Forschung,* 1929, **12,** 1-87.

Gough, H. G. The adjective check list as a personality assessment research technique. *Psychological Reprints Monograph Supplement 2,* 1960, **6,** 107-122.

Gough, H. G. *Manual for the California Psychological Inventory.* Palo Alto, California: Consulting Psychologists Press, 1964 (2nd ed. 1965).

Gough, H. G. An interpreter's syllabus for the CPI. In P. McReynolds (Ed.), *Advances in psychological assessment,* Vol. I. Palo Alto, California: Science and Behavior Books, 1968. Pp. 55-79.

Gough, H. G., & McGurk, E. A group test of perceptual acuity. *Perceptual and Motor Skills,* 1967, **24,** 1107-1115.

Hall, W. B. The development of a technique for assessing aesthetic predispositions and its application to a sample of professional research scientists. *American Psychologist,* 1958, **13,** 510.

Hall, W. B., & MacKinnon, D. W. The prediction of creativity from personality inventories. *American Psychologist,* 1965, **20,** 740.

Hathaway, S. F., & McKinley, J. C. *Manual for the Minnesota Multiphasic Personality Inventory.* Minneapolis, Minnesota: University of Minnesota Press, 1943.

Helson, R. Childhood interest clusters related to creativity in women. *Journal of Consulting Psychology,* 1965, **29,** 352–361.

Holzinger, K. J. The relative effect of nature and nurture influences on twin differences. *Journal of Educational Psychology,* April, 1929, **XX,** 241–248.

Knapp, R. H. Stylistic consistency among aesthetic preferences. *Journal of Projective Techniques & Personality Assessment,* 1962, **26,** 61–65.

Knapp, R. H. A stylistic comparison of Picasso and Cézanne. *Sciences de l'Art,* **1969, VI,** 1–2, 6–11.

Krippner, S. The paranormal dream and man's pliable future. *Psychoanalytic Review,* 1969, **56,** 28–43.

Lerner, I. M. Polygenic inheritance and intelligence. Memorandum, Institute of Personality, Assessment, and Research, University of California, Berkeley, 1969.

Lynes, R. The artist as uneconomic man, *Saturday Review,* 1970, **99,** 25–27.

McGurk, E. Susceptibility to visual illusions. *Journal of Psychology,* 1965, **61,** 127–143.

MacKinnon, D. W. The personality correlates of creativity: A study of American architects. In G. S. Neilsen (Ed.), *Proceedings of the XIV International Congress of Applied Psychology, Copenhagen, 1961,* Vol. II. Copenhagen: Munksgaard, 1962, pp. 11–39.

MacKinnon, D. W. Personality and the realization of creative potential. *American Psychologist,* 1965, **20,** 273–281.

MacKinnon, D. W., *et al.* An assessment study of Air Force Officers. Technical Report WADC-TR-58-91, ASTIA Document No. AD 151040, 1958.

McNemar, Q. *Psychological statistics,* 3rd ed. New York: Wiley, 1962.

Meier, N. C. *The Meier art tests: 1. Art judgment.* Iowa City: Bureau of Educational Research and Service, University of Iowa, 1940.

Morris, C. *Varieties of human value.* Chicago: University of Chicago Press, 1956.

Murray, H. A. *Explorations in personality.* London and New York: Oxford Univ. Press, 1938.

Murray, H. A., & Morgan, C. *The thematic apperception test manual.* Cambridge, Massachusetts: Harvard University Press, 1943.

Nichols, R. C. The national merit twin study. In S. G. Vandenberg (Ed.), *Methods and goals in human behavior genetics.* New York: Academic Press, 1965. Pp. 231–245.

Rochmas, A. Aesthetic sensitivity. Unpublished B.A. thesis, Harvard University, 1965.

Rorschach, H. *Psychodiagnostics.* Bern: Huber (New York: Grune & Stratton), 1942.

Rosenberg, M. *The masks of Othello.* Berkeley, California: University of California Press, 1961.

Shields, A. *Journal of Aesthetic Education,* 1970, **4,** 2, 133–143.

Stark, S. Suggestion regarding drama, inner creation, and role-taking (empathy). I. Dramatic. *Perceptual and Motor Skills,* 1968, **26** (Monogr. Suppl. 6).   (a)

Stark, S. Toward a psychology of knowledge: VI. The sublime, the mystical, and the inner creative. *Perceptual and Motor Skills,* 1968, **27,** 767–786.   (b)

Strong, E. K., Jr. *Vocational Interest Blank.* Palo Alto, California: Stanford University Press, 1938.

Taylor, C. W. *Widening horizons in creativity.* New York: Wiley, 1964.

Thorndike, R. L. Some methodological issues in the study of creativity. In A. Anastasi (Ed.), *Testing problems in perspective.* Washington, D.C.: American Council on Education, 1966.

Thurstone, L. L. Primary mental abilities. *Psychometric Monographs,* 1938.

Vandenberg, S. G. (Ed.). *Methods and goals in human behavior genetics.* New York: Academic Press, 1965.

Witkin, H. A., Lewis, H. B., Hertzman, M., Machover, K., Meissner, P., & Wapner, S. *Personality through perception,* New York: Harper, 1954.

Woolf, V. *A room of one's own.* New York: Harcourt, 1929.

Index